C000225181

PLAYBOYS spies AND PRIVATE EYES

INSPIRED BY ITC

This paperback edition first published in 2017 by Quoit Media Limited,
Brynmawr, Llanfair Caereinion, Powys, SY21 0DG

For more copies of this book, please email quoit@quoitmedia.co.uk

ISBN 978-1-911537-03-8

Copyright © 2017 Alan Hayes and Rick Davy and respective contributors

Cover Design and Internal Illustrations © Shaqui Le Vesconte, 2017

This first reprint published July 2019

The right of Alan Hayes, Rick Davy and respective contributors to be identified as the authors of this work has been asserted in accordance with the Copyright, Designs and Patents Act 1988.

All rights reserved. No part of this publication may be reproduced, stored in or introduced to a retrieval system, or transmitted, in any form, or by any means (electronic, mechanical, photocopying, recording or otherwise) without the prior written permission of the publisher.

A CIP catalogue record for this book is available from the British Library.

Printed and bound in Great Britain by Clays Ltd, Elcograf S.p.A.

Published by

QUOIT MEDIA LIMITED

www.quoitmedia.co.uk

QUOIT

in association with

HIDDEN TIGER

www.hiddentigerbooks.co.uk

Edited by Alan Hayes and Rick Davy

Foreword by Annette André

All profits from this book will be donated to the Born Free Foundation
www.bornfree.org.uk

Table of Contents

Annette André (*Foreword*) is a popular and well-regarded actress who made her name during what can only be described as the Golden Age of Television. No stranger to ITC shows, she appeared in four episodes of *The Saint*, as well as having memorable appearances in *The Baron*, *The Prisoner*, *The Persuaders!*, *Return of the Saint*, and of course as Jeannie in *Randall and Hopkirk (Deceased)*. She also appeared in many other classic TV series from *Crossroads* to *The Brothers*, from *The Benny Hill Show* to *The Avengers*, as well as films such as *A Funny Thing Happened on the Way to the Forum* and *Up Jumped a Swagman*. Annette is also a successful theatre actress, with a string of West End performances to her name. She lives in California with her husband Arthur and her beloved animals, and is a hands-on volunteer for the Born Free Foundation.

Shaqui Le Vesconte (*Illustrator*) trained as a graphic designer, dabbled in illustration, and ended up being bemused and frustrated by both disciplines. For Hidden Tiger, he illustrated the books *Two Against the Underworld*, *Avengerworld* and *Dr Brent's Casebook*, and is now incarcerated in a school in deepest Sussex, catering to the reprographic and occasional design demands of 1,500 girls and a somewhat smaller, though no less idiosyncratic, number of staff. The pay may not be as good, but the rolling tableau of young bodies past the office window is a damn sight prettier than what a person of advancing years and borderline senility is used to. Possessing a quirky and self-effacing sense of humour, especially when it comes to biographies, Shaqui may yet pass away with a smile on the lips.

Elaine Spooner (*Afterword*) is the daughter of Dennis Spooner who created and wrote for some of the best-loved TV shows of the 1960s and 1970s. She graduated from the University of the Arts, London, and has since worked as a writer and production editor for the heritage and culture sectors. She lives in London with her husband Phil.

Foreword • Annette André

The past is a foreign country; they do things differently there. I read that in a novel donkey's years ago and didn't really understand what it meant until I started writing my memoir and discovered that the past is indeed a place with a mind of its own.

Calendar time and the sequence of events in your life often don't jibe, and it seems as if you're continually playing a newsreel in reverse to get things right. But one thing I'm certain of in the story of how I got from there to here is that pure luck played a major role. I was in the right place at the right time to be a part of what has come to be called "The Golden Age" of British television.

None of us in front of the cameras or behind had a clue that the telly we were turning out in the '60s and '70s had a shelf-life or that shows like *Randall and Hopkirk (Deceased)*, *The Saint*, *The Prisoner*, *The Avengers* or any of the dozens more, so popular in their day, would be in constant replay a half-century later!

What stands out for me all these years later, was the atmosphere of fun and the camaraderie that seemed to pervade the shows I did at ITC under Lew Grade. Both Mike Pratt and Ken Cope were pranksters and the shenanigans they invented to make me break-up in the middle of a take made our producer, Monty Berman, old before his time. One of Ken's favourite gags was to make me react to him when he'd appear suddenly in a scene I was doing with Mike. Since only Mike could see Ken, I had to act as if he weren't standing next to me or crossing between us. At the best of times, it took all the concentration I could muster not to be aware of him. But then, without warning, Ken would tickle my knee out of camera sight and I would jump like a rabbit, then collapse with laughter. The poor director would yell "CUT!" and Ken, the picture of innocence, would ask, "What happened?"

By the way, in case you hadn't noticed, Ken's hairdo mysteriously went from a Beatles–type cut in the first two or three episodes to a more conventional style for the rest of the series. He was wearing a wig at the producer's insistence and had it back to front until he and the hairdresser sorted it out.

When it came to pranks, Roger Moore was every inch Ken's equal. We filmed *Randall and Hopkirk* at the Elstree Studios along with *The Saint*, *The Avengers*, *The Champions* and *Department S*. Very often we'd be shooting our series on one stage and on the adjoining one Roger would be filming *The Saint.* Quite early one morning, I was shooting a highly emotional scene with Mike in my bedroom set, when the wardrobe door suddenly flew open and Roger stepped out saying, "Hope I'm not intruding".

Roger and I hit it off right out of the gate when I was cast as a guest star in *The Saint* (the first of six). We both had wacky senses of humour, partial to practical jokes (whoopee cushions included), and over the years we traded "Gotchas" to the delight of cast and crews. But there was a serious side to Roger when it came to work. I was uncertain if I should take-on *Randall and Hopkirk (Deceased),* afraid that starring in a series would typecast me. Roger took me to lunch and pointed out all the pluses but with the caveat that I had to keep my head on my shoulders and not let the spotlight blind me to the fact that I was still one of many who were responsible for making the show a success. Roger practiced that philosophy in every role he played and I'll be eternally grateful for his advice and support.

I awoke early one morning in May 2017 to hear the BBC announce Roger's death. The news literally took the wind from me, as he had been a force in my life since 1964 and I'll miss him for the rest of my days. He was not just an engaging actor and a director but one of the last of a fading breed, a gentlemen. Roger remained a good friend until his passing; we kept in touch mainly by email.

"The Boys", as I called Ken and Mike, were dreamboats to work with – kind, gentle when I was fragile and feeling overworked, and always supportive. Mike was a very talented musician as well, and we'd often meet up in his dressing room during breaks in shooting and he'd entertain us singing and playing his guitar. Of all the shows I've done over the years, I still have a special feeling for *Randall and Hopkirk* and "The Boys".

I've been a lifelong animal lover and advocate for their care both in captivity and in the wild. For more than twenty-five years, I've been an active supporter of the Born Free Foundation (BFF), founded by Virginia McKenna and her husband Bill Travers, stars of the film *Born Free,* and run today by their son, Will Travers. Years ago, I went to hear Ginny and Bill give a talk on their efforts to close zoos in the UK that mistreated the creatures in their care. I was hooked instantly, and began giving talks on the BFF's many projects to rescue and protect wildlife wherever threatened. Along the way I became close friends with Ginny and Bill and expanded my efforts to include investigating zoos and circuses to expose inhumane conditions. The BFF remains a vital part of my life.

We're a superstitious lot, actors are, and so in theatres the world over the lights are turned off after the last performance, except for one left burning stage centre. It's called the ghost light, and it's there for all the spirits who had trod those boards to find their way back. I'd like to think that one day, in the very, very, distant future, I'll find a ghost light waiting for me. There's nothing I'd like better than to hear my cue, hit my mark and do it all over again.

Preface • Alan Hayes

If you asked the average TV viewer today about ITC, no doubt you'd get a blank look. They'd probably think it was an app for a Smartphone, or some obscure government department that had been created for no other reason than to upset people. In many ways, this is not surprising, as the heyday of the Incorporated Television Company is long past, and its days as a producer of diverting fare for television and the cinema are over. However, between the 1950s and 1980s, it was a powerhouse of those media, having been set up in September 1954 by Lew Grade, Val Parnell and Prince Littler as the Incorporated Television Programme Company, with an eye on winning a regional franchise in the soon-to-be-launched ITV.

The company was initially unsuccessful in its application to become a broadcaster, and seemed destined to operate as an independent producer of television films. Fate intervened, though, and ITP were called in when one of the franchise winners, the Associated Broadcasting Development Company, found themselves too short of finance to commence transmissions. Consequently, a new company was created, initially called the Associated Broadcasting Company, a name which was soon changed due to it sharing an acronym with a fellow ITV company to Associated TeleVision (ATV). This became the parent company of ITP, who were already making a mark domestically and internationally with their film series *The Adventures of Robin Hood* (1955 to 1959). In 1957, they took their first steps into more contemporary drama when they inherited production of *The New Adventures of Charlie Chan* from the American company Vision Productions, which had created the series and made the early episodes in the USA.

What came next was to kick off two decades of television entertainment in the action genre, the heroes being variously secret agents, international jetsetters, playboys, private detectives and troubleshooters. The first of these gave a clue that ITC series would not often be humdrum or pedestrian; the action hero in this show was invisible!

From *H.G. Wells' Invisible Man* in 1959, through the adventures of the likes of John Drake, Simon Templar, John Mannering, McGill ("with a big M and a big G"), the Champions, Jason King and Department S, Jeff Randall and Marty Hopkirk (Deceased), and many others, the name ITC carved its way into the public consciousness, a watchword for escapism, thrills and quality television. Sometimes, it went beyond that, with series such as *The*

Prisoner, which challenged the viewer and broke new ground in TV drama while remaining true to the company's ethos of entertaining audiences.

Looking back on the ITC catalogue isn't just an exercise in nostalgia, though undoubtedly you will read of many fond memories regarding it within the pages of this book. Particularly now, when several of these decades-old series have been spruced up and issued in High Definition on Blu-ray, it is clearer than ever that, despite the sometimes modest budgets which necessitated camera trickery to hide the fact that Simon Templar wasn't *really* on the French Riviera, these series were made by skilled craftsmen - writers, producers, directors, designers, composers, camera operators, and countless more - and were graced with the cream of the British acting profession, and stars from the international scene. In many ways, the vision of Lord Lew Grade went beyond the limitations of television, which was at the time locked into low resolution line structures and (until 1967 in the UK) monochrome. The shows that he commissioned could compete with feature films made for the silver screen (indeed many series had episodes repackaged for international cinema screenings) - and today, restored to modern standards from their film elements, they don't seem wildly out of place alongside new television drama output - not something you could say of vintage videotaped productions, regardless of how prestigious they might have been at the time. Such was the level of professionalism invested in series like *The Prisoner*, *Randall and Hopkirk (Deceased)*, *The Persuaders!* and their stablemates that they have transcended their era and its technology.

Playboys, Spies and Private Eyes - Inspired by ITC brings together a selection of essays written by fans of these series, a heady mix of professional writers and talented amateurs. The chapters are approached through the eyeglass of personal experience - what each series means to the writers, how they touched their lives and inspired them to do interesting things. In many ways it is as much a celebration of the fan experience as it is of the great adventure shows that we all grew up watching.

There are 35 essays in the book, and these are divided into sections, one for each series, in chronological order. A handful of series - such as *Interpol Calling*, *Ghost Squad*, *Man of the World* and *Espionage* - are not featured, as it proved highly difficult to find potential writers with strong memories of these series from their television transmissions. Likewise, *Gideon's Way* does not figure, but this is more because, as a straight police series, it didn't really fit the theme of *Playboys, Spies and Private Eyes.*

Each section begins with a stunning, specially commissioned illustration from artist Shaqui Le Vesconte, who has also designed and produced our breathtaking cover. We are delighted to be able to present so many unique, high standard pieces of artwork in this book, and as far as we are concerned, there are four Champions, not three. Shaqui, your Nemesis badge is in the post…

Moving on to our authors, potted writer biographies can be found on the reverse of each section front page. These are designed to introduce our contributors and inform readers of other works that might be of interest.

It's been a pleasure for Rick Davy and me to co-ordinate this project, and it is one that has been made all the more easy and pleasurable by the standard of the writing and enthusiasm of those involved. We are also delighted to have Annette André on board and thank her for her lovely foreword and for suggesting the Born Free Foundation as the recipient of proceeds from the sales of the book. Likewise, we are grateful to Elaine Spooner, daughter of writer Dennis Spooner – a legendary contributor to ITC series and more besides – for her afterword and support for this project.

The ITC series featured in this book are worthy of celebration, from the best and most popular to the ones that maybe didn't quite hit the heights hoped for them, or those that have become unfairly forgotten. And celebrate we will.

We hope that the chapters of this book will provide entertainment, thrills, spills, fun and an occasional laugh, much like the shows that together we are paying tribute to.

And if *Playboys, Spies and Private Eyes – Inspired by ITC* convinces you to buy a DVD, a Blu-ray, another book, to pick up that piece of memorabilia that you always wanted but never got around to grabbing, or donate further to the Born Free Foundation, then all the better.

This book wouldn't be here without the likes of Lord Lew Grade and all those other talented men and women who turned ideas into scripts and scripts into TV gold, so many years ago. We salute them.

The New Adventures of Charlie Chan

1959

Simon Coward is a software developer from the south of England who has lived in the Midlands for 35 years. He made the first website devoted to the series *Ace of Wands*, and created the original *Lost Shows* site for ITV's *Raiders of the Lost Archives* campaign. For six years he wrote a fortnightly column about old TV for the MNA newspaper group, and for a short while dipped his toe into broadcasting by researching, writing and editing *The Ads Show* for Big Centre TV. For Kaleidoscope Publishing he co-edits their series of television Research Guides, and is regularly involved in the production of their autobiographical titles.

Something Old, Something New

Simon Coward

I remember coming home in short trousers, sitting down with an ice lolly and watching an episode of *The New Adventures of Charlie Chan.* I was fifty-six years old.

With that as an opener, you might have guessed that I have no great tales to tell about discovering *The New Adventures of Charlie Chan* as a child, no stories of re-enacting the episodes with friends in the playground at school while doing unforgivable things with our fingers at the corners of our eyes, and no memories of late nights slaving over the pages of a fanzine.

It would be nice, helpful even, if I could just recall watching *The New Adventures of Charlie Chan* when I was a nipper. But hell, I'm not *that* old. Mind you, I'm not so young either, but even so, as far as I can tell just three episodes were shown in my lifetime by my ITV region. I remember nothing of this, but as each one of this trio was scheduled as the final programme in that day's broadcasts, then even if being on well past my bedtime wasn't enough, I was only 18 months old by the time the last of these was aired. So, I'm pretty sure that *Chan* didn't form my first exposure to the world of ITC.

I've wondered what did. By sheer weight of numbers, and the fact that during my lifetime it was shown exclusively at an hour where children could see it, it might well have been *The Adventures of Robin Hood.* But I've really no idea whether the arboreal antics of Richard Greene and company take that particular crown, it could just as easily have been Gerry and Sylvia Anderson's *Supercar* or *Fireball XL5*, or perhaps something my parents were watching which I caught more or less by accident. So many of these series were broadcast, and some several times, that they – and the later series more aimed at grown-ups – were a seemingly never-ending yet ever-changing backdrop to my childhood.

I also wondered just how many there were, and so I had a go at counting them. I reckon that by my tenth birthday, I could – just theoretically, not in real life – have watched more than seventeen hundred broadcasts of British-made ITC shows, the equivalent to more than three a week for that decade. That's just one channel, one ITV company. If you include the programmes made in Canada and Australia that would add a further five hundred and take it well past four every seven days. So even allowing for a proportion of those being on before I was old enough to make sense of them, or shown too late for me to be allowed to watch them, there are still more than enough to have ensured that they're part of what courses through my veins, they're part of me. But, for the first half-century of my life, they didn't include *Chan*.

I can remember my mum explaining to me who Charlie Chan was, and that he called his eldest boy his 'number one son' but I can't for the life of me work out what prompted this conversation in the first place. I was probably too young for the films at the time, so why? A comedy sketch or sitcom, perhaps, where someone said something like, "Who do you think you are? Charlie Chan?" I'm clutching at straws, I really don't know. It's such an odd thing to remember. Well, half-remember.

So, for two-score years and sixteen, nothing. I suppose much of what little I did know about the series came by that odd TV-researching osmosis where stuff you're not even looking at permeates after years of poring over the pages of old *TV Times*.

Hang on a minute, one of the editors of this book is having a word: "You'll need to explain that last bit, me old mate."

Alright then. For years, decades even, I've nibbled at the edges of this TV research lark. Not as a living, not for money, but just to find out a bit more. When I was a teenager, the nearest reference library to where I lived had microfilmed copies of *The Times* newspaper. While such information would now be available at the click of a hyperlink, I remember hunting down transmission dates for series such as *The Avengers* and noting the "Steed... and Tara..." subtitles the paper printed for the series – not realising that unlike those employed in the colour Rigg episodes, these were invented by someone at the newspaper itself. Sorry for the digression, it's just the heady fragrance of nostalgia in the air.

Anyway, later I discovered places that had either microfilmed or hard-copy editions of *TV Times* and *Radio Times* and I'd note down cast information for various series on index cards. I don't recall ever doing this even once for *Charlie Chan*, mind you, but you get the idea.

Sometime in the late 1980s I got involved with Kaleidoscope, a group which now describes itself as "Britain's longest-established television heritage organisation", and I ended up helping with the events they ran and the TV reference guide books they published. At some point, when all these guide books were formed of over a hundred separate Word Perfect® documents, I suggested putting all the information they contained into a database system, which I then ended up building. And yes, even *The New Adventures of Charlie Chan* would be in there, but at this stage no cast, no credits, just episode titles, transmission dates and whether the episodes all still existed (they did) and on what format (35mm black-and-white film). Is that enough, can I get back to my tale now?

So, where was I? Yes, osmosis. So, without really trying, you get to know that like most of its feature film ancestors, the television Charlie Chan was played by a white American in what they now call 'yellowface' make-up, while his son was played by a genuine Chinese American actor. In this case it was J. Carrol Naish and James Hong – and I see that the latter, at the time of writing, is not only still with us but quite extraordinarily busy.

So all those years, all those ITC episodes to watch, appreciation societies to join, and fanzines large and small to read. But no *Chan* amongst them.

In case there's any doubt, let me make it clear that all that watching and collecting and researching was not part of a quest in which *The New Adventures of Charlie Chan* was some sort of unholy grail that I was pursuing. I think I can safely say I didn't give its absence a second thought. Well, maybe I did, but I certainly didn't give it a third one.

So time passes, and it's 2016, and I'm sitting with a friend in a pub. He takes a DVD case out of his bag. "I bought this at a comic mart a few weeks ago," he says, and I can see that the DVD case sports none-too-professional artwork and the legend "The New Adventures of Charlie Chan". "Would you like to borrow it?"

It would have seemed uncouth to refuse.

It's hard to imagine that there's anything legitimate about this release, if I dare even use that word. The recordings look to be transferred from domestic videotape, though there's no sign of commercials or the usual on-screen paraphernalia that today's broadcasters insist we peek through. The picture quality is reminiscent of the second- or third-generation video copies of rarities that passed around in the 1980s, but I could cope with it then, and it is a series I've not seen before…

So what's Naish-ville like? I suppose this would be a better yarn if I said that the series was a forgotten gem, that my life had changed in oh so many ways, and that I'm writing this because it was now my mission to spread the word, brothers and sisters. But really, it's just OK. It's both as expensive and as cheap and cheerful as you'd expect an ITC show of that vintage to be. The stories measure slightly above normal on the predictability and sentimentality scales, but as the episodes are only 25 minutes apiece, it's no great chore to watch.

And of course, I checked the on-screen credits against the info in that database and made the appropriate adjustments, in most cases before I'd even watched the episode. Those who know me won't be at all surprised about that.

H.G. Wells' Invisible Man

1959

Jon Older graduated in English and Drama in 1975. After four years working as a Stage Manager, Jon joined Granada Television in Manchester in 1980. Moving to HTV West in Bristol he became a freelance Assistant Director in 1984. He has worked extensively in the UK in film and television drama, but also in America, Canada, France, Germany, Belgium, Norway, Spain, Japan and South Africa as Assistant Director, 2nd Unit Director and also as Director. His production credits include *Death in Paradise, Poldark, Silent Witness, Beowulf, Da Vinci's Demons, New Tricks, Wolfblood, Primeval, Ashes to Ashes, Doctor Who, Foyle's War, Taggart, Lexx, Starhunter* and *Robin of Sherwood.*

Tell Him I Can't See Him

Jon Older

Accompanied by ominous music, a camera tracks swiftly along a series of bubbling retorts and beakers, rising swiftly to push in on a low-angled shot of a strange figure in a lab coat, slowly turning into camera to reveal a man with a completely bandaged topless head and two vacant eye sockets showing the emptiness inside the wrappings, as the titles *H.G. Wells' Invisible Man* fill the screen.

That opening used to scare the living daylights out of me. It is one of the earliest television images I can remember from the 1950s. I can remember watching an early children's science fiction series called *The Red Grass* at the end of the 1950s, and I was aware of something called *The Voodoo Factor* (which apparently still exists complete in the archives, Network!) that I definitely wasn't allowed to watch. I even have a very vague impression of catching a few glimpses of *Quatermass and the Pit* at around the same time. (Actually my earliest memory of scary television is of being in bed and hearing the scary music to *Quatermass II* in 1955! I was two years old and I knew nothing about the show – just that it was something really, really scary).

I think I must have caught up with a lot of *H.G. Wells' Invisible Man* in re-runs, as it always seemed to be on late at night during my childhood. Having seen the entire series much more recently, it's hard to understand why it was even scheduled in a mid- to late-evening spot on its original transmission, when it's as harmless and un-scary as an episode of *The Adventures of Robin Hood* or *William Tell.* Though the end credits state that the show is "Based on the character created by H.G. Wells", this was a very benign version of the Griffin character in the novel, whose invisibility causes him to go mad and seek world domination. Indeed, even the reason for the invisibility is completely different, brought on by injections of a drug in the book, and accidental exposure to unknown radiation in the television show.

One has to wonder why exactly the producers thought it even necessary to reference Wells at all. Universal Studios had held copyright on the title since its 1933 film made a star of Claude Rains in the title role, producing several sequels like *The Invisible Man Returns* (1940) and *The Invisible Man's Revenge* (1944). (The Mexican Calderon company also released their own Spanish-language *El Hombre Invisible* in 1958, very freely adapted from the Wells story, but it's doubtful that Universal perceived it as a threat to their franchise). The 1958 TV show has more in common with a film like *The Invisible Agent* (1942), wherein the original scientist's completely sane son volunteers to work for the US government against the Nazis, as its very own invisible Richard Hannay.

In fact, *H.G. Wells' Invisible Man* has more of a kinship to the later half-hour *Danger Man* series starring Patrick McGoohan than the Wells text, in that both were produced by, and had some scripts written and directed by the legendary Ralph Smart. Smart, a British born producer who died in Australia in 2001 at the age of 92, saw a kinship between the slightly rebellious anti-heroes of both series, in that although Brady was swiftly co-opted by the British government to work on its behalf, he didn't always do things the way he was expected to. If one was to simply take away the invisibility aspect of the show, it almost mimics the same basic template as *Danger Man*, with Brady operating as a more domestic version of John Drake, tangling with spies, foreign agents, and villains in all manner of lively adventures. (Other links between the two shows are the presence of assistant director David Tomblin – later to produce *The Prisoner* for ITC – who worked on both, *Invisible Man* being one of his earliest television credits, lighting cameraman Brendan J. Stafford, and film editor Spencer Reeve).

Every episode of *H.G. Wells' Invisible Man* has the end credit "Suggested for television by Larry White". For years I've wondered about this mystery man, in particular why he got a name check on Smart's show. I could find next to nothing about the elusive Mr White, only that he represented the literary interests of Universal-International at the time of the show's conception in 1958. He formed his own production company in later years – Larry White Productions – and was still active in the 1980s, as executive on the *Goliath Awaits* mini-series from Columbia Pictures Television, starring Christopher Lee, Mark Harmon and Eddie Albert. It was only while I was poking around on IMDb that I realised that not only had I worked for Larry White, I'd met him too! He was one of two American producers (Hugh Benson was the other) at the helm of *The Master of Ballantrae*, which HTV West shot in the UK in 1984 as a co-production deal with Columbia. He spent very little time in the West Country during the shoot but I wish I'd done my homework and made the connection at the time. I'm sure he'd have been completely bemused by a scruffy young 3rd AD wanting to interview him about *H.G. Wells' Invisible Man*. (Incidentally, the show's on-screen credits cite Incorporated Television Programmes as the production company behind *Invisible Man*. ITP, like Official Films, the distributors of *Colonel March of Scotland Yard*, was a subsidiary part of ITC).

In *Secret Experiment*, the heavily revised and rewritten version of the original un-screened pilot (Smart directed the pilot but gave the second attempt to Pennington Richards who said, in an *ATV Star Book* feature in 1960, "This is the toughest assignment I have ever faced"), we get to see how Peter Brady's experiments with invisibility at the government's Castle Hill Laboratories accidentally render him transparent after he's performed the same action on a hapless guinea pig. Not as hapless as the poor mouse that got recast from the pilot, the same guinea pig also gets to levitate in the episode *Flight into Darkness*! (Brady appears, via some borrowed stock footage from Hammer's version of *Quatermass 2*, to be working for aliens from an asteroid orbiting in space, but that's neither here nor there.)

The sheer genius of producer Smart is that he deals with the whole improbable concept setting up the show in the first couple of minutes, rather than by devoting hours to giving the character an origin story. His masterstroke, however, is that, aside from seeing an anonymous pair of eyes looking through an observation slit at the previously mentioned fantastic disappearing guinea pig, we never get to see what Peter Brady looks like – and thus the star of the show is never seen, never credited, and most importantly, never paid as a series leading man! It wasn't until around 1965 that we finally found out that actor Tim Turner was the voice of Brady (Robert Beatty performed the role for the pilot film, and apparently Lee Patterson did one episode too but it sounds like Turner to me) – obviously at a much-reduced rate than that for a leading man actually appearing as himself. (Some sources claim that towards the end of the production run Turner actually performed under the bandages as well, but it's highly unlikely that Smart would have asked him to do so as it would have undoubtedly meant paying him a lot more money for an anonymous role). Possibly in return for his selfless voice-over services on the series, Smart granted Turner an in-vision role in the episode *Man In Disguise*, which begins with him bizarrely pretending to be Peter Brady. He then later has the schizoid experience of having a threatening phone call with himself (at least he was saved the indignity of also wrestling with himself at the episode's conclusion). Coincidentally, the story gives a prominent role to Robert Rietti – who also made much more of a successful career for himself as *the* go-to voice-over artist in the 1960s film and television industry.

When swaddled in bandages and dark glasses on screen, the role would be played by a variety of dummies, props, stuntmen and stand-ins – not all of whom would have exactly complementary waistlines. A little chap by the name of Johnny Scripps would often appear (or not) in the series, whenever a partially clothed but apparently headless Brady was required, wearing a frame on his shoulders to fill out the invisible man's chest. (Incidentally, regarding those dark glasses – I still haven't worked out how Brady manages to wear them at all as his ears appear to be so tightly bandaged to the sides of his head that there's nothing for the glasses to actually rest upon. They must have stuck them to his head.)

With the advent of CGI-driven spectacles like *Hollow Man* and *Memoirs of an Invisible Man* still many years in cinema's future, Smart's show had of necessity to rely heavily upon live action effects work to portray its illusions, most of which holds up extraordinarily well, even today. Only very occasionally can any give-away wires be seen (over the 26 episode run, only on a handful of occasions can you spot the shadow of the puppeteers and their apparatus in any of the 'floating' scenes) turning book pages, floating sunglasses around a room, opening and closing doors, or lifting and throwing furniture about. Often in the episodes chats with Brady are suggested by having various other actors converse with a smoking cigarette hanging in mid-air. (How exactly he's mastered the art of speaking so clearly with a smoking cigarette between his lips isn't dwelt on.) It's a simple enough wire effect but would have been a non-starter in the current anti-smoking era of television.

Not surprisingly, due to the costs involved in shooting and processing them, true photographic effects are rarely used, and tend to be stock shots from the pilot episode – such as when Brady first unwraps his bandaged head to reveal nothing underneath. It's actually flawed in execution because as the bandages unwrap, they disappear momentarily behind the background plate, when in fact we should be able to see them all the time. It's quick enough not to matter the first time around. Unfortunately, it's a shot that the show would use again and again.

Some of the stunt work on the show is quite eye-opening, particularly the stunt driving where Brady is in command of stealing a villain's car, or – as in the episode *The Locked Room* – a motorbike and suspiciously large sidecar. To achieve this particular televisual illusion, the bike was obviously rigged to be controlled from inside the sidecar, but even so, to control the rig with restricted vision, at speed, in London traffic (despite how relatively empty the 1950s streets all look) with no apparent traffic control, is no mean feat, and I raise my hat to the anonymous stuntman who was given the task. Looking at all of the invisible driving sequences in the series – and there are a lot, in all kinds of different circumstances – I have no doubt that much of the stuff was potentially dangerous and I'm equally certain (being a 1st AD myself) that we wouldn't be allowed to do the stunts in the same way today. *Point of Destruction* features an extended sequence with the invisible Brady, at the wheel of his Austin Healey convertible, being chased by two enemy agents along country lanes that are completely covered in frost and ice. It's really quite hairy and in fact the driving double for Patricia Jessel actually connects with an action police car when it blocks her path and the car slides into it for a (surely unintended) low impact shunt. In almost every instance, the illusion of a driverless sports car is completely convincing – apart from, perhaps, Brady's explanation in the same story of how he avoided getting shot while driving by controlling the car from the front passenger seat...

As well as the constant parade of very familiar actors from the 1940s and 1950s who constantly guest in the series, one of the joys of the show is seeing how well (and sometimes how badly) some of them could invisibly manhandle themselves when apparently being beaten up or arrested by Brady. The late Michael Goodliffe gives himself a first-rate beating up when he throws himself into the fireplace during the concluding moments of *Secret Experiment.* (It's certainly an aspect of the art of acting that probably wasn't being taught in drama schools in the 1950s.) In *Blind Justice*, Leslie Phillips does a brilliant job of knocking himself back onto the bonnet of a car, then throttling himself before being arrested by the pursuing police. In footage from the pilot film, incorporated into the episode *Bank Raid*, actor Brian Rawlinson has a great time duffing himself up and throwing himself around in a field when supposedly under attack from Brady. With a wire stiffener in the back of his overcoat he then frog-marches himself back to his car. In *Flight into Darkness*, the normally staid and sensible Geoffrey Keen manages to eject himself from a theatre box, before manfully struggling with himself in the corridor outside. Naturally, he straightens his hair once the invisible man lets him go. The inimitable Larry Taylor (credited rather poshly as Laurence Taylor) thrashes himself not once, but twice in the episode *The Gun Runners*, which is also notable for its (for the time) extremely violent pre-titles sequence that sees a young mother and father machine-gunned down in the street, while their young son looks on. Of course, there's no blood but it's an odd sequence that really doesn't have any other equivalent in the series and raises an eyebrow even now.

In *Strange Partners*, one of the weaker episodes involving a pretty ineffectual plan to get Brady to murder Patrick Troughton (concealed under a rather unconvincing not-very-well make-up), Brady gets to play several scenes with a Great Dane called Juno. He even gets to acquire the promiscuous hound at the end of the episode after its previous owner gets carted off to jail. Juno obviously impressed everybody concerned because she swiftly got herself cast opposite John Steed in *The Avengers* over at ABC. There's one sequence in the episode *Picnic with Death* that even involves a horse performing as if it has the invisible Brady on its back. With perfect timing, the horse trots up to a parked car, turns around to face someone sitting in the car, pauses while Brady has a quick conversation, then trots off again to pursue the villain! (I'm still not sure how they did that, without any cheating cutaways to play with.)

Just occasionally the series was played for laughs, but rarely with any great success. *The Vanishing Evidence* gives us a laboured and over the top turn from actor Peter Illing as a Dutch police Inspector trying to nail the lovely Sarah Lawson for killing foreign agent Charles Gray. The only saving grace of the thing is that it gives Hammer veteran Michael Ripper a larger than usual amount of screen time as the sozzled hotel desk clerk brought in as a key eye-witness. (He watches Brady perform an invisible conversation between two hotel room keys.)

It's almost a trademark for all of the ITC filmed adventure series in the '50s and '60s that the principal cast members are never used for much of the location filming, instead being replaced by often not-quite-the-same-size camera doubles or stuntmen. *H.G. Wells' Invisible Man* is no exception to this and it's quite rare to see any guest cast members making it beyond the studio gates. Take the episode *The Prize* for example (one of the most *Danger Man*-like stories) wherein Brady helps an Eastern Bloc writer played by Mai Zetterling to escape custody at the hands of dastardly Colonel Anton Diffring. An extended escape sequence across a border minefield, directed, as much of the second unit scenes for the series were, by Douglas Hickox, features endless shots of a young lady looking not exactly like Ms Zetterling attempting to navigate the deadly mines while Diffring's double and his soldiers take potshots at her, and then at the mines in an attempt to blow her up. All this is intercut with close-ups of Diffring getting shot himself, in a nice warm leafy clump of studio bushes and trees. (Larry White obviously remembered Hickox and his second unit work on the show many years later when he hired him to direct the aforementioned *Master of Ballantrae* in 1984.)

The rest of the series' guest cast reads like a 'Who's Who' of period British talent, featuring the likes of (in no particular order) Colin Gordon, Helen Cherry, Ernest Clark, Adrienne Corri, Eric Pohlmann, John Carson, Dennis Price, Derren Nesbitt, Rupert Davies, Honor Blackman, Ronald Fraser, Edward Judd, Duncan Lamont, Peter Swanwick, Dermot Walsh, Andre Morell, Andrew Keir, Alfred Burke, Barbara Shelley, Hazel Court, a very young Isobel Black, and an even younger (and uncredited) Oliver Reed as an extra in a night club in the episode *The Mink Coat.*

I met Hazel Court back in 1986 when I was working with her husband, the American director Don Taylor, on an HTV West / Columbia co-production called *The Diamond Trap*. Hazel wasn't in the film, she was just enjoying an expenses-paid holiday back in the UK while her husband earned his keep. She looked like everyone's favourite granny by then, but was absolutely adorable – unlike her rather grouchy husband – and was shocked when she found out I knew so much about her acting career in the 1950s and '60s. (Sadly, I didn't recall at the time that she'd been in *The Mink Coat* episode of *Invisible Man*). She genuinely thought that no-one would still remember her. Meeting her was the only good thing about the entire film, apart from having dinner with Brooke Shields, who was also in the film. But I digress…

One trick that a lot of them had to learn was the art of sticking their elbow out to suggest that Brady was leading them along while engaging them in conversation. Lana Morris was particularly good at this in *Death Cell*. Nadja Regin, who played in the *Man in Power* story, wasn't. Lisa Daniely, as Brady's sister Diane (or Dee as he often calls her) probably had to do more elbow acting than anyone else on the show, as well as spending entire scenes talking to herself. She was also the widowed mother to little Deborah Watling, still some years from adopting mini-skirts and taking up residence in the TARDIS as a companion to Patrick Troughton's Doctor Who. (Both of these veteran ladies contributed a couple of commentary tracks on the Network DVD set released in 2008 but, sadly, they don't give away a great deal about the making of the show, other than pointing out the frequently obvious use of the Elstree studio exterior for various useful locations like hospitals and air terminals, etc.)

The amount of use that this and all the many other ITC shows got out of using the studios as exteriors – *Danger Man* was especially guilty of this in both its half-hour and hour formats – it's a wonder that anybody else working there could ever actually get in and out. Prior to the advent of *H.G. Wells' Invisible Man*, the National Studios had been owned and operated for several years by Douglas Fairbanks Jnr, who had shot his own 156-part half-hour show *Douglas Fairbanks Jnr Presents* there. (That show was responsible for another of my earliest TV memories – a brilliant episode titled *The Man Who Heard Everything*, starring Michael Gough as a patient awaiting ear surgery who discovers he can hear and communicate with two aliens until his surgery breaks the connection. The truly unearthly creatures were just depicted as pulsating silhouettes on his bedroom wall. I can see them now.) Lew Grade acquired it from Fairbanks and used it for ITC filmed shows up until Gerry Anderson's *UFO* in 1968. The studio complex (much altered from those early black and white days) is still partly in use today as the permanent home of *EastEnders* and *Holby City* for the BBC.

There's an entertaining commentary track on the Network DVD set for the episode *Shadow Bomb*, between screenwriter Brian Clemens and director Ray Austin (I'm not quite sure why Austin is there as he didn't direct any of the episodes – he was still a stuntman back in 1958) during which they manage to get most of their production facts wrong before eventually stumbling on the correct answers. Clemens reveals that most of the *Invisible Man* episodes were shot in about four days – which seems quite miraculous when you factor in how long it took to rig many of the wire effects during shooting. Austin is also the first to identify the entrance to Castle Hill Laboratories as being the gates to the old Danziger Studios in Elstree – which the two American brothers, Edward and Harry, converted from an old aero-engine factory in 1956. *Shadow Bomb* has an illustrious cast including Conrad Phillips, Jennifer Jayne, Walter Gotell, Ian Hendry (before he got his own show *Police Surgeon* and from that to starring alongside Patrick Macnee in the first season of *The Avengers*) and actor / director Anthony Bushell playing almost exactly the same role he would play as Colonel Breen for the BBC in *Quatermass and the Pit*.

The series final episode, *The Big Plot*, has a horribly up to date premise, in its story of a terrorist group assembling an atomic bomb in secret in a London basement. It suggests that the wars of the future won't be via conventional attacks but through urban warfare with strategically placed bombs detonated to order – and this was in 1959! Of course, Brady defeats them all and rescues the leading lady from atomic destruction (London, too) and that was the end of that. He never did manage to discover an antidote to his invisibility but then it has to be said that over 26 episodes he didn't really try that hard to find it.

H.G. Wells' Invisible Man stands up with the best of the ITC adventure shows from the 1960s in its fast-paced, imaginative stories and, for the time, convincing visual effects. Just like *The Saint, Danger Man, The Baron* and the rest, it took its hero all over the world (thanks to World Backgrounds and their library of exotic foreign location footage) and got him to right wrongs in under half an hour, and usually get back home in time for tea. Fantastic stuff.

If you've not seen him already, you really should take a look at *H.G. Wells' Invisible Man*.

The Four Just Men

1959-1960

Louise Penn works as a professional librarian in London but in her spare time she is a keen archive television, film, music and theatre enthusiast. Her blog loureviews.wordpress.com is now in its sixth year and covers a wide range of topics from adaptations of *Jane Eyre* and *King Lear* through to local exhibitions and book reviews. Her second home is the BFI Southbank, although she has a growing and eclectic collection of films and TV on home media. Current areas of interest in archive TV include BBC period drama, ITV children's programmes, and the works of Dennis Potter.

Formula Sleuthing with Four Just Men

Louise Penn

I will open this view of *The Four Just Men* by giving a bit of a potted history of my own archive television interests and viewing.

I'm a Seventies child.

I came to the archive television world not through the usual channels of *Doctor Who* or *The Avengers* (the former I can take or leave, the latter I have grown to love), but through the rather more prosaic route of the period drama. Dickens, Austen, Eliot, Brontë and, yes, Catherine Cookson were my authors of choice.

I'm basically an archive telly geek, and there isn't much I won't give a fair hearing to. In many years of DVD buying, grey market viewing, and BFI Mediatheque squinting, the only failures I can count are *Clayhanger*, *Jennie - Lady Randolph Churchill*, and sadly, as I loved it as a child, *Agony*.

Alongside the costume pieces I loved I also grew up in 1970s ITC land. *The Persuaders!*, *The Champions*, *Return of the Saint* (Ian Ogilvy was 'my' Simon Templar, not Roger Moore), *The Protectors*. And of course, *The New Avengers*. Glossy action series with superpowers, a touch of romance, and a hefty dose of anything but reality.

The earlier ITC series were of the same stamp; they didn't have the energy and (perhaps) fuller budgets of the later shows, but they have a certain charm. And the fact that I am viewing them through grown-up eyes makes them all the more interesting. Meeting Sir Francis Drake, the Pimpernel, Dan Tempest, William Tell and Robin Hood has been quite a television education.

These were the chaps who were in historical garb but also went that bit further into what might be described as 'boy's own' action territory, and it was all over the television from those early days, and in the comics we read as well. There's no surprise that the ITC action series gripped the imagination right from the very start, and for those of us who grew up with the witty repartee, the well-choreographed fight scenes, and the sassy females of the later material, they represented an escapism lacking from other material of the day (this was when *Coronation Street* still ran on

Northern grit, and where *Play for Today* was the high watermark of the single play).

I'm also deeply interested in classic Hollywood cinema, especially noir and musicals, which brings me to one of the draws of this particular title.

One of the series which attempted multinational casting in a detective milieu, *The Four Just Men* was only really of interest to me to start with as it featured an interesting cast as 'the gang of four' including old-time Hollywood hoofer and sometime screen hard man Dan Dailey (1915-1978), reliable leading British player Jack Hawkins (1910-1973), solid American Richard Conte (1910-1975), and the touch of European exotica in the mix, suave Italian Vittorio de Sica (1901-1974). All of them were making their first appearances in a television series.

The series was programmed to a strict formula: other than in the initial introductory episode, where the quartet were exhorted to 'do good' in the dying wish of their former commanding officer from military days, only one of the four was centre stage to each case (although one of the others might occasionally make a cameo appearance or be on the other end of a telephone). Each amateur sleuth has an aide de camp, usually female, to help them out. These number the gloriously husky-voiced and pre-*Avengers* Honor Blackman (1925-), nice English rose June Thorburn (1931-1967), efficient Lisa Gastoni (1935-) and, er, strident Andrew Keir (1926-1997).

Serving to help or hinder the main man, each assistant has their role in a sequence of basic and underwritten plots based on the sequence of 'Four Men' novels by Edgar Wallace. These episodes are mini-B features, 1950s quota quickies with simplistic characters, stereotypical writing, and a whole lot of escapism. The assistants themselves are surprisingly fleshed out for a show which certainly thrived on a quick turnaround, and it is clear why Blackman in particular soon found lasting fame as Cathy Gale and Pussy Galore.

Who cares if it is unlikely that MP Ben Manfred (Hawkins) would be solving other people's problems in far-flung places when he probably couldn't even remember where his constituency was? Are we really that bothered about reporter Tim Collier's (Dailey) crime-busting skills when we can instead watch him make sparks fly with his girlfriend Nicole? And the elegant hotelier Ricco Poccari (de Sica) will always have secretary and butler (Robert Rietti) to make sure he doesn't put an expensive foot wrong while his businesses doubtless go to the wall, while academic Jeff Ryder (Conte) has clearly never spent time hunched over an ill-lit desk marking student assignments.

The series is based in four countries and spent a lot of time and money on location work, but despite some picture postcard photography, this isn't reflected in what we see on screen. Although the quick-rolling production line of making multiple episodes at once is reflected in the writing, it is no worse than other attempts of the same period such as *The Adventures of the Scarlet Pimpernel* (1956) or *Sherlock Holmes* (1954), which were cheap, cheerful and rather charming.

What is interesting to me as an archive TV watcher (and I'll mainly watch anything, on the grounds that if it is old it must be interesting and if it is interesting it must be worthwhile), is the number of supporting cast appearances. Frank Thornton seems to pop up a lot in a variety of roles. Dudley Foster, Patrick Troughton, Toke Townley, Oliver Reed, Donald Pleasence, Charles Gray, Robert Shaw, Paul Eddington, Kenneth Connor, William Mervyn, Ronald Allen, Jane Asher, Alan Bates and Judi Dench are all familiar faces which appear in *The Four Just Men*, and it is the sheer joy of enjoying these fledgling appearances which make sitting through the weaker entries in the series worthwhile.

Over the thirty-nine episodes we see a variety of cases and mysteries unfold. Ben Manfred has to deal with a traitor in France, an army deserter, a diplomatic crisis, an art forger, bogus Nazi sympathisers, money laundering, secret agents, saboteurs and a displaced orphan. Tim Collier's work leads him to a foiled assassination, a jewellery thief, radioactivity, a mysterious potential murderer, blackmail, a mad confessor, family honour, kidnap, and bullfighting.

Jeff Ryder's legal brain is put to the test with mob rule, an angry hostage, radiation, a dodgy doctor, a missing plane, more insanity, molestation, riots, and gangsters. And Ricco Poccari is puzzled by more art fraud, more jewel thieves, more blackmail, another traitor, a slave market, a racketeer and a whistleblower who ends up murdered.

A third of the episodes were directed by Ealing Studios alumnus Basil Dearden, with the remainder shared between Don Chaffey, Harry Watt, William Fairchild, Anthony Bushell, and – just once – Compton Bennett. Although inspired by the stories of Wallace, as was the 1939 film of the same name, it has very little in common with that piece, other than the coming together of four individuals (played by Hugh Sinclair, Griffith Jones, Edward Chapman and Frank Lawton) who unite to work in secret against the enemies of Britain following the Great War. The 1939 film was directed by Walter Forde, who was a contemporary of Dearden's at Ealing between the wars.

How does the television series stand up these days, and does it fit into my own personal archive collecting and watching? I find its brevity and rushed plots a bonus when considering what to slot into a half-hour of viewing which requires no thought or real engagement (for comparison, I might point to the *Tales of the Unexpected* series (Anglia, 1979-1988) or the run of *NBC Mystery Movie* from the 1970s, bringing the likes of *McCloud, Columbo, Banacek, Quincy, ME,* and another crime series starring Dan Dailey, *Faraday and Company*, to the screen.

As a piece of entertainment, I like it. As a throwback to the history of British, Hollywood and Italian feature film making, I like it. I particularly treasure Honor Blackman's role in which she seems to steal every scene she is in: a definite star in the making. The mysteries and their solutions may be sometimes a little laboured, but the writing – within time limitations – is assured.

I bought the Network DVD on the strength of the names involved and the fact that some of the cases sounded intriguing: indeed, leaving aside the brevity of the plotting and the perfunctory nature of the characterisations, this is not a bad series by any means, although I find the Dailey and Hawkins stories the most successful.

For me, *The Four Just Men* has been unjustly neglected and sidelined when it has much to offer. It has earned its place in my own collection. Indeed, having the opportunity and ability to see these series on home media (not just this one, but also the likes of *Interpol Calling*) gives a glimpse into what passed as entertainment in the 1950s and 1960s. I'm a big fan of what was going on across the Atlantic, in the likes of *Five Star Playhouse* and *Alfred Hitchcock Presents* and these Brit originals fitted in perfectly.

Danger Man

1960-1968

Rachael Baez is a library technician who works at a school by the sea. She discovered *The Prisoner* and Patrick McGoohan through a friend and has never looked back. She also loves the sound of cats purring, plants, road-trips, science fiction, vinyl records and thrift shops. Rachael resides in Australia with her husband and two charming cats.

Matt Courtman has been a fan of *Danger Man* since childhood and has run the *Danger Man* website since the late Nineties. His hobbies include collecting and sharing original *Danger Man* related memorabilia, especially magazine articles from the Sixties. He also enjoys going off the beaten track to find and photograph *Danger Man* filming locations for his website. An IT operations manager and computer programmer by trade, he lives in Cambridgeshire with his long-suffering wife and young daughter, whom he hopes will be one of the next generation of *Danger Man* fans.

Tina Jerke leads a very active fantasy life as a travelling researcher, and she hopes to be able one day to combine her passion for British theatre and television with the more mundane routines of her daily existence, which include editing, translating, and occasionally composing, scholarly articles on both classical and modern (literary) history. Working from her home office underneath a very busy flight path for Frankfurt Airport, she is keenly aware of the dual blessing in the location being a gateway to the wonderland of past and present theatrical delights, as well as a major hub for plane spotters and aviation enthusiasts – who happen to share her other lifelong fascination with the actual contraptions that help her turn at least some of those flights of fancy into unforgettable real-life adventures.

Linda Kunkle Schley is a retired business owner and musician. Growing up with '60s and '70s television in the USA she never was exposed to the shows originating in the UK. In 2009 she discovered Patrick McGoohan and decided to give him a bit of a study, collecting everything that was available on DVD including *The Prisoner* and both series of *Danger Man*. She continues to enjoy retirement, exploring local antique and thrift shops, lovingly restoring a mid-century home, plus keeping track of three feline vagabonds and gallivanting about the Sierras with her husband of 35 years.

The View from My Villa

Rachael Baez

> *"Every government has its secret service branch: America, it's CIA; France, Deuxième Bureau; England, MI5. NATO also has its own. A messy job? Well, that's when they usually call on me, or someone like me. Oh yes, my name is Drake, John Drake."*

The first time I heard those words coming from my television was not in 1960, when the show first aired, but in 2013, some 53 years later, when I first discovered the wonders of *Danger Man* and Patrick McGoohan.

Prior to that, my knowledge of Patrick McGoohan was limited to seeing him steal the show as Edward Longshanks in *Braveheart* and as evil Roger Devereau in the 1976 comedy *Silver Streak*. I had no idea my newfound interest was going to have such a profound impact on me.

Fast forward to July 2013 – winter holidays in Australia. I had a week off work and I was looking for some quality shows to inspire me. I was in need of something different and that show definitely came about in the form of *The Prisoner*. A friend at work who I spoke to on a regular basis about our favourite shows said, "There's one I think you'd like – it's about a spy who quits his job but gets kidnapped because of what he knows and is taken to a creepy village and he can't escape."

My initial response to this promising synopsis was confusion. "But if he's a spy… surely he'd find a way out… Isn't that what spies do?"

After several minutes of him attempting to explain the plot synopsis without spoilers, he finally finished with, "Just watch it. Trust me, you'll love it."

So, going on blind faith and a flimsy understanding of what it was all about, I went ahead and watched the first episode. To say I was blown away would be a massive understatement. I'd never seen anything like it before. After that first viewing, I sat for a moment, speechless. I looked at the DVD cover to check the date of the show's production. 1967!?! Unlike most TV shows produced in the 1960s this didn't have that familiar, dated veneer and often wooden acting. This show was fully imagined, intensely colourful and wildly surreal. I felt as though I was going on a ride and I needed to buckle up. After viewing several episodes back-to-back and realising it was way past my usual bedtime, I sat with my mind buzzing with possibilities. This was *too good*! I felt as though I'd stumbled across a unicorn in a barren TV wasteland… and I needed *more.*

I also needed to know more about the brains behind this brilliant creation and it was then I discovered the amazing man that was Patrick McGoohan. My research odyssey began in earnest at 3.00am on a cold July morning. I was never to be the same.

A few days later, when I re-emerged from my DVD binge-watching and finding - everything - on - Patrick - McGoohan - and - *The - Prisoner* research odyssey (I'm a library technician by trade, so this stuff is in my blood), I went straight to the local video store and found there was *more* in the form of a show called *Danger Man*. In fact, there were lots and lots and lots of *Danger Man* DVDs to choose from. Here I was, in my humble local video store, in the midst of a veritable glitter-shower of Patrick McGoohan goodness, and I stood and marvelled at the fact that a few days earlier I'd been living in universe where none of these wonders had even existed! It was one of the happiest discoveries of my life.

The Patrick McGoohan of the first episode of *Danger Man – View from the Villa* – was certainly a very different man from the one who appeared in *The Prisoner*. I was intrigued to know how it all began and how as a performing artist he got from Point A to Point B and beyond. The early episodes of *Danger Man* were 25 minutes long, shot in beautiful noir-style black and white, complete with dramatic long shadows and an air of Cold War paranoia. It complimented the tone and genre perfectly and everything about it exuded class – the exotic locations, the stylish clothes, the plots and dialogue, which was witty, polite and often amusing. Most of all, it was the main attraction – Patrick McGoohan – that drew me in. I was completely hooked.

At six foot two inches with a lean athletic build and the most beautiful cerulean blue eyes, McGoohan's John Drake moved with grace and agility. He inhabited the role and his many other undercover characters-within-characters with an easy charm. It was no surprise that Patrick McGoohan was chosen for the role by Lew Grade and Ralph Smart. Although the producers of the show had a completely different idea for the character – a sleek, handsome, but cold agent who did the job by any means necessary, using an array of gadgets and guns, and not before seducing a few beautiful women on the way. It does indeed sound like another familiar and iconic character of the era.

McGoohan, however, had envisioned the character as a role model and didn't want to just appeal to one demographic, but to the whole family and was keenly aware of the invasive role TV was beginning to have on influencing the minds of younger viewers.

> *"Television is not just for selective audiences – it's for everyone. It's an intruder in people's homes – and as a guest, should behave accordingly."*
>
> **Patrick McGoohan**
>
> *TV Week Magazine, November 13th 1965*

To say that his own moral beliefs and standards were steering the character of John Drake – as it has often been reported many times over the years – is to be way too simplistic. Having the foresight to take an unconventional risk with a character and not rely on popular and somewhat overused plot devices for the genre (girls and guns) was, for me as a viewer, a refreshing change. I greatly admired this man as a creator and a deep thinker, someone who was willing to go against the grain and do something radical despite the fact that the genre already had a successful formula.

Instead of guns, the character used his wits and ingenuity to succeed in his various missions around the world. Seeing McGoohan's admirable fighting skills during the many bare-knuckled action scenes not only made the show more exciting and watchable, it also made Drake's character more human. He knew the bad guys were bad – but he'd rather see them face justice in a fair fight than an easy death at the end of a gun.

McGoohan also insisted that Drake was not going to be involved in steamy weekly trysts with the female characters in the show. This idea particularly horrified TV executives but McGoohan stood firm on his condition, saying that:

> *"These romantic entanglements are okay for the movies, I guess. But with TV, children or grandmothers might by some chance see the scenes. That would be a bad influence on them."*
>
> **Patrick McGoohan**
>
> *TV Week Magazine, November 13th 1965*

Danger Man's female guest stars, excused of their function of love interest (although I can't help but think there were many disappointed actresses who scored roles) were given a rare opportunity in 1960s episodic television to be interesting, dimensional and actually have purpose in driving the story forward. Drake treated his female counterparts with admiration and respect – odd for the times, yet surprisingly effective, to add interest to characters other than Drake. Female characters not used as mere padding in a time when it was not only common but expected… more things to thank Patrick McGoohan for.

Actresses who worked with him in early *Danger Man* episodes have cited positive experiences and worked with him again, including Angela Browne, who stated:

> *"Well, I was in a play in the West End and I got sent this television script – Danger Man. 'What's this?' I said. Nice part; it was called The Girl in the Pink Pyjamas, and I was the girl in the pink pyjamas. I remember I had to stagger across a wasteland somewhere up in Elstree in pink pyjamas on a freezing cold day. But when I met Patrick – he wasn't so well known then, he'd done a couple of films – I wasn't a fan of his at all, but actually, I fell in love with him; I just adored him and he was so kind to me. I was a kid. I was 21, and he took over the lighting I remember. There was a scene where I had to be lying there, rescued from some terrible situation. I was lying there, thinking, 'What a lovely man,' and between takes he was saying, 'Get more light there, get more shadow there'. He was actually lighting it - at a time when he wasn't actually in charge of anything; he was just the actor. And I loved him from that moment on. So when I was asked to do The Prisoner, I said, 'Oh, yes please!'"*
>
> **Angela Browne**
>
> *Interviewed by Dave Jones, transcribed by Dave Healey*
>
> https://www.theunmutual.co.uk/interviewsbrowne.htm

That's not to say that other women never noticed how wonderful he was… or us for that matter. I say 'us' because, out of being a fan of all things Patrick McGoohan, I've made some great friendships with other fans around the world. What came about as a casual chat online about an episode McGoohan appeared in, has evolved into a three-year message thread of almost daily chatting with two friends from other sides of the globe.

With discussions concerning anything from McGoohan collectables, his sartorial splendour, to episode quotes, incidental music or camera angles, we've shared many late-night and early morning banter sessions, depending on what world time-zones allow. To us, Patrick McGoohan and *Danger Man* are an endless source of inspired discussion and enjoyment in re-watching episodes with friends. To me, it's sharing the legacy of an underrated visionary with fans who have a common admiration. Although he's no longer with us and I never had an opportunity to meet him, I hope, wherever he is in the universe, he knows how truly admired he was.

Patrick McGoohan – you will always be our Number 1.

Fish on the Hook

Matt Courtman

Back in 1992 I was just eleven and late one evening whilst watching television in my bedroom an episode of *The Prisoner* was shown as part of Frank Muir's *TV Heaven*. The episode was *The Girl Who Was Death*. I was mesmerised, and the following Saturday my mum drove me into town and I purchased two video cassette tapes of *The Prisoner* from Woolworths. I remember watching the tapes as soon as I returned home and being somewhat disappointed as the episode *Checkmate* was so different to the episode I had watched earlier in the week. Regardless, I watched the other episodes and soon became hooked, which was surprising as one of them was *It's Your Funeral*!

Soon after becoming a *Prisoner* fan I discovered *Danger Man*, which was being shown on Sunday afternoons on the Bravo channel. I remember eagerly waiting for the first episode and can vividly recall my excitement that Portmeirion was used as a filming location. Every week I would watch the half-hour episodes without fail, then the longer episodes were shown midweek whilst I was at school, and so had to be videotaped. Back in the early Nineties recording a programme from Sky TV was not straightforward and quite often the first or last five minutes of an episode would be missed when the previous programme overran, or my mum had forgotten that the Sky box would need to be left powered on and on the correct channel (and not the shopping channel QVC).

Most children look forward to school finishing, but now I had even more reason to get home, so I could watch the next episode. I instantly preferred the longer episodes with the distinctive *High Wire* theme tune and catchy opening sequence. I also remember how excited I was when I loaded the cassette tape and *Danger Man* appeared in colour, although as only two colour episodes were made, my excitement was short lived. I was now watching McGoohan playing a secret agent in colour and this reminded me of *The Girl Who Was Death*. I had come full circle.

For a short time during my teenage years I joined the Six of One appreciation society and enjoyed reading the materials that arrived each quarter. Now, in the early Nineties the internet existed but was too complicated, too expensive and too unreliable for the average person. I can remember the noise of the modem dialling up only not to connect and, when it did, text and pictures would take an age to load. Midway through browsing, the connection would drop and you'd have to start over. It was a faff and really, there wasn't that much on the internet anyway at that time, so I found the early Six of One publications a good way of communicating with other like-minded people.

The classified section was particularly useful and I remember purchasing, amongst other things, three Six of One *Danger Man* magazines which I still have today. Listed in these magazines were the 86 episode titles and pictures of some of the memorabilia that was originally released with the series. Now this may not seem a big thing, but back then this information was gold dust. I started visiting second-hand book shops trying to find copies of the *Danger Man* novels and annuals and soon began to amass quite a collection.

At school my favourite subject was IT, so in 1997 when I started college I chose to take an A-Level in Computer Science. Part of the course involved programming and website design and in my spare time I decided to create a personal website as I could see the potential of the World Wide Web. I wanted to bring together – and more importantly share – all the information I had gathered on *Danger Man*, *The Prisoner*, Patrick McGoohan and Portmeirion.

At the time my internet connection was provided by Freeserve and this came with a few megabytes of webspace and did what I needed. But before long I had to upgrade and buy more webspace – and not long after I purchased the danger-man.co.uk domain name.

Over the next couple of years I completed my A-Levels and went on to study Computer Science at University. During this time the internet bloomed. Websites like eBay now allowed me to search for *Danger Man* related memorabilia from around the world. At this time there was no PayPal and I fondly remember posting off American Dollars to pay for my latest eBay purchases, none of which ever got lost in the post!

I would update my website (http://danger-man.co.uk/) as I gathered more information and memorabilia, which was almost weekly. I added more and more content on Portmeirion, including a virtual tour, added additional pages on related topics such as Sir Clough Williams-Ellis, and before long my website had snowballed. But my efforts were worth it. I regularly received emails from fellow fans from around the world thanking me for my website. Some even contributed to the site by emailing me their stories, scans of magazine articles and photos. I had achieved what I set out to do; the *Danger Man* website had become a repository of information for all to see, worldwide.

As I grew so did my passion for the series, partly because with age I now understood and appreciated the storylines more. The same is true with *The Prisoner*. I am now a similar age to McGoohan when he reprised his role as Drake and I often think about what Drake might be doing whilst I'm doing the normal nine to five grind.

To be brutally honest I don't think I've ever watched another television series that comes close to the quality of *Danger Man*. Not only was it very well acted by McGoohan and a host of famous actors (many of whom went onto star in *The Prisoner*), but the storylines were relevant and believable unlike some you might see on television today. I am quite fond of other TV series of the time, such as *The Avengers* and *The Saint*, but find some episodes a bit too 'out there'. In comparison, I find *Danger Man* (on the whole) to be more straightcut and sensible, whilst not being any less entertaining and enjoyable.

Around 2010 I decided to revamp my website. There were now many other websites on the internet which focused on *The Prisoner* or Portmeirion which I couldn't compete with. As my passion was with *Danger Man* I decided to focus mainly on that series – also there were no other websites dedicated to *Danger Man* that I could find. Therefore, I thinned out the content, keeping the site true to its title. I also redesigned the layout and colour scheme as I felt it looked somewhat amateur. A colleague of mine was good with Photoshop and he helped recreate the *Danger Man* logo which I use to this day. It was also around this time when I first contacted Rick Davy of The Unmutual website (http://www.theunmutual.co.uk/), suggesting that we became sister-sites. Ever since, we have shared links and information and become good friends.

Most TV series have episodes that stand out either for being especially good or for being downright terrible. Anyone who has visited my *Danger Man* website will soon have discovered that I have an obsession with the last black and white episode to be made, *Not So Jolly Roger*. This is mainly because I like obscure Sixties music and this episode is centred on a pirate radio station. My wife will confirm that finding copies of the obscure songs heard in the episode (which were specially written for it by Rick Minas and Mike Banwell), has at times taken over my life. I have spent many hours sending emails, making phone calls, trawling the internet for information about the music used in this episode without much success, until a few years back when Mike Banwell contacted me and luckily still had some of the original recordings on acetates.

Many other episodes stand out. I particularly like *The Black Book* in which Drake befriends and ends up helping a blackmailer. There is a glimpse of chemistry between Drake and Simone (Georgina Ward). I almost wanted, urged in fact, Drake to run away with her. The almost haunting music by Edwin Astley really sets the mood of the episode.

One of the better known episodes is *Colony Three*, in which Drake assumes the identity of Robert Fuller (Peter Jesson), a civil servant who is about to defect. Drake is taken across the iron curtain to Hamden New Town, which resembles a typical English town with red buses, phone boxes and all the normal amenities. In reality, Hamden is a training camp for foreign spies to become more 'British' in order to blend in and infiltrate the western world. *Colony Three* is considered to be a precursor to *The Prisoner*; people with specialist knowledge taken to a faraway secret village to be moulded or have information extracted. The similarities mean the episode appeals to *Prisoner* fans, as it is possible this influenced McGoohan and led to the creation of *The Prisoner*.

Other episodes worthy of note include *Don't Nail Him Yet, Fair Exchange, The Professionals, A Room in the Basement, It's Up to the Lady, That's Two of Us Sorry, The Outcast* and *No Marks for Servility. The Battle of the Cameras* is another great episode, where Drake's flamboyant playboy style is more reminiscent of that of James Bond. One episode, *The Ubiquitous Mr Lovegrove,* divided opinion when it was first broadcast, so much so that viewers wrote in to complain. The story starts with Drake having a car accident and the rest of the story is the nightmarish dream within Drake's concussed mind. I confess that I had to watch it a couple of times before I fully appreciated the concept, but now find it a very enjoyable episode which would probably appeal to fans of *The Avengers* as it's by far the most 'wacky' of the *Danger Man* episodes.

Even I have to admit that there are some episodes that let the series down. *A Very Dangerous Game* is one of my least favourites; it has far too many gadgets, some of which are laughable. Although it's nice to see *Danger Man* in colour, I find *Koroshi* and *Shinda Shima* a bit dull. It is noticeable that McGoohan's heart wasn't really in these episodes, probably as he was eager to end *Danger Man* and move on to *The Prisoner*. But three bad episodes out of 86 isn't bad going.

Danger Man was filmed at MGM Borehamwood and, later, at Shepperton Studios and many episodes featured some 'on location' filming. One of my hobbies is to visit these locations. I've had some interesting holidays in North Wales looking for side roads, bridges and footpaths that might have once doubled for a border on the iron-curtain. I'm amazed at how some of these remote locations were originally discovered by the production team. I'm also grateful that many still exist and are identifiable, mostly thanks to Anthony McKay's wonderful *A Guide to Avengerland* website (http://avengerland.theavengers.tv/). One of my favourite locations is Penmon Priory in Anglesey, which featured in the episode *That's Two of Us Sorry*. I have taken my family on holiday many times to Beaumaris, Anglesey, so that I could make the pilgrimage to the Priory. Another location that I am fond of is Red Sands Forts in the Thames Estuary, which featured in *Not So Jolly Roger*. I remember writing a letter to Patrick McGoohan in 2008 in which I asked him if he remembered filming at the forts. To my absolute amazement, I received a reply a few weeks later in which he described the forts *"as an abandoned, miserable, faintly-haunted rusting place, difficult to access..."* There went any chance of me convincing my wife that Red Sands Forts would be good for our next holiday!

One thing I am often asked is whether I believe *The Prisoner* is a sequel to *Danger Man*. As this is a question which divides opinion and causes fierce debate (sometimes quite nasty) I'm always careful to avoid giving a straight answer. However for the purposes of this article I'll break my silence...

In some of the later hour-long episodes of *Danger Man* Drake is clearly unhappy with his superiors and some of the things he is required to do. In *To Our Best Friend* Drake has to investigate whether his friend is a double-agent, which puts a strain on that friendship. In *The Man on the Beach* Drake is himself suspected of being a traitor and has to run from his fellow M9 agents. Over the 47 hour-long episodes Drake becomes more sensitive, more compassionate. In *Yesterday's Enemies* he is horrified that a double-agent is killed when Drake gave his personal word that he would be safe. He is also ageing and in a few episodes shows more interest in the opposite sex (though nothing to the degree of Bond). Therefore, given these developments it could be quite feasible that Drake was becoming fed up and was contemplating resignation.

Number 6 has clearly resigned from a top secret job; he wasn't a mechanic, teacher or road sweeper. He can fly a helicopter, knows Morse code, can navigate a plane, all the kind of stuff that a secret agent might know. There are many references, such as in *Do Not Forsake Me Oh My Darling*, when Janet asks her father if he has sent her fiancé away on a mission. In my mind there is no doubt that Number 6 was a secret agent before his resignation.

Whether the two characters are the same, who can say? But for me there are too many similarities for them not to be. Will we ever know for sure? I doubt it. Does it really matter? Not to me. Will the question be asked again? For sure!

I do believe that *Danger Man* would have been a completely different programme if Patrick McGoohan hadn't been cast as Drake. McGoohan adapted the role to fit with his personal beliefs and for me this is what distinguishes the character of Drake from others such as Bond. I would much rather have the integrity and qualities of Drake than Bond.

The success of *The Prisoner* has somewhat overshadowed *Danger Man*. Ask people what television programme Patrick McGoohan starred in and most will say "the one with the balloon". Even some die-hard *Prisoner* fans have no idea who Drake is. But be thankful for *Danger Man*, as it made McGoohan a household name and without its success, *The Prisoner* would likely never have existed.

For me at least, though, McGoohan will always be John Drake.

Yesterday's Heroes

Tina Jerke

John Drake did not come into my life as the result of well-meaning parental indoctrination (or indeed prohibition), nor through the sheer lack of choice in the televisual wasteland of West Germany in the 1970s – even though my early childhood viewing habits did condition me for a life-long love affair with 'classic' British television, as defined by the available selection of ITC re-runs. Programmes like *The Saint*, *The Persuaders!*, and *Space: 1999* sat happily alongside assorted American imports and helped shape my young impressionable mind with their distinct 1960s / early 1970s visual style and their air of adventure and foreign intrigue.

By the mid-Eighties I was the proud owner of a shelf load of VHS boxes but it was not until the 1990s that I found *The Prisoner* missing from the collection, and the DVD set was duly added. That addition, for *some* reason, did not fit in quite as easily with the rest of the gang I had accumulated. I was intrigued enough to invest in yet another new format, although it was by no means an instant upgrade. When the Blu-rays finally did land in my virtual shopping basket, and the fully automated checkout algorithm suggested I "might also like" a related product, this fully informed customer needed no further encouragement. Yes, I am an adult convert, and a fairly late one at that who took the detour via that *other* series – to discover a whole new playground that was at once exactly what I had been looking for and different enough to tickle my imagination – even and especially when I thought I just needed a "quick fix".

Today, John Drake is still good for all that and more: the episodic 'secret agent' format still works, and will always work, but our relationship has grown more complex over the years, as I've continued to indulge my two childhood obsessions of live theatre and 1960s television. Perhaps I should have known that the deeper I would immerse myself in my two hobbies the more connections I would see between the two worlds of traditional and 'electronic' entertainment. I should not have been surprised to find the ties especially strong with *Danger Man*, where the theatrical heritage can be observed not only in the personnel, presentation, working practices, and performances, or perhaps even the occasional convenient / gratuitous use of a West End location, but it is woven into the fabric of the show itself, and into the central character's very essence.

If I had to pick one episode to illustrate the point, it would have to be *Yesterday's Enemies*, which manages to combine all of the above bread-and-butter aspects of the routine production with a self-consciously theatrical quality that is, for one thing, directly addressed in the light-hearted subplot that runs beneath and through the sinister serious tale of the veteran agent turned rogue entrepreneur: the British expat community, including embassy staff members, spies, and their spouses, are staging an amateur production of an Agatha Christie-type murder mystery, and none other than Joan Hickson suggests Drake play the part of the "handsome stranger".

Perfect casting indeed, but it is Drake's self-conscious and exceedingly polite response to the impossible request which adds a layer of irony to the situation that the other characters couldn't possibly be aware of but that we as the external audience can appreciate: "I'm sorry, I'm no actor," is a classic paradox which draws attention to itself as a fictional construct; it communicates both with the other actors in the scene as well as with the audience beyond the footlights – or in this case, the viewers in their living rooms. It is this act of collusion between the actors and their audience which has always intrigued me about live theatre because it acknowledges the existence of the audience and invites their participation. Nothing could appeal more to this member of the audience than to be asked to play an active part in the experience – which is what live theatre does: with every single performance we agree to suspend our disbelief.

We know we are sitting in a darkened room and we are about to be told a fairy tale. We can see the stage, the lights, the curtains the fake scenery, yet we agree to go along with the experiment; we acknowledge and accept the conventions of theatrical story-telling. This pact demands that we ignore the plywood and the lighting grid on the ceiling. Television to an extent eliminated that part of the bargain by hiding the stage craft from our view but what if – not by conscious design – the studio rigging does become visible? This also happens in *Yesterday's Enemies*, and rather than destroying what is not a perfect illusion to begin with, the happy accident for me is a reminder of my own complicity. No, the famous fourth wall is never broken, but I am in on the joke, and it is a remarkable privilege rarely granted by modern TV productions whose definitions of realism vastly differ from the *conventional* approach.

However, the privilege we enjoy, of being able to step outside the fictional world, is not shared by Drake, and this is the third theatrical tie: Drake's mission is to *perform*. His assigned task defines the character; Drake is never off duty. He may be able to refuse the part of the handsome stranger in the blithely self-referential play within a play, but he has no choice in the hand that he is being dealt by his superiors and, of course, the writer. He has been tasked with finding the mole in the organization and neutralising the threat, at any cost. To that end he impersonates, in rapid succession, a journalist, a Board of Trade investigator, a clueless fellow agent and fearless enemy, a physician and an unwitting executioner before he finally takes on the role of the liaison officer who must deliver the ultimate performance and tell a fairy tale to the grieving widow. Drake risks his life in the performance of his task as he walks back into the villain's trap. At the precise moment of Drake's realization that he will have to sacrifice himself in the performance of his duty, the studio ceiling is revealed and, magically, the apparent accident takes nothing away from the *drama* of the situation.

I know I ought to confess at this point to a certain bias for the 'old' way of doing things. My sense of nostalgia will override questions of plausibility or plot development any time, but I cannot deny the sheer pleasure I have since childhood derived from actors and acting, in the simplest, most basic form and my earliest viewing habits have certainly shaped my preferences. What we now describe as "classic" television, that decade and a half when the medium was itself still in its infancy and heavily, self-consciously, dependent on the steady supply of theatrical expertise while developing a set of distinct techniques of its own, to my mind captures – and preserves – the best of both worlds. Of all my beloved ITC heroes, John Drake is the one who most faithfully embodies that bold, adventurous era of transition. Ultimately, I suppose, it could be argued that it was *The Prisoner* which marked the next logical step in the emancipation of the medium, and its hero.

Better Late Than Never

Linda Kunkle Schley

In the autumn of 2009, totally by chance, I lighted on an evening airing of several episodes of Patrick McGoohan's '60s television show *The Prisoner*. More episodes would be broadcast over the following weeks to refresh and perk interest in the new rendition of *The Prisoner* that would premiere in November 2009.

I was ten years old when the original series aired and along the way had never been exposed to it or to what has become known to many as its predecessor, the spy series that starred McGoohan as John Drake, *Danger Man* (or *Secret Agent* as it was known in the United States). I only had a vague idea of who McGoohan was: the warden in *Escape from Alcatraz* (1979), a baddie in *Silver Streak* (1976) and, way in the back of my mind, the father in *The Three Lives of Thomasina* (1963).

Immediately I took a liking to the show, but with the minor distractions of entertaining and caring for my 87 year old father, these evening broadcasts slipped by without me getting a good grasp of the series. Yet, I tuned in, focusing on the rather superficial aspect of Patrick McGoohan's often unruly hair. I became consumed with the study of it and, in time, I was hooked – mostly on the man – and a pretty huge crush ensued, which made me want to find out more about him as a person, his works and career. Much to my dismay, I discovered that he had died in January 2009.

I soon found myself on Amazon.com, and in a short time, I had *The Prisoner* and two box sets comprising the complete *Danger Man* series – 39 half-hours (1960-1962) and 47 hour long episodes (1964-1967). This would be an excellent place to begin my study.

Starting from the beginning, I watched late in the evening, free from interruptions, with headphones and an MP3 player perched on my chest. This method of viewing provided an up close, intimate and private experience. When I was not watching an episode, I read all I could find about the series, referring to the *Danger Man* website (http://danger-man.co.uk/) and to the only biography available at the time.

The more I studied, the more interesting the series became to me. There were many ways and levels to enjoy, from lessons in history to small glimpses of the future setting of *The Prisoner*. Snippets can be spotted in several episodes. With the facility of the pause and rewind function, the series can be scrutinised in a way never imagined at the time. Every detail of face or fabric, gestures, continuity errors were once all too fleeting and lost, but are now at our fingertips if we so desire.

The first thing that came to mind about *Danger Man* was "classic", which takes it right to Patrick McGoohan as John Drake. He sets the tone by his presence, demeanor, speech, chivalry, stature, attire, looks and conduct. It is obvious that Drake / McGoohan takes his job on and off screen seriously. This overflows to the other actors, the result creating a very worthwhile viewing experience.

I took notes on each episode, from plotlines, guests, writers and directors. I had never before studied a television series and it quickly became evident and fascinating to see the same names appear as cast and crew in his works before and after *Danger Man*. It seems clear that Patrick McGoohan forged long lasting and positive working relationships with his peers and was able to call on these people throughout his career.

Aside from the final two episodes, the series was filmed in black and white. This adds a certain timeless artsy quality, somehow befitting to the spy genre. The studio sets in back alleys and other unsavoury places are perfect, with the lighting and shadows creating a sort of action fantasy, adding to the mood, complete with fight scenes, mainly choreographed and performed by McGoohan himself. You come away with the feeling that he was enjoying himself and that he worked hard to make those moments convincing.

Another area where *Danger Man* stands out and holds its own, some fifty-five years after filming, is in its abundance of strong female characters, many on equal footing with John Drake. They range from scientist, CEO, nurse, spy, pilot, reporter, disc jockey, doctor, business owner and colleague – a most impressive list. A few episodes of note in this respect: *View from the Villa, The Sisters, The Contessa, Fair Exchange, Don't Nail Him Yet, Fish on the Hook* and many more.

Drake does not have on-screen love interests in the series, though a few are implied, for example in *Whatever Happened to George Foster?* and *You Are Not in Any Trouble, Are You?* This allows for more character and story development. The lack of frivolous relationships, merely thrown in for filler, is something the studio fought against, but McGoohan stood firm on this aspect of creative control, which in the end made the series much stronger and more believable, then and now. The lack of love interests in the series does not mean there is no sexual tension. If anything, this creates even more between Drake and his female counterparts on and off the screen. Along with more than abundant close-ups that seem to go on forever, Drake has my undivided attention.

As with the many close-ups, there are numerous instances that focus on him using his hands, from assembling a makeshift gun, a radio, tape recorder, to reading microfilm or decoding a message. McGoohan performs the tasks flawlessly under the pressure of time, lights and camera, bringing the viewer into the room. This special talent can be seen in *Not So Jolly Roger, Loyalty Always Pays, I'm Afraid You Have the Wrong Number* and *Koroshi / Shinda Shima*, but not in *Colony Three* with the typewriter repair. Most definitely a stand-in! In a similar vein, Drake makes lighting a cigarette or cigar and holding a drink look like an art form.

At the onset of the series, Drake looks young, fresh, even innocent, on the job with the enthusiasm of youth. As the series progresses, events transpire that are out of his control. He is manipulated by bosses and betrayed by members of his own side. He becomes cynical and begins to question his role and position. Drake is not a perfect agent. He makes mistakes which make him appear human and relatable. He has visible regret for some of his actions, things he cannot reverse.

For those who wish to link John Drake and Number 6 of *The Prisoner*, there is ample evidence pointing in that direction. This could be a study in itself, but I have not gone down that path. I would rather look at it as applying to all of us as we go from being wide-eyed and young to gaining experience and wisdom, which leads to a more realistic view of the world.

As I watch the series in broadcast order, I arrive at *Not So Jolly Roger* (one of my favorites), the final episode shot in black and white. I feel like a child on Sunday evening, dreading the school week to come. There are two more episodes remaining which can be watched separately or in movie form. These final two episodes, *Koroshi* and *Shinda Shima*, feel different from the rest of the series. They are filmed in color, there is a change in style – more fantastic, straying away from the core of what made the series great, from the musical score to the flashy, less believable plot. I say this to point out the negative, but these episodes still have merit and are very much worth viewing. You will see a Japanese tea ceremony, some Kabuki theatre, great fight scenes, a bit of swimming, and some lovely close-ups of those busy hands. You will meet Potter (Christopher Benjamin), who will later reappear in *The Prisoner*, Kenneth Griffith – who is featured in several episodes of *The Prisoner* – and finally Barbara Yu Ling, who crossed over to the next series, too.

By this time in the series, I feel that the heart and soul of its driving force has already moved on to his next project. Because of this, these episodes –

which should be the culmination of *Danger Man* – leave me feeling a bit empty... but *View from the Villa* is up next!

In summary, I love the show, mainly because Patrick McGoohan makes it something special. He set the bar and the rest fell into place. You can sit back and enjoy as pure entertainment, but if you choose to delve into the more intricate details, today's technology will help you do so. And finally, the best thing of all has to be the new friends from around the world that I have made along this journey. Almost sixty years and still having a positive impact on people's lives... I like to think Patrick McGoohan would be pleased.

The Saint

1962-1969

Sheena Samujh Born Blackpool, Lancashire, 1961. Lover and sometime student of the moving image in various manifestations, from zoetrope and early silent movies on, including among much else German Expressionism, film noir and 'B' movies, Hammer and Amicus horrors, and the occasional haunting dreamlike fantasy (*Malpertuis*, *Le Grand Meaulnes*), to television both recent and 'classic'. Vintage British television staples for me include many ITC series, chief among them *Danger Man* and *The Prisoner*, and *Man in a Suitcase*, as well as *The Saint*, one of the favourites of my dear late Dad, Andrew Gray, who died 26th April 2015. This is for you, 'Little Dad,' with love.

Greg Bakun is an Englishman trapped in an American's body. He is a seasoned connoisseur and reviewer of British television. For the past ten years he has been reviewing programmes and media connected to the genre at his blog *From the Archive: A British Television Blog* (www.from-the-archive.co.uk). Recently, Greg began a partnership with the British television preservation society Kaleidoscope to produce their podcast, creatively titled *From the Archive: A British Television Podcast* focusing on all aspects of the state of British television archives and missing episode content.

Knight in a Shining P1800

Sheena Samujh

Leslie Charteris' creation the gentleman-adventurer Simon Templar (also known as Sebastian Tombs, and more famously, The Saint) had been around for some years before he was portrayed by Roger Moore in the popular and long-running 1960s ITC series of 118 episodes over six seasons, between 1962 and 1969; the character first appeared in print in 1928, and became the subject of approaching a hundred books over a period exceeding 50 years, latterly written by others with approval from Charteris.

In my late teens I attempted to read some of the early Charteris *Saint* books, but abandoned this (never to return) as a bad job for various reasons, including the teeth-grindingly awful (in my opinion) portrayal of female characters, and the irritating sidekick Hoppy Uniatz (mercifully not in the '60s series for long), but mainly because I could not help regarding ITC's telly update featuring Roger Moore as Simon Templar as the 'proper' Saint, the one I watched excitedly with my late Dad on first transmission*, and the one I re-watched on DVD with him and Mum many years later, when Dad was disappearing into a fog of dementia, as a kind of reassuring, familiar visual comfort blanket (for us all).

* I should explain that this was from Season 5 (1966) onwards (the first colour season, which I remember in black and white, 'cos we didn't have a colour set until the '70s!) as I was a wee bit too young (honest) to see the earlier seasons when first broadcast... and it may not have been such a bad thing to see some of those early episodes considerably later; don't get me wrong, I think many of them are excellent and some of my favourites are from among those black and white seasons, however, the very first episode *The Talented Husband* is, in my view, a pretty eccentric start, featuring as it does Derek Farr in drag masquerading as possibly the least convincing Irish housekeeper *ever* – 'the Saint meets Old Mother Riley'... I concede that it does have a certain camp charm and Roger Moore and Shirley Eaton make an appealing team.

For me *The Saint* is among those precious television series which have miraculously survived from the '60s and '70s, never intended as anything more than transient diversions, that re-viewed have the power to trigger involuntary memory, transporting one, like a time machine or a magic carpet of the mind, to another time and place as effectively as the taste of cake dunked in a cup of tea does in *Swann's Way*, the first instalment of Marcel Proust's massive *À la recherche du temps perdu* – much more evocatively translated in my view by the literal *In Search of Lost Time* than the more traditional *Remembrance of Things Past* (a work more talked about than read in its entirety. Guilty! It is seven volumes, for pity's sake. Respect if you have persevered through the lot. By the way I am typing this in bed, how très Proustian).

As well as the personal emotional resonance some television can have for an individual due to its associations with particular places, times and people (I miss you, Dad), the social history aspect of TV and films in general from the early '60s when I was very young holds a fascination for me. How quickly the world seems to have changed in those 50 years since I was a small child in Blackpool, Lancashire. The Britain of the period of my birth and early childhood, as viewed in the black and white TV of the time, was a low tech one of high streets of small shops, relatively few cars and still some horse drawn vehicles, steam trains, no personal computers or tablets, no mobile phones, no CCTV, and few burglar alarms (making the occasional spot of essential burglary a lot more straightforward for the gentleman-adventurer than it would be today).

It was a world teeming with rigidly coiffed 'ladies' in fitted suits, gloves and court shoes, and carrying on most occasions a brick-like bulky dark leather hand bag weighing half a stone empty, or 'housewives' wearing shapeless floral dresses and headscarves, going out for groceries daily carrying wicker shopping baskets. The 'chaps' wore suits, overcoats and hats, and polished shoes – even on their days of leisure, taking the family out for the day, or going to a football match.

The Saint himself, as played by Roger Moore, a some-time model, was elegant at all times, even in a fishing sweater and wellies. He did not indulge in a lot of hat-wearing, and he seldom had a bad hair moment; following a vigorous punch-up with a ne'er-do-well, all it took was a casual sweep of the hand through the Templar locks, and his coiffure was once more immaculate.

Of course he also drove that amazing car, stylish but subtle, the sleek white Volvo P1800 with the ST1 plate; it looked very different from most of the cars of the time, and was an appropriate substitute for the dashing white charger of the idealised knight in medieval romances.

That world was also, in TV adventures anyway, one of clear moral divides, heroes and villains; good was good, bad was bad and generally the former still reassuringly triumphed. Even if Moore's Simon Templar (an anti-hero in the early Charteris books due to his habit of thieving from thieves and keeping the swag; he grew out of it) was regarded by some as a bit of a nogoodnik and had run-ins with the authorities, we knew that under the roguish exterior he was a good guy who sometimes had to resort to using the bad guys' own methods against them, the end justifying the means – spectacularly, for instance, in *The Careful Terrorist* (Season 1, episode 3) in which a homicidal, corrupt American union boss is deservedly hoist on his own petard, a bomb intended for Simon.

Fortunately for him, Simon Templar did not resemble his medieval namesakes too closely, an order of celibate, papally-sanctioned, mass murderers and proto-bankers who became extremely powerful, rich and influential in the 12th century, but came dramatically unstuck in the late 13th / early 14th when King Philip IV of France, in debt to them and envious of their wealth and power, turned on them and convinced / bullied the Pope to condemn them on trumped up charges of heresy and blasphemy, with predictably hideous results for many, which I will not dwell on here. If you are of a curious and enquiring frame of mind or have nothing more important to do, and crave to learn more about the history of the real Templars, and the way they have been (mis)represented in various media, I recommend you seek out on the Interweb thingy *Knight Life: Templariana – Knights Templar in Fact and Fiction* (http://www.silverwhistle.co.uk/knightlife/templariana.html), a site I came upon after watching Michael J. Bird's oddly cast (apart from Peter Egan, Michael Sheard, and a Greek actress called Betty) but weirdly compelling Rhodes-set 1980s mini-series *The Dark Side of the Sun* (end of lengthy digression from Simon – sorry!).

A favourite episode of mine in which the Saint definitely dominates the moral high ground, while tackling a *big* social issue, is *The Charitable Countess* (Season 1, episode 12), in which Simon counters a fraudulent charity campaign supposedly fund-raising for doe-eyed Roman street urchins living as beggars, induces a sense of shame in the perpetrators, and ensures a more fulfilling future for the snot-nosed little oiks / lovable cherubs (delete as preferred) than scavenging through the rubbish bins of the picturesque city of Stock Footage.

Which leads more or less smoothly on to... suspension of disbelief. Viewing as a small child, I believed *totally* that Roger Moore was really in all of the exotic locales in which the episodes were set. I was blissfully unaware that in the stock footage or back projected inserts the people were often dressed in outmoded styles and the vehicles were similarly well past their sell-by date, and I would neither have noticed nor cared that Simon on occasion disembarked at an airport from a plane other than the one we earlier on just about saw cruising above the grainy clouds. It did not bother me in the slightest that the taxis in which Simon travelled through crowded European cities frequently appeared to be floating a few feet above street level.

The 'exotic' locations (let's face it, not being my home town seemed exotic to me then), whether real or faux, were an exciting contrast with Blackpool. Oddly enough, Simon Templar never touched down in Blackpool in the course of one of his adventures – unlike defrosted Edwardian gentleman-adventurer Adam Adamant. Respect to Adam.

As I developed into a slightly more sophisticated television viewer, and became aware of the techniques (some more convincing than others) used to create an appropriate backdrop and a sense of the atmosphere of a location without actually travelling there, if anything spotting the fakery made favourite programmes even more entertaining and, re-viewing them now at a remove of many years, endearing. It can also be quite fun spotting the same familiar streets, panoramic cityscapes, or grainy aeroplanes used across different series.

While probably not strictly politically correct, a great deal of pleasure can also be had from the performances of stalwart Brit character actors as variously villainous or lovable incarnations of 'Johnny Foreigner', a phenomenon not, of course, restricted to *The Saint* (such representations were, ahem, 'of their time'); an outstanding example to relish from the Saint being gleefully over the top Warren Mitchell as greedy but (reluctantly) loyal Marco in three Italian-set episodes, with spray on five o'clock shadow and a one size fits all Greco-Italian-Spanish accent. Pure, er, class.

While we are still just about suspending disbelief… in 1966, I was five years old. And I can still recall being scared rigid by *The Convenient Monster* (Season 5, episode 6). This featured in the cast Suzan Farmer, Laurence Payne, Caroline Blakiston and Fulton Mackay, however it was not them that frightened the wits out of the five-year-old me, but the tale of a fake Loch Ness monster used as a cover for nefarious / bonkers activities under a nearby castle. The thing is, the episode actually has quite a convincing menacing atmosphere with mysterious foggy night-time beach scenes, monster footprints in the sand, and a *dead dog*! At that age, the violent death of something four-legged and furry in a television programme upset me far more than the death of a person. (Is that weird? Oh, well.)

I was so scared that, even now, just the mention of the title can produce a reflex frisson down the spine. How Proustian is that? And was there, in fact, a real monster lurking about in the depths all along, just biding its time? That ending... mmm? It is still one of my favourite episodes.

I will stop waffling on soon, but first a brief canter through a few more of my own favourite episodes from among the 118; some appeal due to storyline, some for the cast, and some 'just because':

~ *The Covetous Headsman* (Season 1, episode 4, 1962, B&W) – Barbara Shelley in danger in Paris, echoes of wartime intrigue, a genuine sense of threat, a long-separated sibling vainly hoping for a joyous reunion with her brother. Excellent stuff.

~ *The Russian Prisoner* (Season 5, episode 3, 1966, colour) – a defecting Russian academic in jeopardy in Switzerland, a 'fake daughter' plot, plus Yootha Joyce (shades of Rosa Klebb), Sandor Elès, Anthony Booth, and humorous but shrewd Swiss cop, Inspector Oscar Kleinhaus, played by the not klein Guy Deghy, returning from a Season 1 episode, *The Loaded Tourist.* A true character actor fest, this one.

~ *The Saint Plays with Fire* (Season 2, episode 11, 1963, B&W) – neo-Nazis, Justine Lord, and one of my character actor faves, Tony Beckley, always great in my opinion whatever he was in. Long gone, and sadly way too young (at 50, in 1980 to a malignant illness; apparently possibly an early AIDS casualty but this was before anyone really knew what AIDS was, so it is not certain). Tony Beckley also appeared earlier in Season 2 in episode 6, *Marcia*, but I prefer this one; I like this episode *just because.* So there.

~ *The King of the Beggars* (Season 2, episode 9, 1963, B&W) – back to the historic city of Stock Footage / Rome, with Maxine Audley, Oliver Reed and Warren Mitchell (again); this time the story involves a protection racket. More beggars! More Warren! (Mitchell here reprises his Season 1 role from *The Latin Touch* and *The Charitable Countess* as the colourful local character Marco). And young Ollie Reed! What more can one say?

Finally, I just have to include a mention of how pleasantly surprised I was very recently to come upon Roger Moore's Saint being referenced even now as the epitome of suave cool; for evidence please see, if you have not already, the final episode of Season 2 of BBC 1's *Boomers*, a comedy of 60-somethings refusing to go quietly which features some of my favourite *living* character actors (yes, some of the performers I like are still alive) including Alison Steadman and Philip Jackson – and June Whitfield is in it too, still hanging in there!

In the Season 2 finale, greige, mild-mannered, and generally very un-Simon Templar-like Trevor discovers courtesy of a lifestyle consultant that his 'power colour' is orange, and that wearing it will give him instant dynamism.

So take a guess at what signature theme is sampled each time Trevor deploys his orange clothing-fuelled power of super cool assertiveness? All together, now:

DE-DA, DA, DE-DAA, DAA, DAAAA!

The World Through A Halo

Greg Bakun

She had great big beautiful eyes. The biggest I'd ever seen. She was beautiful before I ever knew what that word meant. Then, there was the racing. Fast cars, a slick racetrack. It all had a very international feel. Things did not seem like what I was used to in my life in suburban Minneapolis, Minnesota. When I saw this television show, the world became bigger, a lot bigger.

I was six or maybe seven years old when I encountered this scene I just described. All my life, up to that point, I would be watching cartoons and other things that children would watch. Suddenly, I saw something very different. What was I watching? It was *The Saint* starring Roger Moore. As it happens, some of the ITC series appeared on my local TV stations when I was growing up. *The Saint* was shown on occasion in the afternoon. I was probably waiting for something like *Sesame Street* to start but this was on TV and got my immediate attention. Why would that be? Like I said, my world became bigger. It became international, not that I would have understood what that meant at the time. I enjoyed the accents, not because they were different or funny, but because they sounded intelligent. The locations were intriguing and the cars looked fast and sleek and I'm not just talking about the ones on the racetrack.

I don't know if *The Saint* was the first British television series I saw but it would have been one of them. I have stated on my British television blog that *The Avengers* or the BBC series *Butterflies* were among the first British shows I encountered but I do believe *The Saint* would have been the catalyst that started me on the journey I've been on for the past 35 years or so.

Series like *The Avengers* had been playing on another local station in my area. Please keep in mind, I am in the US. We didn't get a lot of British television series on commercial television stations. This station mainly played the black and white Emma Peel series which has been a strong favourite for me ever since I was a child. Maybe I have a slight crush on Emma Peel but it would be the gentlemanly attributes of John Steed with his bowler hat and umbrella that kept me interested. I had never seen anyone like that in my life. A major problem with *The Avengers* episodes on the local St Cloud TV affiliate KXLI channel 41 was that it aired every night at 10.00 or 10.30pm. I was in grade school so that was late and for some reason my mom would let me stay up and watch at least half of it every night. So many great memories.

Of course, I need to bring up the one British show that had the greatest impact on me, which was *Doctor Who*. That's a given. It had such an impact on my life and introduced me to so many friends; I will be forever grateful. Yet, this article is not about *Doctor Who*, it's about *The Saint*, so let's get back to it.

As we all know, The Saint is a man by the name of Simon Templar. He was created by Leslie Charteris in 1928. Templar is a thief with dealings with the underworld but generally uses the knowledge he accumulated and his contacts in crime to help people who are in desperate situations. Obviously, there have been books but also films, comic books and radio series. *The Saint* was extremely popular. Simon Templar was described as "buccaneer in the suits of Savile Row, amused, cool, debonair, with hell-for-leather blue eyes and a saintly smile..." Enter Roger Moore.

Perhaps not just Roger Moore but the ITC series. Now, I am going to be honest. The notion of what an ITC series is was very different to me than probably to most people. Even today, when I think of ITC, I am not thinking about such stalwart series as *The Saint*, *Danger Man*, *Man in a Suitcase*, *Strange Report*, *The Champions* and *The Prisoner*. I think of *The Muppet Show*. I cannot see the opening ITC Ident from 1973 with that bombastic music and not expect it to end with Kermit the Frog coming on screen to scream at me, "It's The Muppet Show!!" It's going to be stuck with me forever. I wonder what Lord Grade would think of that?

The Saint as a TV show started in 1962. From the very start, because it was a production for Lew Grade, it was shot on film with an eye on the US market. I always thought that was smart on Grade's part with all of the shows he produced. Of course, he was a very smart man. *The Saint* ran for six series for a total of 118 episodes. The first four series were shot in black and white while the remaining two were made in colour. It is in fact the first of the colour episodes, *The Queen's Ransom*, that was the first episode not be based on Charteris' work.

Oddly, after I'd seen *The Saint* when I was young, I didn't go back to it for some time but by the time I did I was already watching whatever British television I could. For some reason I was mesmerized by the way a lot of British television was produced: interiors shot on videotape in a studio while exteriors were often shot on location and on film. There is something wonderful about this look that I still love to this day. When I watch an episode of *Public Eye* and perhaps the whole episode is on videotape (including on location exteriors), I get a little disappointed.

I wanted to see more and more of this style of programming. Lucky for me, we have in the US the Public Broadcasting System, PBS. So much of the programming back in the day for PBS was provided by the likes of the BBC, Thames, LWT, etc. I didn't have to look far to get my fix. I didn't understand what much of it was about but I watched. I watched series such as *Butterflies*, where I couldn't begin to understand the complexities of an underappreciated housewife contemplating having an affair but I loved it. Every moment of it. I loved the look of her house and loved the VW Beetle painted with the Union Jack on its roof. I have happy memories of watching *Only When I Laugh*, thinking it was *Fawlty Towers* because Peter Bowles has the slimmest of passing resemblance to John Cleese; they both had a moustache. During the day at school, I would be just waiting to get home to watch whatever programs were being shown that night on my local PBS station. During this period, *The Saint* would pop up now and again in syndication in my area. Sometimes I'd watch it and sometimes I wouldn't. It really depended on what mood I was in at the time. Let me explain.

Is it too simple for me to divide *The Saint* simply into its black and white and colour episodes? When I want to watch episodes of *The Saint* for myself, it depends for me on what type of story I want to watch. The black and white episodes seems to be more straightforward crime stories or at least Simon Templar's role is more straightforward. When we get into later colour episodes some elements become more fantastical such as *The House on Dragon Rock*. I really do feel there is a distinction between the black and white and colour episodes. I love both but sometimes I am not in the mood for one over the other. I feel the same way with *The Avengers*. Somedays I want lavish filmed episodes and other days I would prefer studio bound stories shot on videotape.

Some of the iconic elements do stick out for me, cementing my love for *The Saint*. Obviously, the stick figure with the halo over its head. It is so simple. I do wonder how many people, if polled randomly today, would get what that was. That stick figure goes all the way back to the beginning. What doesn't go back to the beginning is the theme music for the ITC series that was written by Edwin Astley. It is the perfect pairing with the look of the series, the music, and the time this series was produced. Being pedantic, I prefer the slightly revamped version of the theme from the colour series onwards with the magical middle eight... or whatever you call it.

I love this series because it checks so many boxes for me. This is English action adventure. In a way, I think it does all the stuff a young boy watching would love to do. Our hero, played by Roger Moore, drives fast cars, continually gets knocked out, gets into punch ups, and saves ladies from danger but he is a quintessential English gentleman. In a way, no different to John Steed but yet very different. Simon Templar is more contemporary and is very much a product of his time, from how he likes his women to the cars he drives. I think he is more defined in that way than John Steed. As I've mentioned, one of the appeals of this show, along with many of the ITC series, is its international scope. I feel some people may take that aspect of the series for granted, so permit me to elaborate.

I am from America. As most will probably no doubt agree, much of the US media, including the production of its television series, lives in a bubble. So many programs are US-centric. Even series set in the vacuum of space often are US centric. So up to that point in my young life when I first saw *The Saint*, most programs I'd seen were set in the US, and even *The Avengers* was solely set in the UK. *The Saint* would be set where the story needed to be told; sometimes the UK but on other occasions it went to Berlin or Rome, or elsewhere. It is probably more accurate to say the show had a European setting, but to me this was international. The way these other countries looked from how the road system was laid out to how advertising was placed on the walls of old buildings opened my eyes and was inspiring to me. Places like New York seemed gritty and dirty while seeing London or Rome was seeing history and the world from a wider perspective. It was like going on holiday to the places I knew I would never get to see in person.

Finding friends who liked British television was, as you can imagine, not easy. When you are an outcast to start with and you like oddball things, it can be a tad difficult to find people who liked these shows. *Doctor Who* wasn't even remotely popular at my school so you could imagine how well *Yes, Minister* or *Rumpole of the Bailey* would have gone over. I eventually was able to meet people who were like-minded. Through *Doctor Who*, I was able to find people who liked what I liked. This wasn't through school but through fan clubs that existed locally that I was able to get involved in during my teenage years.

The thing that stands out for me with what I could only call my obsession for British television is that I am a collector and an archivist. I love to collect British television. When I was young and watched it on the PBS stations, I would record as much of it as I could on VHS. I still have some of these tapes. Not in my wildest dreams would I have ever thought that so much content from the BBC, ITC, LWT, Thames, etc, would be available on a home video format. Let alone getting it in the quality that DVD provides. When I started to watch these programs, no titles were being offered on VHS by companies so the thought of owning every episode of

Doctor Who seemed like science fiction, let alone now being able to buy more obscure series like *The Plane Makers, The Troubleshooters, Hugh and I, Till Death Us Do Part, The Organization, Muffin the Mule*, or even *Ghost Squad*. The more obscure the title, the better for me. Collecting these programs when they come out on DVD is an addiction. It's obviously not just the obscure stuff but also more mainstream I like owning, for example, all of *The Saint* on DVD.

To me, Roger Moore is Simon Templar. There are some actors, who for me, are the definite article of that character. This isn't a slight on Ian Ogilvy for *Return of the Saint*. I actually haven't seen it yet but I will get to it eventually. Roger Moore had a way to infuse his own personality into the characters he was playing. Perhaps Simon Templar and James Bond are two examples of how he did this so well. It should also be pointed out that Simon Templar is not James Bond. I don't mean this as saying the characters are connected but I think it is easy for people to think that Templar and Bond are so similar because of how Roger Moore played them. I see them as two different characters played expertly by Roger Moore. They had similar attributes but Moore played two distinct characters.

It's extremely silly and sentimental for me to say that I never expected a time when Roger Moore would not be with us. Even typing those words out, I am blushing with embarrassment because death is something all of us will experience eventually. Roger had been with us and we had been with him. Roger was accessible; he never turned his back on the James Bond franchise and he never turned his back on *The Saint*. He was always available to the fans in some ways, including doing his one man shows that never made their way to me, but I know many people who were able to experience his wonderful stories first hand. To me, it was Roger Moore who seemed international. He had views, wit and intelligence so much bigger than where he was from. He often was jokingly self-deprecating about his skills as an actor but that was OK because he was so much more than an actor. He became an institution that we all loved which went far beyond James Bond and far beyond *The Saint*.

Remember when I said it was tough to find people interested in what I was interested in? That was a long time ago. As I am sure for just about everyone, the Internet has brought a lot of fans together to share their love of these programs and we all cheer together when a new title is announced to be released by a studio just as we all complain together if they get it wrong. For years I had been trying to find my place in this community because I felt like I wanted to say something about the programs I love.

Ten years ago, I started *From the Archive: A British Television Blog* (http://www.from-the-archive.co.uk/). It was started as a writing exercise for me as I was studying at the time for my Masters degree and had been writing ten page papers every week. I wanted to find a way to continue this routine because I think it is a good skill to have; I decided the blog would fill that void. I never could imagine how the blog would change my life, not overnight but over time. I have met a number of people who are fans of these programs I love but also people who worked on the restoration for their home video releases. Many times when I write about the restoration of a release, inevitably I will get someone who worked on the release or knows something about it write to me to either correct me or fill me in with more information, sometimes "off the record". I am proud of that. I am also proud that all the major video labels in the UK send their content for me to review.

Finally, I am very proud of the fact I work directly with the British television preservation society Kaleidoscope on a number of things, including producing their podcast. The podcast focuses on my absolute favourite topic which is missing episodes of any British television series. I could write a number of essays just on this topic alone. On the podcast, we've interviewed people who have found missing material, people who helped set up archives and we've been able to play material that has just been announced as discovered.

My journey with the accumulation and enjoyment of British television is far from over, and yet I look back and can't believe how lucky I have been. Opportunities have presented themselves to me and I have met and befriended amazing people along the way who mentored me in this subject and gave me their time and knowledge to enlighten me. Words will never be able to fully describe how incredible this has been!

Oh, as for the woman with big beautiful eyes and the racing setting. Did anyone figure out what I watching? It was an episode of *The Saint* titled *The Checkered Flag.* It was a memory that stayed with me for a very long time, but I was unable to accurately place. It took me years to track down the episode it came from but I was so happy when I did, for in those long-held recollections was the genesis of my love of *The Saint* and British television in general. And the memory did not cheat!

The Sentimental Agent

1963

David Mackenzie is a software developer for the self-service kiosk industry in Dundee. He has been a fan of the ITC stable of shows for more than twenty-five years since first watching *The Prisoner* in the early 1990s. Aside from appreciating cult television, David is a keen LEGO builder and frequently exhibits his models at events around the UK. His long-term building project is to complete a model of Portmeirion, otherwise known as The Village from *The Prisoner.*

Meeting Carlos Varella

David Mackenzie

In 1992, while on a family holiday to Wales, we visited the village of Portmeirion (you can see where this is going!). There was a shop there devoted to *The Prisoner*, which at the time was a series I was completely unaware of. I asked my Dad what it was about – I was fifteen then – and he explained it was about man kept prisoner in a village and that in each episode he would try and escape.

Later that year, Channel 4 broadcast the series and I wanted to watch the first episode so I could see what it had to do with Portmeirion. As you may have suspected, I was completely hooked by the series and it started me on a 25-year journey where I end up writing an article about *The Sentimental Agent* for a charity book!

As *The Prisoner* was being screened, it turned out quite a few people in my class at school were also watching it – an early indication that it was a special series.

Now, by this time I was already aware of a few ITC and similar shows, particularly *Randall and Hopkirk (Deceased)* and *The Saint*. I cannot remember actually watching them, but I do know that at the time I had certainly seen some specific episodes, so I must have seen them during terrestrial screenings during the 1980s.

In 1997 I joined the *Prisoner* fan club, and through meeting other members at events it really expanded my knowledge and appreciation of the ITC genre.

In the years between then and now I have become very good friends with some lovely people, regularly staying at Portmeirion with them. Although it was fundamentally *The Prisoner* that brought us together, it is today almost forgotten among all the other shows that we appreciate and enjoy.

The ITC stable is broad and I have learned about and seen many shows I would otherwise never have even been aware of – one of which is *The Sentimental Agent*. I recently decided to introduce myself to it to see how well it matches up to other ITC shows, and whether I could spot similarities to those shows and their episodes.

The premise of the series is that Carlos Varella, a well-heeled businessman, runs an international import-export company in London, assisted by his secretary Suzy Carter and Chinese manservant Chin. His business connections lead him to become involved in various scrapes in exotic places around the world. The series had been born out of an episode, perhaps not coincidentally entitled *The Sentimental Agent*, of another ITC adventure series, *Man of the World*. This episode had featured Carlos Thompson in a similar role, as a character called Borella, and this turn impressed to the extent where a series was quickly spun-off for the debonair Argentine actor to front.

The first episode, *All That Jazz*, sees Varella asked by MI5 to manage a visiting jazz band in order to determine how they are transmitting secrets abroad. I guessed fairly early on that it was somehow connected to the music (spoiler!). There are at least two *Danger Man* episodes (*The Actor* and *Not So Jolly Roger*) that come to mind featuring secrets encoded in music or recordings, both of which post-date *All That Jazz*. I can see here that this basic premise has been reused and refined.

As the series progresses, we learn that Varella is well-connected and is often called upon by his many contacts to resolve problems they have. He happily takes these on due to his natural sense of justice. He sometimes involves Ms Carter and Chin, who appear willing to do whatever is necessary as part of Varella's plans.

This sets the blueprint for many other ITC shows in which the hero is always one step ahead of the baddies and executes his plan perfectly. In that regard, I could argue that *The Sentimental Agent* is something of a cliché trailblazer!

The series is very much of its time, perhaps more so than other ITC series, but as Varella has many business interests and connections there is plenty of variety in the stories presented throughout the series.

Varella's sense of justice is shown most clearly in the episodes *Never Play Cards with Strangers*, *The Scroll of Islam* and *A Little Sweetness and Light*.

~ In *Never Play Cards with Strangers*, Varella and Chin expose two Bridge players who have scammed a couple on a cruise arranged by an associate of Varella. In preparation for bringing the criminals to justice, Varella visits a bookshop and asks the horrified owner for a book on how to cheat at Bridge – as if it were the most heinous crime imaginable. With Chin undercover as a waiter, Varella beats the cheats at their own game and, in what seems like a scene from a bygone age, the scammers promise never to do it again.

~ In *The Scroll of Islam*, Varella assists two scientists to photograph a Moroccan sheikh's sacred scroll so they may study it. However, Varella gets the blame when the scientists steal the scroll. He decides to steal it back and, at great risk to himself, return it to the Sheikh.

~ In *A Little Sweetness and Light*, Varella's representative on a Greek island is killed by a local gangster who is not happy that Varella's business activities are hampering his own ambitions. Varella heads to the island to solve the murder and sort out the gangster once and for all.

In all these episodes, Varella's actions are driven by the ideal that a man is nothing without his reputation and a desire to right wrongs that are not his fault. He does all this with the expected wit and charm of a true ITC hero.

The final four episodes see Ms Carter's boyfriend Bill Randall take over the business in Varella's absence. Sadly, the reason behind the change in front man was that Carlos Thompson, for whom English was a second language, had been struggling with his lines, causing production to fall behind schedule.

I found Randall to be somewhat of an accidental hero, not unlike Jason King perhaps. He takes on the issues of Varella's many friends in an awkward and haphazard way and seems to 'get lucky' in resolving them.

~ In *The Height of Fashion*, Randall finds himself with a warehouse full of horse blankets after another deal falls through. He clumsily attempts to meet with fashion designer Sally Clare after Ms Carter appreciates their high-quality fabric. I found myself thinking that Varella would charm his way into Clare's office and have the blankets sold in no time at all.

~ In *Finishing School*, Randall investigates the apparent kidnapping of a young girl. It turns out the kidnapping was arranged by the girl herself and her boyfriend in order to get the ransom money the girl's father would pay. It becomes obvious fairly early on that the kidnap was a setup and even when Randall is outside the caravan where the couple are hiding, he still does not seem to work out what is going on!

These episodes highlight the difference between Varella and Randall. Varella is always one step ahead of both the bad guys and the viewers – Randall is always a few steps behind.

In retrospect, I can see in the series the genesis of some ITC hallmarks: Varella is a dapper, self-supporting fellow and, rather like Simon Templar, or Brett Sinclair and Danny Wilde, he somehow finds himself in an adventure each week. He is also a person who is called upon by his many contacts and acquaintances to solve mysteries or sort out situations they find themselves in.

It also has the charm and sense of fun that many other ITC shows share. I find Carlos Thompson to have a great screen presence, so it is a shame to learn that his time on the series was not easy for him. (However, he retained a connection to ITC, as husband of actress Lilli Palmer, one of the stars of

The Zoo Gang in the 1970s.) Clemence Bettany as Ms Carter and the legendary Burt Kwouk as Chin are very watchable as well and effortlessly portray their characters. John Turner plays Randall exceptionally well, though I found the character mismatched with the rest of the series.

One thing that viewers of all ITC series can do is to engage in what one might call 'ITC spotting' – to notice an actor, a phrase or a similarity which is from another ITC show. As has been well documented over the years, there was certainly an ITC stable of actors, studio sets, music, sound effects, and locations (mostly in Hertfordshire and Buckinghamshire) and watching any ITC show will illicit that sort of 'spotting'. *The Sentimental Agent* was no exception, with around half of the crew working on the series being familiar names, although cast members familiar to me were fewer and further between.

Overall, I think *The Sentimental Agent* is an important, if unmemorable, series in the ITC canon.

Thankfully, we live in the age of the DVD, in which even shows with limited appeal like *The Sentimental Agent* are released and made available for a price where it is worth taking a punt on an unknown show. In days gone by one would have to have waited for a TV screening to enjoy vintage series, if they were ever re-screened at all. Indeed, *The Sentimental Agent* had not received such a television revival during my lifetime.

In this particular case, the DVD set I bought included a lovely interview with Burt Kwouk about his ITC work, further piquing my interest in other shows.

Beyond *The Sentimental Agent*, the world of ITC has had a significant role in developing the other interest in my life – LEGO. Many years ago I decided that I wanted to build some models of Portmeirion. After several failed attempts using paper and card I found success with Danish building bricks.

At this time I was not expecting in any way to become 'involved' with the adult LEGO community, but have since met many new friends and now regularly exhibit all around the country.

Interestingly, when I display my Portmeirion models they are often recognised by the attendees at the shows and it's great to chat to them about *The Prisoner* and other ITC shows.

Indeed, that they are still remembered by the general public is a fine tribute to the craftsmanship of all the directors, actors, writers, cameramen and propsmen who created them.

The Baron

1966-1967

Robert Morton, born in the late 1960s, saw his potential as a writer fuelled when still at school, when his English teacher told him that his essays were like novels, and were taking too long to mark! After a college course in journalism, he became a motoring columnist at a local newspaper, and later contributed articles to the national motoring magazine *Auto Trader* and numerous other publications as a freelancer. In recent years, a switch to working in design and marketing has seen writing take a back seat, though he still writes occasionally for local newspapers.

Max Pemberton, having had a lifelong interest in film and television, has served as UK TV Schedules Guide for About.com and movie, DVD and film music reviewer and Associate Editor for *Films in Review*, New York, NY. At the time of writing he lives on an island in the Mediterranean with a wolf.

Meet The Baron

Robert Morton

He is known as THE BARON... a man whose career is a crescendo of breath-taking thrills. Master story-teller John Creasey created him, and Hollywood's Steve Forrest portrays him. He is tall, handsome, debonair... a man who knows the world and loves adventure. He finds that adventure through his business as an international arts and antique dealer. It's a business that thunders him in to exciting, danger-laden, unusual thrills stemming from the fabulous wares he handles and the people he meets.

That's how the ITC publicity department 'sold' our hero throughout the world. For me, my foray into the ITC action series came much later than this mid-1960s production; it was *Space: 1999* that had me hooked, being the first show from the studio that I watched as a child. *The Baron* was produced over a decade before I was born.

My first memories of *The Baron* are from the HTV afternoon repeats in the early - 1980s. I was immediately hooked, and proceeded to research the series for a Journalism Course essay that I had to prepare.

The Baron, whose real name was John Mannering, was a Texan rancher (purveyor of the Baron brand) turned fine arts dealer with exclusive establishments in London, Washington and Paris, who was also a secret undercover agent for British Intelligence, helping them out whenever a crime took place involving valuable pieces. The series became the first live action ITC show to be produced entirely in colour – and as such would have instant appeal in the United States.

Cast as the leading man was six foot three inch Texan Steve Forrest (born William Forrest Andrews), who had appeared in a number of minor film roles as well as numerous 'guest appearances' on US TV series such as *The Twilight Zone, Alfred Hitchcock Presents, The Virginian, The Fugitive* and *Burke's Law.* He was the younger brother of Hollywood movie star Dana Andrews, who had earlier worked in Britain as star of *Night of the Demon* (1957). Script supervisor for the series was to be Terry Nation. Whilst the series was still in pre-production, Terry approached his friend and fellow scriptwriter Dennis Spooner to come and join the team.

My first task at this time was to track down Dennis Spooner and hopefully get an interview, before attempting the same with the show's producer Monty Berman. This proved relatively easy and a glorious afternoon was spent in the man's company.

My first question was how the concept came before Lew Grade's ITC empire. Dennis explained that ITC had already filmed a series based on books by John Creasey (*Gideon's Way* starring John Gregson) and this was a period when adaptations were in fashion (possibly due to the success of *The Saint*). A lot of authors were looked at with a view to basing a series on their work, the theory no doubt being that an instant audience was waiting in the shape of their readers.

With *The Baron* there were no constraints in script approval (such as those which had been imposed upon *The Saint*) and this meant that significant changes could be made. Creasey's original creation was a British 'Raffles' type character, a reformed jewel thief who went from breaking the law to helping the authorities and fighting crime. A major change imposed in order to make the show more attractive to the US market was to change the nationality of the main character from British to American.

When ITC boss Lew Grade announced that *The Baron* was to become the first UK drama series to be filmed in colour he was able to sell it to the ABC Network in America, putting the show straight into profit. This was the norm at the time: programmes were pre-sold (a number of episodes were scheduled for showing on a certain date, or dates, before they were made), which Dennis saw as a problem for the actors involved, and the production as a whole, as episodes would have to be completed to tight, rigid deadlines. It became apparent that any show starring one lead put an enormous strain on the actor playing the part. He would be filming all day, and learning lines all night for shooting the next day. As it took ten days to film a show, and the series showed weekly – every seven days: "We could not fall behind in deliveries and we could not lose shooting time."

One way around the production problems was to have an 'assistant' able to carry some of the scenes. That way it was possible to structure the writing of the show – and, with the use of a second filming unit, to literally double the amount of screen time filmed. Consequently, the actor Paul Ferris was cast as Mannering's assistant David Marlowe.

Once production was underway, the first four episodes completed – *Red Horse, Red Rider, The Legions of Ammak, Samurai West and Diplomatic Immunity* – were sent to ABC in the US to gauge an opinion.

Dennis told me he had already embarked on a number of rewrites for the *Diplomatic Immunity* episode and in the process introduced two new characters, though purely in guest roles. The first of these was SBDI (Special Branch Diplomatic Intelligence) agent Cordelia Winfield, played by 26-year-old actress Sue Lloyd. The character was designed to inject a little humour into the script and act as a counterpoint to the Mannering character, who was played very straight and seriously by Steve Forrest. The second new character was the head of SBDI, John Alexander Templeton-Green, played by veteran actor Colin Gordon. Mannering would receive his 'assignments' from Temp (as Mannering would refer to him) and in return would receive diplomatic immunity whenever he needed to travel abroad.

The US Network's executives were anxious that these characters be used again – Sue Lloyd had, in fact, just starred in *The Ipcress File* with Michael Caine, and so, in their terms was a 'name'. Therefore, producer Monty Berman instructed Dennis to embark on further episodes using these characters. Again, it was at a time when the spy genre was at its height, *The Man from U.N.C.L.E.*, James Bond, and countless copies and spin-offs were rating highly. So it was inevitable that *The Baron* started to lean in that direction. As a result of this Paul Ferris was gradually dropped, only appearing in a few episodes before disappearing completely. It was after all, about *The Baron* and was not a 'group' show, like *The A Team* or *Mission: Impossible.*

My time with Dennis was becoming a dream-come-true; what a gent he was to allow me such time, in what was then a busy schedule for him. We continued to discuss further complications arising from the American involvement.

Issues came to light insofar as they had not contracted Sue Lloyd, or Colin Gordon, to appear in the series originally. They – presumably – already had prior commitments, so could only be used as and when they became available. They were not 'resident' – as such – in the series.

I queried with Dennis why the disappearance of the Marlowe character was never explained. As ever, his reply was made obvious to my naïve mind, changes in the make-up of TV series at the time being almost impossible. Although ITC had a certain amount of control in the transmission order when it came to the UK and the US, it was nigh on impossible in the rest of the world. In most markets, episodes of ITC series were screened in the order that film prints became available from other territories that had purchased the series. Participating countries would have their prints swapped over by the distributors. So, for instance, a typical transmission order for the rest of the world might read: Episode 23, 4, 17, 7, 29, 11 and so forth.

Dennis explained that there was also the economical factor to consider: to cover a transmission order for everybody buying the series, then maybe a hundred prints of each of the 30 episodes would have to be made. Even at £200 a print you would be talking in terms of £600,000, and this was the equivalent of more than half the cost of the whole series.

My time with Dennis was a wonderful experience and one I shall never forget; he had me hooked on his work. Sadly, Dennis passed away on 20th September 1986. This is the first time that the *Baron* part of the interview has ever been transcribed in print (my course-work eventually concentrated on *The Adventurer*!)

Back to *The Baron* and its other attraction to a teenager in the 1980s: John Mannering's car! The British car manufacturer Jensen, realising the benefits that Volvo had reaped with Simon Templar's P1800 on *The Saint*, were only too happy to supply *The Baron* with one of their CV8 Mk II sports cars with the powerful 6.2 litre V8 Chrysler engine, bearing the (unregistered) index number BAR 1. It paid off and sales of the CV8 increased greatly until it finally went out of production in 1966 to be replaced by the Interceptor.

Watching this series back after close on twenty years, all episodes hold up pretty well. *The Baron* featured John Mannering involved in the world of antiques, whether trying to unmask a scheming insurance agent, trying to obtain rare collectibles, helping a friend who is being blackmailed and forced to sell her valuable collection, or trying to sell a fake Renoir, the adventures took him from London to behind the Iron Curtain, from New York to Switzerland.

If I had to chose my top three episodes, they would be:

~ The show's solitary two-parter, *Masquerade / The Killing* (later released as a feature *The Man in a Looking Glass)* by Terry Nation and Dennis Spooner, in which The Baron is invited by Sir Frederick Alton to his country home. When he enters the house he hears a woman crying for help and goes to help but he's knocked unconscious. He wakes up to discover that he has a twin double. The glorious Hall Barn, Beaconsfield, an oft used TV location, saw service as 'The Gables', and the story was bolstered by sterling performances from guest stars Bernard Lee ('M' in the James Bond films) and John Carson.

~ *The Seven Eyes of Night*, by Terry Nation, in which The Baron is at the centre of an elaborate double-cross which revolves around the sale of the Seven Eyes of Night, a necklace once owned by the Empress Josephine. A great performance from guest star Patrick Allen, whom I once saw in Swindon town centre, walking down the road, under the influence, shouting at the top of his voice to passers-by: "Don't you know who I am? I'm a famous actor!!!"

~ *Countdown,* also by Terry Nation, in which The Baron comes up against a rival antiques dealer when a long-lost antique sword resurfaces. However, only one of them plays by the rules. Edward Woodward (*Callan, The Equalizer*) guested here as Arkin Morley, who is after the sword and has our hero abducted and imprisoned in a railway goods truck.

There are many other episodes that remain entertaining more than half a century after they were made, and that the people who made it, while for the most part no longer with us, will be remembered for this and other ITC series.

Prize Bull or Bum Steer?

Max Pemberton

In common with *The Saint* and *Gideon's Way*, *The Baron* was an ITC series that re-invented a popular literary character for television. The protagonist in John Creasey's original stories was a reformed British jewel thief who used his skills and connections to investigate and solve antique related thievery and confidence trickery. For television, his character was changed by the producers to that of an American antiques dealer with shops in major capitals across the globe and a nickname derived from a cattle ranch in Texas once owned by his grandfather and used 'The Baron Brand'. He no longer had a criminal background and in fact, apart from being cast as an American, bore more of a resemblance to another of Creasey's literary sleuth creations, The Toff. The Toff, however, was not such a catchy title to sell to the American market, which was a primary consideration for ITC mogul Lew Grade. The re-characterisation also allowed for the casting of an American lead, Steve Forrest as John Mannering, the titular Baron, and an excuse for his jet-setting lifestyle and affluence.

Being of a 'certain age', I do remember the series when it was first broadcast. I would've been around nine years old when it was broadcast in the north of England in black and white and exciting and glamorous it was, too. Well, I certainly saw it in black and white. Although it was the first non-puppet ITC show to be made entirely in colour, another requirement of the desired American market, colour television broadcasting in Britain did not start properly until 1967. The ITV network (on which ITC's shows received their British screenings) would not switch to colour for a further two years.

The most striking memory I have from that time would be the opening titles and music, something of course ITC always did so well. In this case we were offered a staccato, machine-gun opening with static shots of a man with a briefcase alongside postcard views of various international locales like Rio, Rome, Paris, then a gunshot sound effect, a bullet hole in the middle of the screen and sharp cuts to a man viciously attacking someone (from a camera point of view), ramping up the music, and a girl backing away in terror, her scream masked by the sound of The Baron's car, a Jensen CV-8 Mk II, roaring down a motorway before striding into Edwin Astley's brilliant militaristic, brassy no-nonsense title theme. What a hook that was.

After that it was standard ITC fayre, much like *Danger Man* and *The Saint*. Even as a youngster I could spot the difference between the standard establishing shots of exotic locales and then the transition to the studio. *The Baron* may have travelled the world but in reality never went too far from the Elstree Studios' backlot which, with a strategically placed potted palm, could double for any European, Middle-Eastern, Asian or South American destination. When I first moved to Cyprus ten-plus years ago I remember sitting at a roadside cafe, busy traffic, scooters beeping their horns, surrounded by swaying palm trees and old colonial buildings and thinking I was in an establishing shot from an ITC show. Such was the impression these shows left on me.

Initially *The Baron* was given a male assistant, David Marlowe, played by the adequate but unmemorable Paul Ferris, but after Sue Lloyd, who had just made her international debut in the Len Deighton spy thriller *The Ipcress File* with Michael Caine, was introduced in the first episode it was decided to bring her back as regular, glamorous co-star, romantic interest and 'damsel in distress' Cordelia Winfield. Poor old 'David' having been written out after eight episodes continued to crop up occasionally as his filmed episodes were scattered throughout the series giving the impression that he was there for the entire run, even appearing in the last broadcast episode. Like a *Star Trek* red shirt he would be missing for weeks on end only to suddenly re-appear in Mannering's shop to get bopped on the head, gassed or incapacitated in some other way that would never happen to the glamorous Cordelia. Sue Lloyd, who was brought back for the ninth episode recorded (actually broadcast third), eventually went on to appear in 23 of the 30 episodes.

Her character was a little bit of an enigma. She had been introduced, in the first episode, initially as an agent for a British governmental department run by a 'spymaster' character called Templeton Green ('Special Branch, Diplomatic Intelligence') played by Colin Gordon, who would later play the bespectacled Number Two in *The Prisoner*. John Mannering was also recruited on occasion on assignments for Templeton Green and thus became an antiques dealer and part time spy, but Cordelia's character seemed stuck with Mannering whether she was working for Templeton Green or not and they sported a flirtatious relationship much like John Steed and Mrs Peel. Anything of a sexual nature was hinted at, but of course no impropriety was ever shown as this was British television in 1966, after all. Continuity, or lack of, also didn't help. In an early episode the two make their escape from an Eastern Bloc country by swimming across a river. Episodes later when the two have to flee from a ship to a nearby island she claims she can't swim, which of course adds more tension to their escape as the inflatable raft they've commandeered gets machine-gunned and she *has* to swim for her life. I also noted her title credit, listed after that particular week's guest stars, started in the second broadcast episode as 'also starring Sue Lloyd as Cordelia' and then later 'with Sue Lloyd starring as Cordelia' and at the time not knowing what the difference was. I know it's only a subtle difference but noticeable nonetheless. I can only assume with hindsight that this was salary and billing related, though I'm still not sure. Maybe it was an objection from Steve Forrest to the 'starring' credit. The series also featured the regular 'Rogue's Gallery' of ITC actors and stuntmen, some appearing, as per their other shows, in more than one episode as different characters. ITC was essentially its own repertory company.

Retrospectively the show is a bit of an oddity. Although enjoyable at its time it now seems very formulaic, predictable and contrived, which it no doubt was, using similar storylines, sometimes the same storylines, as *The Saint*. The American lead to be able to sell to the American market, a practice which would continue with Joel Fabiani in *Department S*, Richard Bradford in *Man in a Suitcase*, Stuart Damon in *The Champions*, Robert Vaughn in *The Protectors*, Gene Barry and Barry Morse (known for his role in the long-running cult show *The Fugitive*) in *The Adventurer*, *Mission: Impossible*'s Martin Landau and Barbara Bain and Barry Morse again in *Space: 1999*, Brian Keith (and Barry Morse again!) in *The Zoo Gang* and, the crème de la crème, Tony Curtis in *The Persuaders!*. But Steve Forrest, although he tried gallantly, seemed at odds and out of place with his environment and with his co-actors and, reportedly, they too with him. This, plus the confused, muddled and unsure concept, resulted in it running for only one series.

That one series however comprised 30 episodes, virtually thirty hours of television, which is still quite an achievement. And it did its job. It was exciting entertainment for its time when you consider that in 1966 in the UK there were only three television stations available to watch and you had to choose, there was no videotaping option, and it is still fun and enjoyable now when watched in context. All the ITC shows are time capsules for their period and capture an age we shall not see again. Also of note is its title theme and score from Ted Astley. He scored almost every ITC show, but *The Baron* had his very own distinctive themes and fight music, and with at least two fist fights per episode you remember these things.

Evidence of the show's lack of appeal also shows in that there was no toy version of his car, the aforementioned and very distinctive Jensen CV-8 Mk

II. There were Corgi Toys of *The Saint's* Volvo P1800, Bond's DB5, the Batmobile, Steed's Bentley and Emma's Lotus, even a non-specific Oldsmobile 88 with the *Man From U.N.C.L.E.* logo on the bonnet (sorry, 'hood'). Dinky Toys also brought out Lady Penelope's pink Rolls from *Thunderbirds* and the Mini Moke taxi from *The Prisoner*, but no model of *The Baron*'s Jensen. And I really wanted one. Maybe it was because there was no logo as such the makers could utilise. *The Saint* had his 'stickman', Bond his 'OO7'. All *The Baron* had was... well... *The Baron*, and a picture of a guy holding a briefcase. Having said that, there were no models of McGill's Hillman Imp or John Drake's Mini Cooper either but surely the Jensen was glamorous enough to deserve a model.

The Baron also gave us one of the most iconic visuals that pervaded nearly every ITC adventure series, that of the white Jaguar plunging off a cliff. The stunt was filmed for the show at considerable expense and from several angles. The footage was subsequently re-used in *Department S*, *Randall and Hopkirk (Deceased)*, *The Saint* and others, and became a running gag. Again, like the *Star Trek* red shirt, whenever you saw a character in any ITC show climb into a white Jaguar you knew it wasn't going to end well. Apart from Ian Ogilvy that is. And he got a model…

Man in a Suitcase

1967-1968

Al 'Smudge' Samujh – fascinated by television and film ever since watching old movies and programmes on a tiny black and white set with his grandad many years ago. As he got older, as well as enjoying viewing and re-viewing old favourites, he became interested in all aspects of how television programmes and films are put together: writing, direction, production, design, camera work, as well as the star actors, character players and stunt performers. This led to attending events where it was possible to discuss television and cinema with the people who worked in the business and to meet up with other television and film enthusiasts, making many friends along the way. The fascination continues…

Geoff Dodd is a frequent contributor to the *Guide to Avengerland* website as well as various other film and TV forums. He is a co-organiser of the annual *Dead Man's Treasure Hunt* location tour and lives in Hertfordshire.

Mike Gorman hails from Leigh in the North West of England and is a huge fan of most things ITC, James Bond, horror and sci-fi, and the music of John Barry and David Arnold. He creates unofficial, original comic strip stories – created using Photoshop – including crossovers with other ITC characters, and shares them for free at his Facebook page *Mike's Man in a Suitcase Archive & Revival* (https://www.facebook.com/mikessuiitcase/), where ITC fans can discuss the strips and find information and images from the series. He lives with his wife and step-daughter and two attention-seeking dogs.

Learning the Trade

Al Samujh

Dedicated with the greatest respect to the memories of
Richard Bradford and Sidney Cole

Some years ago now, just before my college days, I remember talking with a good friend and his parents and we got onto the subject of old television. We were throwing titles around for discussion when suddenly one popped up that I didn't recognise, *Man in a Suitcase*. "Ah," said my friend, "that's the one where the chap shrinks and can fit inside a suitcase. It's a Gerry Anderson puppet show." He was right on that point, it was a Gerry Anderson show he was describing, but – as his Dad said – it wasn't *Man in a Suitcase*. Unfortunately, I was no further forward as, although the title had been thrown into the general debate, no one could really pin down what *Man in a Suitcase* was – the title was there but memories were fuzzy…

Fast-forward not quite a handful of years. The bug that had bitten me so many years ago still had a good hold. I was at college studying English, History and Law, the option of doing Theatre Studies having been dismissed by the family's entreaty that I train for "a proper job" first. But I still loved old films, vintage TV and actors and acting. The advent of cult TV releases at a 'reasonable' price on VHS (£10 a tape) had stretched my pockets, but grown my collection. We were but a handful back then – appreciation was still for 'anoraks', in the nomenclature of prejudice – and we met up once or twice a year to share our enthusiasm with that handful of like-minded souls.

Then, suddenly, things changed… I don't know whether regional TV companies were sensing something was in the wind and were saving their pennies for what was soon to be an arduous, expensive, and in some cases tragic, licencing round, but in the mid 1980s somebody, somewhere must have decided that daytime TV was too expensive. Into the schedules crept vintage TV – cheap, 'filler' TV; those shows that I remembered from childhood began to re-appear in the schedules. An initial path had been laid by *The Avengers* (of which I only truly remembered the multi-coloured playing cards credits from my smaller days) and *The Prisoner* on early Channel 4. But now action adventure series like *Randall and Hopkirk (Deceased)*, *The Champions* and *The Baron* were beginning to appear in the ITV Regional afternoon listings. Our region even went as far as repeating *Fireball XL5* in the early mornings of the school holidays.

The VCR, which as a student with no fixed income I had funded through vicarious credit in a family member's name, was now working overtime! As often as I could I sat in front of the recorder and started it off myself – and woe betide any family member or friend who acted as a stand-in if they missed or clipped anything! Scanning the *TV Times* (also self-financed, so that I could have first call on it) a dim recollection of that conversation of years gone by was triggered when the series playing changed and there, in a small column entry, was described the first episode of *Man in a Suitcase* – a playlet entitled *Brainwash*. The VCR was set, interest was piqued after all those years, and I awaited the results on my return from college that afternoon...

With the hard-earned luxury of my own VCR (each tape swathed in warnings to my brother *not* to record over it after a devastating loss of my only tape of *The Prisoner* a couple of years before) I was able to lock myself away after teatime and get down to discovering what *Man in a Suitcase* was about. The first thing that struck me was that this new bloke – McGill – was a world away from the slick, polished world of Roger Moore's *The Saint*, for example; this chap was fast, and hard – so hard in fact that he could get beaten to a near pulp and still keep his cigarette between his lips. Now this was impressive even to a non-smoker like myself. I considered myself 'grabbed'.

That first story, *Brainwash*, was a tour-de-force with our hero, played by the soon to become much admired (in my book) Texan, Richard Bradford, was up against one of Britain's finest acting talents of the time – Colin Blakely. Blakely played an ostensibly civil henchman to the main protagonist of Howard Marion Crawford, but the core of steel-hard ruthlessness at Blakely's character's heart meant we knew who the real ringmaster was. This series was clearly something else and some distance from the glossy adventures of *The Persuaders!* and so many other ITC series.

If the show stood out from the off, then its second episode *Man from the Dead* brought it head and shoulders above the rest. Properly the first episode in McGill's saga, this one gave us a fully formed back-story, and the character of the man alone with his gun and his suitcase was fleshed out further. This was the point – McGill was a real person and the relationships around him had truth as well. He had his highs and his lows; in *Man from the Dead* he lost the girl (again) and these lows were compounded in *Variation on a Million Bucks*, where he lost a good friend and the lover from his past who he had only just recently found again.

So, after knowing nothing about this mysterious show from the '60s, here I was, utterly hooked. So what now? I began to take notice of what was behind the show and developed a more critical eye as the stories continued. No series can be perfect, and there were a few lapses in quality along the way – more so, in my opinion, towards the end of the run. However *MIAS* (as I was by now abbreviating the title to) gave us some excellent tales:

~ *The Girl Who Never Was* – where we see the human side of the hardened agent in dealing with a shell-shocked former soldier;

~ *The Man Who Stood Still* – a brilliant character study as McGill gets mixed up between old rivals;

~ *Day of Execution* and *Which Way Did He Go, McGill?* – two strong, revenge-based stories, which gave breaks to a very young Donald Sutherland;

~ *The Whisper* – another powerful outing with Bradford's favourite guest star, Colin Blakely.

There were some mis-fires too:

~ The over jokey (to my taste) *Jigsaw Man* with Paul Bertoya as a responsibility-shirking student;

~ *The Boston Square* – which left me wondering how style-setting *Prisoner* director Don Chaffey could create something so leaden;

~ *Blind Spot* – for me, not even Felicity Kendal could save this one!

However, the good far outweighed the bad and I even had soft spots for some of the more colourful and eccentric plots such as *Three Blinks of the Eyes* and *Property of a Gentleman*. However for some reason I missed out on *No Friend of Mine* in this run and didn't catch up with it until a fair few years later. But the show still inspired me – I became almost evangelical in my championing of the programme to friends who hadn't seen it. The *MIAS* bug bit me hard.

Some years after the repeats, in the era of appreciation societies and fan magazines, I began to think that if I could get enough information together I might be able to do something similar for McGill aficionados. But where to start? This was, or appeared to be, very much a distant cousin in the ITC canon – not much information appeared to exist, or readily came to hand. *MIAS* was nowhere near *The Prisoner* in the cult status and publicity stakes, so what to do…?

I discovered an address – unreliable, as it turned out – to try writing to Richard Bradford. Many months passed and no reply. Where else then? My appreciation had given me a keen eye for the credits of the show, "Created by Richard Harris and Dennis Spooner". Alas Dennis was taken from us not long after this repeat run ended. However, there was a chap called Richard Harris working on *The Darling Buds of May*. A quick letter to the *Darling*

Buds Production Office, a wait of a month or so and a reply, "Dear Mr Samujh, Yes, I am the Richard Harris who many years ago co-created *MIAS* with Dennis."

My first 'in' – and I was highly pleased to correspond with Richard Harris a couple of times. He explained that the show's format consisted of a single sheet of paper, the main character's name came from a football star of his youth and that he and Spooner were never further involved as they simply weren't asked after Lew Grade brought in an American script editor to assist overseas sales. Richard said that the script editor had changed the title, the nationality of the lead (McGill was originally English) and that he and Spooner never received a penny from their creation of the format.

One of the luckiest breaks in research was getting in touch with director Peter Duffell, who was then working on Gerry Anderson's *Space Precinct*. Peter was as keen on classic British films as I was and he opened my eyes to various avenues of research, and new films, sending me his thoughts on micro-cassettes. In return I sent him his episodes of *MIAS*, which he thought stood up fairly well, and he himself circulated them to actors he'd used in the series, so that they could see their own performances. The real coup was when Peter casually mentioned that if I was really that keen on *MIAS*, perhaps I should talk to the show's producer, Sidney Cole.

Sidney Cole was a name I knew all too well, he being the supervising film editor at Ealing Studios at the height of the Ealing Comedies. Judging from the age of those classic films I'd rather suspected that Sid would have gone to the great studios in the sky by the time I was researching *MIAS*. I couldn't have been more wrong. At the age of 87 Sid was still comfortably settled in his home a stone's throw away from Ealing Green, chosen because it would be a short walk to work back in the day. Peter arranged for me to spend an afternoon with Sid, to chat about his work on *MIAS*.

As it happened, our chat ran the gamut of Sid's career, from how he came to Ealing, his work in co-founding the ACTT trades union, working with refugees from McCarthy-ism in the early days of commercial television and finally moving on to produce *Danger Man*, the origins of *The Prisoner* and his work on *Man in a Suitcase* (notice which came last here!).

Sid told me that the day before he'd been rehearsing his interview technique with another Ealing icon, Michael Relph and they'd joked about the modern values of what were 'ten a penny' posters which they could have taken home from Ealing by the armful. He regaled me with tales of having a quick drink with Patrick McGoohan and Don Chaffey at the end of a hard day on *Danger Man*, which would frequently develop into a whisky fuelled pub-crawl around the lanes of Hertfordshire. I sat rapt as Sid told me how one day Patrick McGoohan had walked into his office and asked, "Sid, why does it always have to be the way you say?" gaining a response, "Because I'm the Producer, Pat," that would be one element in his star's decision to break away and produce his own series.

For Sid, *Man in a Suitcase* was not without its ups and downs. His star's pursuance of the Method school of acting sometimes put him off-kilter with his more theatrically trained English supporting casts, to the extent that Richard became a sort of 'Marmite' figure – you either loved him or hated him. I collected a number of views from his fellow actors, but I have to say that the majority seemed to have found him to be OK, although Mark Eden expressed a common observation, "He did mumble a bit." Only one person of those canvassed for an opinion categorically said that they would never discuss the show, such was their strong feeling about its star.

A story on a lighter note was that of the time Sid was waiting to hear that *MIAS* location filming had commenced one particular morning. A somewhat panicked report came over the 'phone that only half the unit had turned up. Sometime later another call came, from another caller, that they were sat waiting for the other half of the unit. It didn't take long for Sid to fathom out that both teams were in fact at the location after he asked his secretary to find out precisely where they were. The location in question was a hill; one half the crew had gone to one side of it and the others to the other! Thankfully the twain did meet and filming was able to commence.

One of the more pleasurable aspects of researching any film or TV show is when you engage in a conversation that develops into a broader aspect. Such was the case with *MIAS* director Freddie Francis. After our initial correspondence the topic widened to include *MIAS* guest star Jennifer Jayne, who had been a good friend of Freddie's, and who co-wrote one of his 'horror' movies *Tales That Witness Madness*. Although Freddie hadn't been in touch with Jennifer for a while I had a pleasant surprise some weeks after our chat when a small bundle arrived from him – it was an assortment of printed matter about Jennifer, which Freddie had kept for many years. A lovely man. When I said I was unable to make his BFI Lecture, surely enough, about four weeks later, a cassette tape of his interview arrived in the post with a little note. What marvellous fringe benefits!

I recall writing to scriptwriter Kevin Laffan about his time on the show. It wasn't necessarily the easiest of times for him as one of his scripts suffered heavy re-writes and the company wouldn't accede to his request to have his name taken off as a result. Again the correspondence widened and I learned what the creator of *Emmerdale Farm* thought of what the producers had done to his show in modern times, as well as helping him to investigate fringe outlets for his more recently written plays. *MIAS* certainly led me down many and various avenues in my quest for information.

So what did *Man in a Suitcase* do for me? Well, as the title of this essay says, it taught me about the trade. I paid much more attention to production as a result and I rapidly became aware of the politics of association within the industry, learning that so many of the backstage crew were friends of Sid's and fellow former alumni of Ealing Studios. I began to follow, and be able to quickly identify, directors' and other technicians' particular working styles. I learned that research was fun and that so many people out there were only too happy to talk about their fascinating careers. I became a little bolder, and when Bravo repeated the ITC shows in the 1990s; I put myself forward to create their *Timewarp Text* pages to accompany their *MIAS* screening.

To borrow from the late, great C.J. of *Reginald Perrin* fame, I didn't get where I am today without *Man in a Suitcase*. It got me immersed in the wider ranges of my hobby, rather than just sitting watching the shows. After working my own patch on *MIAS* I dipped my toes into other waters and began to contribute to other fan publications. I started to attend the various conventions around other films and shows that I enjoyed, finding many new friends along the way. Of course, the advent of the internet has made these circles even wider. Even now, new information or pictures come to light – or new friends and associates arrive who share this mutual interest.

Mac was a proper hero – a flawed hero with human foibles, failings and desires; but above all Mac was *my* hero. Sadly, we recently lost Richard Bradford, but for my money he left something unique within the ITC catalogue, for which I personally will be forever grateful, and I'm sure that his work will be appreciated for a very long time to come.

Where Did You Go, McGill?

Geoff Dodd

My introduction to this finest of ITC series came when I was a teenager during the ITV regional repeats in the mid-1980s. I had already seen *The Avengers* and *The Prisoner* on Channel 4 which had further stimulated my interest in all things 1960s, whether it be film, TV or music, and signed up for Six of One, The Prisoner Appreciation Society and Stay Tuned / On Target, an *Avengers* fanzine produced by Dave Rogers. I would regularly seek out any other magazines that carried articles on TV programmes from that era (not as easy as it sounds at that time, as people of a certain age will testify) which led me to visit some very dubious book shops and as a result became aware of other series from the ITC stable, such as *Strange Report*, *Gideon's Way* and *Randall and Hopkirk (Deceased).* Other ITC fare such as *The Baron* and *The Champions* were already on my radar, courtesy of my local channel, Granada, by the time I settled down late one Sunday night to watch my first episode of *Man in a Suitcase*.

Now, I'll be the first to admit that it isn't the catchiest of programme names, indeed I thought it was some sort of travel series when I first saw the title written down in an article, but having enjoyed immensely all the other ITC output, I was certainly going to give this one a go. Strangely, Granada chose to start their repeat run with the episode *The Sitting Pigeon* rather than the usual *Brainwash* or *Man from the Dead.* Maybe not as strong as those two instalments but one which probably occupies a top half spot in most fans' chart run-down of favourite episodes. This episode doesn't have the greatest pre-credits teaser for a series introduction either – police car follows man down the street, they pull him over, he questions whether they're really police officers and they take him inside their car before driving off to go and see their boss, Inspector Franklin. Not the most scintillating of enticements, I'll grant you. And yet… there was something about that opening scene, something that drew me in and even before Gilley tells Percy to "Tread on it," and we get the crash of the opening piano salvo of the instantly familiar theme tune, I knew that this was going to be my favourite programme. I was already hooked.

Having recorded all the ITC episodes that I could since my parents purchased a VHS video recorder (a Fisher Studio Standard, no less), I was, of course, recording *The Sitting Pigeon* as I sat there glued to the screen. Now, one by-product of my watching these vintage shows had been an interest in where they had been filmed. Of course, when watching *The Prisoner* and wondering where it had been filmed, I didn't have long to wait to find out as newspapers and magazines of the time were carrying articles about the show and often mentioned Portmeirion as being used for the location of The Village, but I had a desire to discover where those pretty villages used in *The Avengers* and the ITC shows were located. I'd already started to notice that certain locations cropped up in more than one episode of a series and sometimes in other shows too. Where was that big white house with the pillars outside? Where were the two grassed triangles at a crossroads? And where was that bridge that Tara King jumped off and which seemed to be in everything? I needed to know and so, as I sat watching McGill and Rufus Blake driving around London I was already wondering where these places they were visiting were located.

At the end of the episode I sat there not quite believing what I'd just watched. I was mesmerised by Richard Bradford's performance and wondered why I hadn't seen this programme or heard of him before. Everything about it was perfect – the premise of the show, McGill's appearance and attitude, his insistence on driving a Hillman Imp rather than a flashy car, a believable plot, the familiar faces of the guest actors, the incidental music and the theme tune – it was everything I wanted in a show. It was now well after midnight, but I needed to see more McGill. This would be a formality in this digital, on-demand age, but simply wasn't possible back in the mid 1980s. So I did the only thing I could – I rewound the tape and watched it again from start to finish, something I'd never done before for any show and nor have I since. It was every bit as good the second time around and that was it – *Man in a Suitcase* had knocked *The Prisoner* off the number one spot in my personal TV chart.

The next day I watched it again and started counting the days until the following Sunday when the second episode was due to be broadcast. This time I managed to resist the urge to watch it again immediately after transmission, but I certainly watched it again the next day. I duly recorded all the episodes that were broadcast, again not a straightforward task. There was no 'series-link' option in those days – you just had to scan the TV listings to see when the show would next be on and these shows were certainly moved around the schedules. The Granada Sunday night transmissions didn't last very long before the series moved first to a late-night, weekday slot and then to afternoons. I can remember scrambling to get a VHS tape into the machine when I was watching TV as the announcer informed viewers that due to a live broadcast ending prematurely, they were going to show an episode of *Man in a Suitcase.* Disaster narrowly averted this time but I wasn't quite so lucky when the time came for me to leave home and start work. I left instructions for my mother to record my favourite show as I wouldn't be able to afford a machine of my own. Unfortunately, she couldn't oblige and wrote to me apologising for this catastrophe (I've still got the letter somewhere). I returned the following weekend and talked her through the procedure to ensure that there was no repeat. Help was at hand though, in the shape of HTV (Wales), who were also airing the show but were a couple of weeks behind the Granada schedule so I was able to record the missed episode and remain on course for the full set of 30.

As the weeks unfolded the show just got better and better – the explanation of how McGill came to be in his current predicament in *Man from the Dead,* the Bradford tour-de-force that is *Brainwash,* the hard hitting ending of *Burden of Proof,* the political intrigue of *The Boston Square* and *Somebody Loses, Somebody... Wins?* (we'll skip over that episode, shall we?) all reinforced its credentials at the top of the chart. However, throughout the broadcasts I kept wondering where these episodes had been filmed. Sure, it said "Made at Pinewood Studios" in the closing credits but where else did they go?

One episode in particular intrigued me – *Which Way Did He Go, McGill?* The farm occupied by Joy Hallows and especially the (then) fairly modern house where Jerry Norman lived looked like idyllic places to live and I wanted to know where they were and what they looked like now. As mentioned earlier, I'd moved away from the north-west and was now working down in London. I eventually came to live in South Hertfordshire which, unbeknown to me, was a fertile area when it came to location filming for the filmed shows of the 1960s. I was still getting my quarterly Six of One magazines and so I was pleased to read in one of them that someone was researching the locations used in many of these series with a view to publishing a guide. A guide to filming locations? This was music to my ears. That person was, of course, Anthony McKay and his *Guide To Avengerland* was duly published. I was equally pleased to discover that there was an annual event that toured some of the locations used, based around the *Dead Man's Treasure* episode of *The Avengers.* I was thrilled to see that the location of Joy Hallows' farm had been identified but was disappointed when I visited for the first time and found that being private property, very little could be seen from the road. One down, but the location of Jerry Norman's house still eluded me.

I found my first 'Avengerland' location in 1992, the diving board seen in *The Bird Who Knew Too Much* episode of *The Avengers,* something I was able to pass on at my first Treasure Hunt the following year. I was able to discover one or two more but living where I did, I was in the catchment area for location filming for crews out of MGM Borehamwood and Elstree studios and not Pinewood. In 1998 I started in earnest to hunt for the Norman house, taking trips over to Buckinghamshire and driving around places close to the studio in the hope that I would stumble across it. Things got a bit easier the next year when I bought my first home computer, but I was still drawing a blank. On the face of it, it shouldn't have been too difficult as the houses looked fairly modern (and therefore unlikely to have been demolished since filming) and the layout, with the curve of the road leading to a dead-end just beyond the house in question, should be fairly easy to match on a street atlas. It wasn't. I began to think that the house had fallen victim to developers after all.

I was still finding locations closer to home and my forays into Pinewood territory had yielded results for locations featured in other shows, but not the one that I wanted most. The advent of Google Earth which gave you an aerial satellite view of a location was proving useful, but despite spending countless hours poring over these images and nearly ten years of searching, still nothing matched. I was regularly checking the websites of estate agents in Buckinghamshire and Berkshire just in case the house was being put up for sale, but nothing. A change of tack was needed.

Later in the episode, McGill speaks to the concierge at a 'luxury apartment block' which was once the home of George Hastings. Having become more familiar with how location filming was organised at that time, I thought it unlikely that Richard Bradford would be allowed to venture too far away from the studio for such a short scene as he was only filmed leaving, with the interiors shot back at the studio (locations generally had to be within an hour's drive of the studio so that in case of inclement weather, the actors could return to the soundstage and resume filming there). So, it stood to reason that this distinctive apartment block was more than likely very close to my target house, especially since Earle, played by Donald Sutherland, visits there as well, riding the same motorbike which he used earlier to get to Norman's house. In all likelihood, these scenes were shot on the same day and shouldn't therefore be too far apart.

Shifting the focus of my search, I now began searching for the apartment block rather than the house and it wasn't long before I had a result. A flat was up for sale in the Burnham area of Buckinghamshire which looked very like the block seen in the episode. It was May 1st 2008 and I'd been searching for this for nearly ten years. I quickly looked at the map and was disappointed to see that it was a location I'd previously discounted on the map as the road layout didn't match. Sure, the curve was there but there was no dead-end. A quick check on Google Earth gave me a slightly angled view of the apartment block which at least gave me hope that this was at least the same block used in the episode but frustratingly, the images of the surrounding area were strictly overhead shots denying me the chance of investigating further from home. Of course I was going to have to mount another expedition.

The following day I left work early and headed straight for Burnham. Turning left into The Fairway, I immediately saw the apartment block to my right and instantly knew it was the same one that McGill had visited. I got out and took a couple of pictures before returning to my car and continuing along the road, around the curve. The road stretched out ahead, certainly no dead-end here but then I noticed a house with a distinctive chimney to my right. I was sure that this house was the one seen in the background as Earle arrives at Jerry Norman's house and lights a cigarette. But what of Norman's house itself? Surely I couldn't have missed it? The answer soon became clear. Alighting once more, I began to take some more pictures but was approached by a local resident who enquired as to what I was doing – one of the very few occasions when I have been, despite photographing locations for more than 20 years. I explained to him that the road had featured in a TV show (he seemed very impressed that Donald Sutherland had visited) and he told me that I was actually standing outside the house I was looking for. The reason I had missed it was because the house had been altered beyond recognition, with the front extended and a substantial loft conversion. My inability to match the road layout to the map was also explained – the dead-end had been opened up and the road extended to make it a through road not long after the *Man in a Suitcase* crew had filmed there and so it too now looked completely different. My quest was at an end.

Since that day I've been able to find further locations from the show but that is the one that has given me the most satisfaction and has inspired me to keep hunting these places down, even if they appear difficult and are time consuming. In this case, persistence certainly paid off. I've also been fortunate to be able to visit many other locations from the show, some of them not open to the public – including a second visit to Joy Hallows' farm where I was allowed in and was able to take as many pictures as I wanted. The show continues to win over new fans with various DVD releases around the world and hopefully I've played a small part in adding to the enjoyment of the series by tracking down some of the locations and increasing our knowledge of the production.

A Fuzzy Thing Happened...

Mike Gorman

Back in 1986 (and me of a youthful 18 years) we had regional TV; not just for local news as we have today, but each particular region would often have many differences in its schedule compared to those of other ITV companies. Daytime programming was particularly diverse across the regions, and it was in the afternoons that various ITC shows would pop up. One channel would be showing *The Baron* while another screened *Randall and Hopkirk (Deceased)*. On Sundays in this particular year, I was avidly following *The Champions* on Granada Television in the North West of England.

One day whilst perusing the *TV Times*, I noticed that the Yorkshire area would be broadcasting *Man in a Suitcase*. By fiddling with a spare channel button, we were able to tune into Yorkshire Television. It was fuzzy but watchable.

Now here was an ITC series I'd heard of but knew absolutely nothing about. I had never seen an article or clip, nor knew who starred in it. It sounds odd now but in those days there wasn't really anywhere to visit to investigate, at least as far as I knew. I didn't even really know what it was about, so I made a mental note to watch.

The 1.30pm transmission of *Man in a Suitcase* on Yorkshire clashed with *The Champions* on Granada, so I duly set the timer on my video recorder and, following my fix of super-powered espionage, settled down to see what this *Man in a Suitcase* was all about.

To say that this mysterious series was a revelation to me would be a vast understatement. This was an ITC show and although it had many similarities with the company's other shows, with familiar actors and directors involved and recognisable lighting and sets, pretty much everything else was unique. Refreshingly so.

The episode that Yorkshire decided to air first was the second one produced, *All That Glitters*. Channels regularly ran series completely out of order unless it was pretty essential that you had to see the pilot first.

At the start it was just like any other series; a quaint English village, a dramatic incident that led to a fade to the title sequence, which was the first major plus point. From first hearing, that pounding rhythm accompanied by the animated title sequence (more muted and less garish than other such ITC sequences), Ron Grainer's theme has remained my favourite of all time.

The opening scene wasn't much different from the norm. But then I met McGill.

Up to this point, the ITC leading men that I'd encountered were all good-looking, suave, charming and likable. Although McGill fitted the first of these traits, the rest (at least initially) were conspicuous by their absence. Here was a man who appeared surly, rude and suspicious. Only later in the episode *Man from the Dead* would we learn the reason why. But for now it was a mystery to me.

Richard Bradford is more than watchable. He was an actor who could make the simple act of walking into a room interesting. His McGill is a real, three-dimensional character, who checks out his surroundings and the people he meets with equal interest. He sizes them up and treats them as he sees fit.

The next revelation was a shocking one. ITC heroes are virtually invulnerable. Fight scenes are swift, with them usually coming out on top. If they are knocked out, they recover quickly with a swift palm to the head placing their hair neatly back in place. Not so McGill. Over the course of the series, he is seen stunned, he staggers and bleeds, he bruises visibly and has difficulty shaking off the effects of a good whack to to the head. And in *All That Glitters* (and other episodes to follow) he is shot and hospitalised. The final scene depicts him unconscious in a hospital bed! This was unheard of in the ITC world. Needless to say, I was hooked and wanted to see more, to know more about this guy who seemed to care a lot about money but yet had an inner integrity and sensitivity toward those deserving of it.

As the weeks passed I continued to watch and learned why McGill was the way he was. His only companion was his suitcase, which was a mirror of himself. It was used (and useful), battered but reliable, and always there when needed.

Once the series had ended I sought out more information about it but there didn't seem to be much available. The odd, brief article in a magazine was about the most I found. Virtually nobody I met had even heard of it. Being something of a loner anyway, this wasn't much of a surprise to me!

And so time passed and the world changed. And so did I. I collected the video (and later DVD) releases and it remained with me, like McGill's suitcase; something I loved and watched but I was isolated in my appreciation. I would write the odd short story that nobody else read and that was it. Marriage and fatherhood happened. Then I joined Facebook and learned that it was possible to make your own page on any subject you wished to, so I created *Mike's Man in a Suitcase Museum* (https://www.facebook.com/mikessuiitcase/). I filled it with as many photos as possible (thousands of screencaps that I'd taken from episodes, along with other material that I had stumbled across). I just wanted to share as much as possible with as many fans as possible.

I later renamed the page *Mike's Man in a Suitcase Archive & Revival*, the reason being that although the page is an archive for the series, I learned how to use the wondrous Adobe Photoshop and started to create my own revival of McGill in the form of strip stories using photographs culled from the series and many other sources to make brand new adventures. I created crossover stories with other ITC series such as *The Prisoner* and *Department S* and received some complimentary comments.

I chose *The Prisoner* and *Department S* for these crossover stories for very different reasons.

McGill and Number 6 of *The Prisoner* were, to me, quite similar characters, and running through both series is the theme of betrayal. McGill was set up and used as a fall guy by friends and colleagues whom he had trusted, and when we first meet McGill he has been living with the consequences of their actions for six years. As the show progresses, he constantly finds himself used and betrayed by employers and old friends alike. Number 6 is also used for all manner of nefarious schemes and is stabbed in the back by almost everyone he encounters.

I thought it would be interesting (to say the least) to bring these two characters together with their shared background of suspicion and distrust of the world around them. Naturally, the story itself – *Prisoners and Pawns* – is one of our heroes being manipulated as events spiral out of their control.

The *Department S* story – *Deadly Harvest* – arose out of my desire to place McGill in a storyline that was most unusual for *Man in a Suitcase*, but mainly to ally him with a very contrasting character. And you can't really find more of a character clash than the one you get by bringing McGill into the presence of the ultra-flamboyant Jason King!

The story is primarily a *Department S* yarn with an outlandish premise, but McGill – somewhat surprisingly – fits in quite well with this very different type of adventure.

It was enormous fun to combine these different series and I think the end results make for entertaining reading. Who knows what other ITC characters McGill will find himself teaming up with (or battling against!) in the future? Suggestions on a postcard, please!

I'm blessed to have a wonderful partner who supports my efforts to keep Mr McGill alive and kicking. She is also well aware of the dearth of merchandise out there, and because of this she has had *Man in a Suitcase* items such as T-shirts, mugs and pens made for me, and has even printed my strips in book form to adorn my shelves!

One thing that I had always wanted to see was a big hardback guidebook to *Man in a Suitcase*, filled with colour photos and episode synopses. My partner said, “Well, do one yourself then.” So I designed one and she had it made. It was expensive but well worth it to have a large book, packed with pictures, that I can dip into whenever the fancy takes me. And it’s unique as it’s the only one in existence!

Man in a Suitcase is the only ITC series for which my enthusiasm has never waned. It’s always there and I’m always eager to create more original strips for McGill, to formulate situations for him that wouldn’t have been possible on television but which keep the spirit of the original intact.

Hopefully, I’ve succeeded in some small way. I’m not making a big difference but I hope I’m keeping the *Man in a Suitcase* flame burning, even if it’s only a dim light. At least it’s lit.

The Prisoner

1967-1968

Robert Fairclough is a film and TV journalist and blogger and a regular contributor to *Doctor Who Magazine* and *SFX*. He is the author of books on the iconic TV series *The Prisoner*, and co-author (with Mike Kenwood) of definitive guides to the classic TV dramas *The Sweeney* and *Callan*. His biography of the actor Ian Carmichael was one of *The Independent*'s Top 10 Film Books of the Year for 2011.

Annette Hill was brought up in Lytham St Annes, Lancashire. She learned piano from the age of six and by eight had set her heart on becoming a teacher. She subsequently trained at Bretton Hall College and has taught music in Doncaster since 1987. Alongside her love of music, Annette developed a passion for TV, beginning with the Tom Baker *Doctor Who* era. She became production assistant on *Time Screen* magazine which led to her introduction to *The Avengers* and various ITC shows such as *The Prisoner*, *Randall and Hopkirk (Deceased)* and *The Champions*. She co-wrote *A Guide to Avengerland* and visiting locations where these shows were filmed has continued to be an exciting pastime.

Jon Older graduated in English and Drama in 1975. After four years working as a Stage Manager, Jon joined Granada Television in Manchester in 1980. Moving to HTV West in Bristol he became a freelance Assistant Director in 1984. He has worked extensively in the UK in film and television drama, but also in America, Canada, France, Germany, Belgium, Norway, Spain, Japan and South Africa as Assistant Director, 2nd Unit Director and also as Director. His production credits include *Death in Paradise*, *Poldark*, *Silent Witness*, *Beowulf*, *Da Vinci's Demons*, *New Tricks*, *Wolfblood*, *Primeval*, *Ashes to Ashes*, *Doctor Who*, *Foyle's War*, *Taggart*, *Lexx*, *Starhunter* and *Robin of Sherwood*.

Rick Davy is a researcher from Wales (originally from London) and is owner of The Unmutual Prisoner and Portmeirion Website. In 2017 he wrote *The Prisoner – The Essential Guide*, and in 2014 the biographical content of the book *George Markstein and The Prisoner*. Rick was also involved in the 50th anniversary Blu-ray / DVD special edition released by Network, contributing text commentaries for all 17 episodes in addition to other content. An aficionado of several ITC shows, he also co-ran the *Randall and Hopkirk (Deceased)* fan club Faithful Unto Death.

The Persistence of Memory

Robert Fairclough

The older I get, the more nostalgic I get about the pre-internet age. If you wanted to know something, you really had to work hard to find out about it.

As with music, if you wanted to research a TV series over ten years old you were up against it. Records not by the usual suspects that were always 'in print' could only be found second-hand, and even then you had to know where to look. Looking into 'vintage' television was even harder – there was hardly anything: an afternoon or late night repeat if you were lucky; usually on ITV, as they seemed more relaxed about repeats than the BBC. Happily, by the late 1970s magazines were beginning to appear whose writers offered valuable info about TV that had been and gone – *TV Sci-Fi Monthly, Starlog, Starburst.*

I think I first heard about *The Prisoner* through an article in *Starlog*. I remember pictures of an angular-looking guy standing by an old-fashioned penny-farthing bicycle, a younger guy in a top hat and large white balloons. Curious. Phrases from the article that stuck in my memory talked about the whole production team (whatever that was) being on drugs (whatever they were) and no easy answers. All this ambiguity must have struck a chord somewhere, because later on I remember being intrigued that the man behind *The Prisoner*, Patrick McGoohan, had written the foreword to a book called *Fantastic Television*. Even then, this was considered something of a coup – equivalent to persuading Bowie to write the introduction to *The Guinness Book of Glam Rock.*

Over the next few years, *The Prisoner* would be name-checked so many times by cult TV friends older than me, that when I found out that an episode was being shown in a late-night slot as part of the *Best of British* TV summer season in 1982, I was determined to sit down and see what still excited people, sixteen years since *The Prisoner* had first been shown.

I think it's true that most of your most important influences come into your life when you're young. Usually, they stay with you because they open your eyes to new ways of thinking about the world, or tell you something about yourself, or both. In the darkened front room of my parents' house late one summer night in the early 1980s, *The Prisoner* comprehensively blew my mind.

It's hard to imagine now a time when every TV show on the air didn't resemble a feature film. The biggest TV show in my life at that time was the BBC's evergreen SF serial *Doctor Who,* shot on the then industry standard of three large video cameras, in a studio, with the occasional outing on to film for exteriors. There wasn't even an awareness that TV could be made any other way: it was just how it was. Things like *The Saint* and *The Rockford Files* – all shot on film – were the exception on British television back then, and even then didn't really possess what could be described as a cinematic sensibility.

> *A crash of thunder. A deserted runway. The music creeping up slowly on the soundtrack. In the centre of the screen, a small car races straight towards the camera like a bullet from a gun. Crash close-up to the angular, implacable face of the driver, McGoohan himself, as the series' theme crashes in at the same time...*

This wasn't usual. This was the opening of a film rather than a TV title sequence. The revelations went on: in a mixture of stylised camera angles, impressionistic lighting and perfectly judged, propulsive music, the driver delivers a resignation letter and returns to his fashionable address. The whole back story was laid out with devastating economy. Narrative and cinematic ambition fused together perfectly. And the colours were so vivid, the way you always imagine the sunlight was in your childhood.

Preconceptions kept tumbling. After a fade to black the driver – by now identified in the title as 'The Prisoner' – woke up still in his front room but the world outside his window was different, an idyllic looking place that was a riot of baroque architectural styles. As he explored this strange village, the oppositions of the series were spelt out in a voiceover between the Prisoner and an unseen 'Number 2' controller / gaoler. The visual rhythm changed again: here were hi-tech, circular control rooms that wouldn't look out of place in *2001: A Space Odyssey*, and a quivering balloon born under the sea pursuing the Prisoner along a beach – *Alice Through the Looking Glass* in collision with Powell and Pressburger. A final, iconic shot, full of sun flare, of the lonely man on that empty beach railing against the dying of the light: *"I am not a number, I am a free man!"*

Identity, rebellion. Serious themes, intertwined with the unlimited potential of film making, the unlimited potential of art in general... It was all there in that short section of brilliantly edited film, searing into my mind in one of those genuine but rare Road to Damascus conversions we have in our lives. Something had shifted dramatically in me in those few short moments. I was somehow processing all this as, with great wit, the episode proper, *The Girl Who Was Death,* cheerfully tore up the TV action thriller rulebook before my eyes and threw away the bits. There is, of course, a great and forever pleasurable irony in my love affair with *The Prisoner* beginning with a story that, initially at least, seemed the least like the rest of it. This in-built subversion was somehow fitting. *The Girl Who Was Death* is still one of my favourite episodes of anything.

Thirty-five years later I've written a lot of words about *The Prisoner.* It's no exaggeration to say that my life, both personal and professional, would have been very different without that curious late night viewing in 1982. *The Prisoner* opened my mind to art and literature and was the subject of my first book. I've been lucky enough to meet and interview many of the people I admired for creating something so breathtakingly unique, including Kenneth Griffith, the star of *The Girl Who Was Death.* I'm one of the few TV researchers who spoke to Patrick McGoohan in his twilight years, if only briefly (skip to the end for that highlight, if you wish). I heard second-hand that, apparently, Patrick didn't like some of the conclusions I came to, but as far as I'm concerned, with *The Prisoner* that's just as it should be. Never accept.

It would be an exaggeration to say that, fifty years later, the world at large has at last caught up with *The Prisoner,* but television drama certainly has. From *Peaky Blinders* to *Breaking Bad* to *Sherlock,* TV looks like quality cinema. You can watch *The Prisoner* today after any of the above, gloriously restored on Blu-ray, and it fits perfectly; more than that, it doesn't look like it's half a century old. Watch any old episode of *Doctor Who* from the 20th century now, and the staginess of the sets and the emphatic performances look like some short-lived, arty experiment in televised theatre. *The Prisoner* was of its time but timeless.

All those years ago, I had no idea that the series was a stablemate of colourful pulp thrillers such as *Department S, Randall and Hopkirk (Deceased)* and *The Champions* that I fondly remembered from rainy Sunday afternoons in the 1970s. If you like iconoclastic artists like Orson Welles, Bowie or John Lydon, you can recognise in *The Prisoner* the sheer delight people like them take in twisting the most popular of popular culture out of shape to create something genuinely new, thrilling and challenging. On television, McGoohan's restless spirit has informed deliberately unconventional dramas like *Twin Peaks, Mr Robot* and *Westworld,* among many others. An impressive legacy.

Wherever I am now, I'm largely there thanks to *The Prisoner*. Because of it I'm more open minded, question the status quo more and am massively impatient with the increasing bureaucratisation of a society where, it seems, no one has to, or wants to, take responsibility for anything. I often think about how the person I am now really began with those fifty minutes of revelation, long ago on a late night in a 1980s summer. Thank God television was once that powerful.

***

It's sometime in 2001. *The Prisoner - The Official Companion to the Classic TV Series*, my first book, had been commissioned. Holed up in my best mate's spare room, I was researching and trying to type quietly (thin walls). In those days, it was still possible to communicate with people by fax, so, via the local corner shop in overcast Catford, I'd contacted Patrick McGoohan's agents in America. All the evidence suggested that I wouldn't get a response, but I've always believed you should never say never. Still do.

The mobile rang. I didn't recognise the number.

"Hello?"

A gruff, wry voice. *"This is Patrick calling from LA."*

I didn't make what should have been the automatic connection. *"Patrick who?"*

"Patrick McGoohan." Even and unflappable.

People describe their brain freezing but I'd thought it was hyperbole until that moment. This was Patrick McGoohan. The mastermind behind *The Prisoner*. Calling *me*. From America. The chance of a lifetime.

I tried for something significant to say but it wasn't happening.

"How are you, Patrick?" It was the best I could manage.

"Fine, fine. I wish you could see this: the sun coming up over the sea..."

It was clearly early where he was, but he was in good spirits and already out and about.

Then, *"I'm just calling to tell ya I won't be doing any more interviews about* The Prisoner *for the rest of my life. Be seeing ya."*

End of phone call.

It's the shortest and most inept interview I've ever done - it's not even an interview, in truth - but it's still the one I've thought about the most. They say you shouldn't meet, or talk, to your heroes, but even though I'd been disappointing during that conversation, Patrick hadn't disappointed me. How so like that enigmatic and mischievous man to phone up a gauche, aspiring writer to tell him he was done with talking about *The Prisoner*. I've often wondered why he did it but there could be any number of reasons. Maybe he didn't really know why.

I do know one thing. Sixteen years later, I'm still writing because of that phone call.

Thank you, Patrick.

Where Am I?

Annette Hill

I've always enjoyed watching a variety of TV shows and as a child I was a particular fan of *Doctor Who* starring Tom Baker, so much so that I wrote to the BBC and a month later I was thrilled to receive a signed photograph. I went with my family to watch Tom and his co-stars Elisabeth Sladen and Ian Marter switch on the Blackpool Illuminations in 1975 (when I was 10) and I excitedly went to the town's *Doctor Who* Exhibition to meet them and get their autographs.

My primary school in St Annes-on-Sea had an annual summer fair and somehow the school was often able to organise a celebrity to open the event. One year my Dad was chair of the PTA and I got the job of presenting Wilfrid Brambell of the BBC situation comedy *Steptoe and Son* with a pen as a thank you from the school. Another year the comedian Russ Abbott bought one of my Mum's apple pies. Most years we ran the book and comic stall. If I could go back in time I'd snap up all those *Look-in* magazines we had on sale.

My introduction to action TV series came in the form of American imports such as *Alias Smith and Jones*, *Starsky and Hutch* and *The Six Million Dollar Man*. Whilst I enjoyed the action and storylines I also appreciated leading men such as Ben Murphy, David Soul and Lee Majors. The first ITC series I remember watching was *Return of the Saint*. I liked Ian Ogilvy (having never seen the Roger Moore series at that time) and I loved the series' theme tune. I never would have imagined meeting Ian years later (at *Memorabilia* in Birmingham in 2011), let alone sitting in one of the Jaguars used in the series.

In the early 1980s my favourite actor was John Duttine, star of *To Serve Them All My Days* and *The Day of the Triffids*. My bedroom wall was adorned with clippings of interviews and photos of him from *Radio Times* and *TV Times* magazines. One feature included information on the management company that represented John, so I duly wrote off to his agent explaining how much I enjoyed his TV work and I was delighted to receive an autographed photograph.

Fast forward to 1986; I was training to be a music teacher at Bretton Hall College near Wakefield and my boyfriend was editor of a TV magazine called *Time Screen*. This brought about my introduction to a variety of ITC series that I'd never heard of including *Randall and Hopkirk (Deceased)*, *The Champions* and *The Prisoner*. We used the actors' directory *Spotlight* to speculatively contact actors to interview for the magazine and we were amazed when Kenneth Cope phoned us up out of the blue to tell us that he was available to be interviewed that weekend in Liverpool. A hasty preparation of questions was organised and that interview would, when transcribed, form my first article for the magazine. In fact, I only went on to write one more article for *Time Screen* as I much prefer proof reading the work of others!

1986 also marked the first time that I attended a *Prisoner* convention at the series' principal filming location, Portmeirion. I'd never seen the series and Andrew Pixley had some episodes on VHS so I duly watched *Arrival*, *Checkmate*, *Free for All* and *Fall Out* in the way of preparation. My recollections of the event are rather hazy, but Portmeirion was to have a massive impact on my life.

I loved the magical surroundings of Portmeirion from that very first visit; the quirky architecture, the colours, flowers, sea views. I have visited the Village every year ever since and each time it's like returning home. I got engaged there in 1997 and luckily my husband and daughter share my love of Clough Williams-Ellis' creation. For the past fifteen years we've had family holidays there in the summer, sharing a cottage with like-minded friends.

Rob Piercy prints of the Village adorn our bedroom wall and I avidly collect Portmeirion postcards old and new. Breakfast is always eaten out of Portmeirion pottery cereal bowls and, despite having visited the place so many times, I continue to enjoy filling photo albums and creating photobooks of my times there.

My passion for visiting TV locations had blossomed still further after I attended the first *Avengers Dead Man's Treasure Hunt* in 1987. For the fourth *Treasure Hunt – Wish You Were Here* – in 1990, the first *Guide to Avengerland* was produced and this contained all the locations we had by then found for *The Avengers* and ITC filmed series. In the days before the internet and Google Street View, the process of location finding included study of Ordnance Survey maps and Hertfordshire guidebooks and taking off-screen photos from VHS recordings of episodes and taking the prints with us! Tony McKay, Andrew Pixley, Mike Richardson and I made several further location hunting trips down to Hertfordshire, the result being the publication of a more detailed *Guide to Avengerland* in 1993 and another revised edition six years later.

I attended many *Prisoner* conventions over the years and I happily took part in the chess game and election parade re-enactments. Highlights include meeting Kenneth Griffith there in 1990 and the outdoor interview with Alexis Kanner in 1996. Other memorable *Prisoner* events took place outside the Village. *The Last Chance* event in November 1989 was the final opportunity to see The Thatched Barn in Borehamwood before its demolition. Back in the Sixties it had doubled as Number 6's local pub in *The Girl Who Was Death*. Several members of the cast and crew were in attendance but the highlight for me was being able to photograph a wonderful building that is now lost to us. In 1991 the Borehamwood *Priz Conference* had James Bree as a special guest and there was an opportunity to try the paternoster lift at the GEC Marconi building on Elstree Way that he had used in *Do Not Forsake Me Oh My Darling*. Ten years later, the lift was removed from service, and the building itself was demolished in 2012 – another distinctive *Prisoner* location consigned to memory.

In 1993, I went to another convention, this time devoted to ITC film series in general, called *Action 93*. It was held near Shepperton Studios and guests included Kenneth Cope and, memorably for me, the man who pushed the white Jaguar over the cliff (first seen in *The Baron* and then re-used in many other ITC series). Marty's red Mini from *Randall and Hopkirk (Deceased)* also put in an appearance at the event, fortunately never having been pushed over a precipice!

My enjoyment of ITC programmes has continued to this day. Over the years my DVD collection has grown considerably, enabling me to watch series such as *Strange Report* from remastered prints plus others new to me like *Espionage*. Away from the TV screen, I have been very fortunate to meet ITC stars William Gaunt, Kenneth Cope, Annette André and Alexandra Bastedo, among others, at events such as *Memorabilia* and *Autographica* and I loved proof reading Mike Richardson's magazine *Action TV* as it gave me valuable insights into many ITC series.

I still continue to visit TV locations when the opportunity arises. On a week-long family holiday to Paris, I managed to incorporate some places seen in *The New Avengers* and *The Protectors* as we walked around Montmartre and Notre-Dame. In 2015, as part of my 50th birthday celebrations, I travelled to Amsterdam with a group of friends and we went on a location tour organised by Jan Van Leeuwen, a regular *Treasure Hunt* attendee from the Netherlands.

2016 marked the 50th anniversary of *The Prisoner*'s location filming in Portmeirion, a landmark well worth celebrating. Coincidentally, it also marked another anniversary of a more personal nature, since 30 years had passed since my first viewing of the series and my eye-opening introduction to the Village. The feeling of excitement that I experienced on my memorable first visit to Clough Williams-Ellis' breathtaking creation – the filming location from my favourite ITC series – has never left me. The 'I've been there' feeling I get when I watch an episode remains as strong as ever and I look forward to many more location visits in years to come. Where am I? In the Village – whenever possible!

Living in Harmony with The Prisoner

Jon Older

It's quite hard from the viewpoint of 2017 – fifty years after I first saw it - to remember a time when *The Prisoner wasn't* a part of my life. Ever since the autumn of 1967 this most remarkable of all television series has been with me in the form of books, home-made audio tapes, magazine articles, Six of One mail outs and conventions (though it's been a long while since I've been to one of *those*), the Channel 4 re-screenings, the Precision Video and Channel 5 VHS tapes, Japanese laserdiscs (*The Prisoner* in Japanese is surreal), DVDs and now a glorious Network Blu-ray edition of the series. It has been a constant back drop to everything else I've ever done. *The Prisoner* has always been there. "I will not be pushed, filed, stamped, indexed, briefed, de-briefed, or numbered! My life is my own" has informed most of my adult life.

I couldn't explain the huge impact that *The Prisoner* had on me when I first saw it (in black and white, by the way, on Granada TV in 1967. It wasn't until the first re-run that I got to see it in colour, hugely improving an already incredible show). It touched a nerve. Something about it was uniquely different and it had an instant appeal for me that no other show had ever had up to that time – or has had since. I'd been hooked by the visual poetry of *The Outer Limits* and Vic Perrin's lyrical Control Voice narrations. I was already a big fan of other American shows like *The Twilight Zone*, and eventually would be of *Star Trek*, *Mission: Impossible* and *The Man From U.N.C.L.E.* I'd been a fan of *Doctor Who* from the very beginning (I saw the first episode twice, two weeks running, because of the assassination of John F Kennedy in 1963). There were lots of ITC action adventure shows, like *The Saint*, *Gideon's Way*, *The Baron* and *Danger Man* that I really liked, but none of them had the instant, challenging appeal that *The Prisoner* delivered.

The narrative was easy enough to follow (OK – I admit it, I still don't understand the Guardians sitting worshipping Rover in the cave at the end of *Free For All*) and I, like millions of other viewers, was totally confused (and blown away) by the final episode of the series which seemed to explain nothing and appeared to have been written on drugs. (I know now just what a fantastic piece of showmanship writing and directing McGoohan pulled off with *Fall Out*.) All I did know was that I was seeing something that I'd never seen before. I'd been a big fan of *The Avengers* since its video days and I loved (still do) the fantastic adventures of John Steed and Cathy Gale, Emma Peel and Tara King. But I knew that despite its wonderful performances and Swinging Sixties vibe, *The Avengers* was just about telling fairly conventional stories in a heightened, stylish way. *The Prisoner* seemed to be trying to tell me something more than that and I needed to find out what it was.

It wasn't about just the actor. I've spent my entire working life surrounded by actors so it's hardly surprising that I have no illusions about them but I'd always liked McGoohan as a performer prior to *The Prisoner*. I grew up with him on *Danger Man* in both its half hour and hour-long editions. I went to see him on the big screen for the first time in *Dr Syn – Alias The Scarecrow* in 1964 (I still have the re-issue quad poster) – and here's a bit of previously unpublished trivia for all you *Prisoner* fans: Russell Thorndike, author of the original *Dr Syn* novel was also a frequent visitor to Portmeirion in North Wales, and the concluding chapters of his fifth novel *The Amazing Quest of Dr Syn* are actually set in the grounds of an un-named Portmeirion – some thirty years before McGoohan got around to it! Thankfully, I didn't get to see *The Three Lives of Thomasina* the following year as its saccharine tone might have put me off for life. (Another trivial fact – McGoohan originally had a three-picture contract with Disney dating from the 1960s. It took him until 1985 to deliver the last film on that contract, *Baby: Secret of the Lost Legend*.)

I caught up with his earlier films mostly via TV screenings. Great movies like *Hell Drivers*, *All Night Long* and *Life For Ruth*, and not-so-great potboilers from his Rank contract days like *Nor The Moon By Night* and *The Gentleman and The Gypsy*. But PMcG rapidly became someone whose work – for good or bad – I'd strive to see. There've been some lows as well as some highs along the way as anyone who has seen his performance as an American astronaut in the *Armchair Theatre* production *The Greatest Man In The World* can attest to. Admittedly a broad satire, McGoohan's performance is so far over the top as to be back round the other side. He's terrible in it! Yet his performance as a doomed Russian cosmonaut in the same show's *The Man Out There* is first rate and deeply moving. *Brand*, on the other hand, is theatrical and bold and far too big for the television version that was produced in 1959, but it shows the young actor at the height of his powers, and embraces perfectly the themes that he would pursue in later life, in projects like *The Prisoner*.

McGoohan wasn't always good, but he was always fascinating to watch. *Ice Station Zebra* was to have been McGoohan's breakout performance, the one that would have catapulted him into Hollywood as a career action man. Shot during the gap between the putative first and second series of *The Prisoner*, (one story has it that McGoohan wrote most of *Fall Out* on the plane back from America), his portrayal of David Jones, a British secret agent, could almost have been a missing adventure from the backstory of Number 6. But the film wasn't the box office smash that Hollywood hoped for and McGoohan, after completing *The Prisoner* with the most controversial wrap up in UK television history (and make no mistake, *Fall Out* really was a radical way to close an ITC show back in the 1960s) retreated to the States and his career never really again regained the status it had enjoyed in the UK. Later film performances, in David Cronenberg's mind-blowing *Scanners* (the first VHS commercial tape I ever bought) or Alexis Kanner's *Kings and Desperate Men*, or Mel Gibson's *Braveheart*, were equally mesmerising, but it would be McGoohan's unbeatable, resolute, immovable, indefatigable Number 6 that would always be his defining image.

I've worked as an Assistant Director in UK television for over thirty years. I've had the pleasure and privilege of meeting a number of actors and technicians who did work on the series, most of whom, alas, are no longer with us in 2016. Almost to a man, they all expressed amazement that anyone wanted to know anything about this quirky, off the wall show that they had appeared in or worked on so long ago, but were equally happy to dig back into their memories and talk about it. Though I never met him face to face, my first success was getting a written interview with Leo McKern, a truly remarkable Australian actor who – *Rumpole* notwithstanding – never quite achieved the sort of fame he should have done. At the time it was rumoured that he always refused to talk about his involvement in three episodes of *The Prisoner* because of a nervous breakdown he apparently suffered while working on the series. It seems clear to me that poor old (hardly slimline) Leo was probably physically exhausted by the gruelling two-hander that McGoohan put him through as both actor and director in *Once Upon A Time*. He may have lost a few pounds but a nervous breakdown? (*Prisoner* Trivial Fact #3: According to Derek Pykett's excellent history of the *MGM British Studios: Hollywood in Borehamwood*, a supporting artiste, one William Rutherford Lumley from West Hampstead, was actually found dead near the *Prisoner* dressing room block, in February 1967.) Anyway, McKern couldn't have been that upset by the experience – and the episode is quite unlike any other episode of adventure TV from the 1960s – because he returned within months to take part again in the series' delirious final instalment. He was remarkably happy to chat about the show when I got through to him when he was working at The Royal Exchange in Manchester in 1978 in a production of *Uncle Vanya*.

Many years ago I took a train up to London to meet with Jack Shampan, the unheralded but absolute genius set designer for the show. Jack was the most modest and unassuming of men and looked like he should have been running a hairdresser's or selling Woodbine in a little corner shop somewhere in Islington. He entertained me for several hours at his house in North London and it was a genuine thrill to just sit in an armchair with him, taking tea from the very same tea trolley that Angelo The Butler used in the series (*Prisoner* Trivial Fact #4: My ex-wife in Cape Town is a great friend of Wolfgang Weissenstein, who played Number 2's Butler in the totally forgettable and ill-judged remake of *The Prisoner* from AMC and Granada in 2009, shot in Cape Town Studios and Namibia). We talked about movies (Jack's credits included *Modesty Blaise* and a couple of *Carry On* films), set design and his incredible experiences shooting McGoohan's show. Jack was maybe *the* true, unsung hero of *The Prisoner* and his fantastic set designs are indivisible from the show's lasting success and longevity. I don't think he was ever really recognised enough for his huge contribution and sadly it's much too late now as Jack passed away in 1989.

I knew, and worked with, the late George Baker for many years, beginning with his guest spot on *Robin of Sherwood* as Marion's dad, and then for several years on *The Ruth Rendell Mysteries* series, when George played Inspector George Wexford. Over the years George and I became quite good friends and he often used to throw impressive dinner parties in his cottage in Romsey during the shoot. One of my favourite evenings was getting to watch my VHS of *Arrival* with the New Number 2 drinking several large brandies and telling me all sorts of stories about PMcG while he handed out generous portions of his home baked dessert. It was also during my time on that show that I encountered the lovely Norma West, who played Number 6's Observer in *Dance of the Dead*. She recalled her time on the show with much affection and even allowed me to photocopy her personal copy of the script.

Other *Prisoner* personnel I've talked to over the years include Assistant Director John O'Connor. I once had to pick his car up from a garage on a job we did together – *The Master of Ballantrae* for HTV West in the early 1980s. It was like driving around in a giant ash tray! John loved to smoke big thick cigars. He was always really hard to draw out about his time on *The Prisoner* but he did tell me that it "was one of the hardest jobs I ever worked on". John was the 2nd AD on the series, a role that doesn't usually require much time to be spent actually on set. However, John features in dozens of on-set stills taken during the shoot, and he even gets to play a disgruntled gardener with dialogue in the *Checkmate* episode. With the number of units they constantly had shooting during the 1966 Portmeirion visit, it's pretty obvious that it was a case of all hands on deck to get all the material shot in time. (Speaking of cases and hands, *Prisoner* Trivial Fact #5: It's John O'Connor's hands that throw our hero's passport into his case in the opening titles as the pre-credits sequence was slowly completed during the main unit shoot at MGM Borehamwood.)

I've also spoken to Anton Rodgers, Mark Eden, stuntmen Max Faulkner and the lovely, late Peter Brayham (Peter was the one that gets dumped into the horse trough by PMcG in *Living in Harmony* after a prolonged – and originally censored – fight sequence), Rachel Herbert, set dresser Ken Bridgeman, John Laurimore, Rosalie Crutchley, and both Nigel Stock and Zena Walker (who turned up together on an early episode of *Crown Court* at Granada). Nigel was nice but Zena was a bit scary and didn't seem to recall much about working on *The Prisoner* at all.

I also once worked as 1st AD to director / producer Peter Graham Scott, who was more than happy to tell me that McGoohan was basically "a thick Irishman who got lucky", despite the fact that the "thick" Irishman was the one who asked Peter to direct *The General* at short notice when somebody else dropped out of the running. Peter was a very amusing man and I'm sure he really had a great deal of respect for PMcG when he wasn't just trying to wind me up (he directed several episodes of *Danger Man* too). His most famous instruction to me when we were shooting second unit scenes at sea off the coast of Dartmouth for *Master of Ballantrae* was "Jon, get that f**king battleship out of shot" as it hove into view out of a fog bank behind our three-masted rig, the ill-fated *Marques* (she sank shortly after the film had wrapped, off the coast of Bermuda, with the loss of 19 lives).

The one person I really regret never meeting – apart from McGoohan of course – was David Tomblin. (I did get to work with his Art Director daughter Jane once, though. She was much better looking than Dave was.) Tomblin was so central to the whole *Prisoner* enterprise, not only as McGoohan's business partner in Everyman Films, but as Producer, as co-writer of the set-up episode *Arrival*, as co-writer and director of *Living in Harmony* (one of the best episodes of the entire show), and I suspect not infrequently as unofficial 1st AD on one of the many units shooting the series. I'd love to have sat in a pub with him and just talked about his hugely successful – and long – career in UK television, from *H.G. Wells' Invisible Man* to *The Prisoner*, *UFO* and *Space: 1999*, and then his mega career as a movie 1st AD on *Raiders of the Lost Ark*, *The Empire Strikes Back*, *Gandhi* and all the rest. I'd love to have asked him about those early days of pre-production, after McGoohan pulled out of a fourth series of *Danger Man*. I'd love to know why Leslie Gilliat went on the early recce to Portmeirion but subsequently pulled out of working on the show. I'd love to know who really came up with the idea of a giant, white bouncing ball to patrol The Village in place of the robotic beefburger that arrived off the back of a truck at Portmeirion. So many questions he could have answered. But sadly that particular meeting never happened.

As to meeting McGoohan himself, well it was obviously destined never to be. Barely weeks prior to my joining HTV West, McGoohan had actually been working in the West Country for the company on their remake of *Jamaica Inn*! By the time I'd landed in my new job, he'd already been and gone. All I have to show for it is an original copy of the shooting script. I'd almost had another chance prior to that when I was living in Manchester, when the Royal Court Theatre had announced that PMcG was to return to the UK to star in a new production of *Moby Dick*, to be directed by Michael Elliott. (McGoohan, of course, had been in the original stage production of Orson Welles' *Moby Dick – Rehearsed* in 1955 at the Duke of York's Theatre in London.) I still remember the incredible excitement I felt, thinking that I'd actually get to see McGoohan perform live on stage! But it never happened. For whatever reason, PMcG pulled out of the show and made his eventual return to the stage in America shortly afterwards in 1985 in Hugh Whitemore's play *Pack of Lies*, playing (of course) a British intelligence agent. There was one more close call. In 1991 I got invited to meet director Alvin Rakoff at the Cinema Verity offices in Shepherd's Bush, with a view to working on an upcoming project that they then had in pre-production. It was a good enough meeting but for whatever reason I didn't get the job. It was only after I'd eventually watched *The Best of Friends* that I realised that this was the show that I'd interviewed for – and it had starred John Gielgud, Wendy Hiller and, of course, Patrick McGoohan…

I made my first trip to Portmeirion shortly after the first transmission of *Fall Out* in 1968, and have been back many times since, pacing over every inch of its famous landscape and marvelling at how really, *really* small it all is – and all the time getting more annoyed by the fact that it was barely two hours away from where my family then lived, in the 1960s, in Wrexham, North Wales, and I could have been watching them shoot the bloody thing if I'd only known about it – and been a bit older, with a car, and some money. I could even have joined that revered group of (now) mostly dead original crowd artists. People who actually worked on the show for £2.10 a day and all the tea they could drink. I've been there with college friends, assorted girlfriends, my mum and dad, on my own and even stayed there with a particularly nuts Canadian producer who was totally blown away by the place – and she'd never even seen *The Prisoner* (I made her watch *all* of it; we split up shortly afterwards).

I read Drama and English at uni and did my degree dissertation on *The Prisoner*, tracing its influences from novels like *Brave New World* and *Nineteen Eighty-Four* and attempting to show just how bloody radical the series had been back in 1967. I'm sure it was a bit of a cheat really when all my fellow deep-thinkers were writing about incest in the Brontë family or how Shakespeare was secretly an Italian or something. I think I've actually still got it in a box somewhere.

It used to be my party trick when I was at university that I could recite from memory every one of the seventeen *Prisoner* scripts to anyone who was daft enough to ask me. Simply by years of listening to my off-air tapes over and over again (this was prior to the advent of home video, you understand) I eventually learned them all by heart. I'd also laboriously typed out transcripts of all the shows from my off air-recordings and copious notes scribbled during the original screenings and re-runs. So I'd challenge anyone to pick a script at random, give me a line and I'd tell them the next one. I got a lot of drinks out of that useless ability, but it wasn't a great deal of use in trying to date any women. These days of course I still pop in an episode if my spirits are needing a bit of a lift, but I don't listen to or watch it anything like as much as I did thirty years ago. But I can still give it a pretty good shot if you want to test me.

I was in at the formation of Six of One. I'd never been a member of a fan club in my life. But having endured years of slightly patronising and sympathetic looks from my school friends for my obsession with *The Prisoner*, when Dave Barrie's announcement was broadcast by ATV Midlands at the end of their 1976 re-run, I jumped at the chance to meet anyone at all who thought as much of the show as I did. So I got on the train (I didn't buy my first car – a Triumph TR7 – until 1981) and headed off to Cheltenham to meet with Dave, Roger Goodman, Judie Adamson and a handful of other enthusiasts and that was where the Appreciation Society was born. For a few years it was great. Not only did it bring quarterly mail-outs, telling me things I'd never known about the production, but it also gave me regular treats like photocopies of call-sheets, stills I'd never seen before, access to actual 16mm screenings of episodes themselves (this was the *only* way to actually see the series again at that time) and an annual convention in the grounds of The Hotel Portmeirion itself. For many years it was a great resource – a far cry from the rather elitist and small-minded organisation it seems to have become today.

I've collected just about whatever there is to collect regarding *The Prisoner*. Don't forget this was before commercial companies latched onto the fact that there's money to be made exploiting fans and their enthusiasms, so there was actually very little original *Prisoner* merchandise to collect. But I've got my original (photocopies) of the seventeen shooting scripts, I've got the Dinky Mini-Moke Taxi in its original box. I've got the original ITC publicity brochures. I've got hundreds of production stills from the show. I've got the paperbacks (and hardbacks) based on the show and of course the much more recent script books and *Prisoner* Fact Files magazines. I've even got a two page hand-written letter from the late Thomas Disch when he was kind enough to reply at length to my gentle criticisms of his original novel based on *The Prisoner*. (I was politely outraged that he'd changed so much of the details. He admitted to me that he'd never actually *seen* the series when he was asked to write an original novel based on it.) I've got the original RCA Victor 7 inch vinyl single [1635] of the Ron Grainer theme (in its sleeve of course) and I've got the various LP and CD soundtrack releases from more recent years – including the most recent release from Network, a soundtrack album on vinyl! Who saw that making a comeback? One day I'd love to track down the original Everyman Films progress reports for the show as they'd definitively tell us the true production history of the show. (There are a number of photocopied call sheets from the shoot in circulation, but they only ever represent what's intended to be shot on a given day. The progress reports show what actually happened.) A handful of photocopies have surfaced over the years but I'm willing to bet that they're all languishing somewhere in a forgotten cardboard box in somebody's attic.

For years I had the image of Patrick McGoohan zooming around sunny Sixties London in his S2 Lotus 7 and I knew that one day – *by hook or by crook* – I would have to own one. It took a few years longer than I thought it might, but eventually, after I moved from Granada TV in Manchester down to HTV West in Bristol, I finally had the funds to pick one up second-hand. It was both a joy and a nightmare to own. From a practical point of view it was freezing cold in the winter. I once spent a very long, very miserable night parked in a lay-by outside Bath waiting for the AA to arrive, watching the snow pile up on the bonnet. You also can't get anything in one – and these were the days I needed to carry boxes of walkie-talkies and all manner of things to work with me, wherever we were shooting. I once memorably blew the side exhaust clean off the car on the way to a *Robin of Sherwood* location. I was even daft enough to let Ray Winstone take a spin in it (but only around the field where base camp was parked up). My new favourite party piece was driving up to the HTV studios on Bath Road and simply driving underneath the security barrier, much to the annoyance of the little man in the booth. And yes, I did drive up to London and recreated the drive from the opening titles – across Westminster Bridge, past the Palace of Westminster, hanging a right into the Abingdon Street underground car park, down Pall Mall and eventually ending up parked outside 1 Buckingham Place (on double yellows). And this was in the days when Stag Place still had its stag and the high rise office blocks still stood across the road. Much as I loved it, in the end my 7 just had to go. The sub-frame cracked and it was going to cost me too much to fix it so I sold it on to a dealer in Salisbury for almost the same as I'd paid for it. These days I drive a much more civilised Honda S2000, with a heater that works.

I can still recall the exact moment when and where I was when a friend of mine called me in 2009 to ask me if I'd heard the news – the terrible news – that Patrick McGoohan was dead. Number 6 was dead. Died in Santa Monica after a short illness. Probably the only real hero I'd ever had. I was devastated and I'm not embarrassed to admit that I really did tear up a little bit. Why? For somebody I never knew? For somebody who had just played at make-believe all his life? It wasn't just that. I'd lost an ideal. Somebody whose fictional creation had genuinely touched a deep nerve in me.

I never understood why I reacted so strongly to *The Prisoner* when I first saw it in 1967. It was only in later years that I fully understood what McGoohan had been trying to say with the show and how it had affected me so much that I had ended up trying to live a life grounded in its philosophy by trying to avoid and escape the traps that modern Western life seeks to shape and fit us all into constantly – "the helpless consumer consumed in the feast" according to Roy Harper's tribute song *McGoohan's Blues*, on his 1969 *Folkjokeopus* album. By subtly encouraging us all to conform and buy into a system that thrives on exploiting us all for mainly monetary gain – to unquestioningly repeat the patterns that previous generations have set down for us – the System ultimately seeks to control us all.

The Prisoner has always been a central, but mainly a fantastically enjoyable, part of my life. It always will be. I can't imagine a time when I won't want to watch it all over again. *The Prisoner* taught me all about the importance of the individual in an ever increasingly centralised society. That a quirky, experimental (and some would say failed) TV show could do that is a mark of how truly inspiring and transformational Patrick McGoohan's crazy idea would finally prove to be.

My Favourite Waste of Time

Rick Davy

"Where is it you're going today?" asked an attractive lady in her mid-twenties. "Oh, I'm walking round what used to be a film studio, but now it's a housing estate; there's nothing left of the studio now," replied her suitor.

I still struggle to get my head around the fact that the lady in question didn't run off in the opposite direction screaming, "This man is bonkers," for the two individuals described above are myself, and my now wife, not long after we first met.

The fact that it wasn't the first time I'd walked round such locations with a group of like-minded individuals wasn't something that needed to be mentioned at the time, but whenever anyone enquires as to *why* one would want to do this, it's fair to say an appropriate answer would be, "Oh that's just one of things you do if you love *The Prisoner*."

The journey started for me, as it did for many others, in 1983. At the age of ten, my television diet was a mixture of children's series and low-budget science fiction. Occasional forays into adult series served little purpose other than to allow me to stay up later if I pretended to be interested in watching it (think *That's Life!* on a Sunday night – meaning I could still be up at gone 10pm, for example – "Sausages!").

"There's an old series being repeated tomorrow night; you might like it." Those were the immortal words uttered by my then 19-year-old brother on a Sunday in early September 1983. I was hoping it might be as good as *Sapphire and Steel*. It more than was, and unlike *Sapphire and Steel* I would actually understand what was going on in this new mystery series.

A fast-paced and unpredictable action-adventure thriller on one hand, and a thought-provoking allegorical conundrum on the other, I soon realised that *The Prisoner* was vastly different to any other series in television history. As was the case with many other people, it had a profound effect on me when I first saw it, and again as for many others it is a show into which I have become absorbed over the years. For some it is just another ITC show, one show in a list of many with a nice mix of action and fantasy. But to me it is so much more than that.

It had a message, and the message is as real today (if not more so) than it was when I first saw it. People talk about it being something of a 'Cold War thriller'. When I was ten I didn't know my Cold War from my Boer War, so

I didn't categorise it as that in the slightest. From my perspective, *The Prisoner* is life, and the Village is all around us. Patrick McGoohan is all of us; he lives on through *The Prisoner* and *The Prisoner* lives on through each of us.

I realise that's perhaps a bit deep for a book like this. Sure, I can regale you with tales about becoming close friends over the years with members of the cast and crew. I can amuse you with funny anecdotes from the series' production. I can tell you how I made countless friends through my interest in the series. But what *drove* all that is the fact that the series had something important to say. It spoke to me. A TV series, that many would see as a waste of time, affected me more deeply than any piece of music, or art, or film, or news, has done before or since.

Like many people, I spend an unhealthy amount of time arguing with people on the internet. Whilst most people's internet fracas relate to Brexit, or other political matters, my arguments mostly revolve around the minutiae of a fifty-year-old television series. Some might regard this as a waste of time. Maybe they are right. The signs were there from early on…

When I was ten, and armed with around half the episodes on VHS… Ah, I should probably explain here. Our top-loading AKAI was very unreliable – I had attempted to record all 17 episodes, but it had this habit of recording no picture and white noise as the soundtrack around half the time, and one didn't know it had done this until after the recording had been completed. Sometimes the sound would record but with no picture other than pure fuzz, which was fine for *Hancock's Half Hour* (*The Economy Drive* is just as funny with no images) but not so much for *Living in Harmony*.

I loved that AKAI though; it seemed so futuristic, something so 'adult' at such a purely childish time. I remember school sick days (or 'heating is broken at school so you've all got the day off' winter blessings). Along with Lucozade and Golden Cup or Texan chocolate bars, neither of which exist today (although, if you take off the bottom layer from two Double Decker bars and join them together, you get a Texan!), nothing says more to me than days off of primary school than the AKAI. We didn't have too many tapes, mind, and what we did have I had an aversion to recording over (in case it messed up the tape), so random things would be kept and loved and re-watched: the *Rising Damp* movie for one, a selection of 1982 editions of *Match of the Day*, *The Young Ones*, and nine episodes of *The Prisoner*.

Anyway, as I was saying, when I was ten… I made my own board game for the series. Nobody else at my primary school, other than my teacher Mr Milroy, had even heard of the series let alone seen it, so only my other brother (who at 15 had sat with me whilst I watched each Monday evening) and I could play it.

This total immersion was a sign of things to come (Quiz Question – What is the connection between the phrase 'total immersion' and *The Prisoner*? Answer given at the end of this chapter – no cheating!).

Move forward some thirty-four years and in 2017 I find myself, in the space of a month, writing this chapter of this book, writing the foreword to another, writing a column for a fan newspaper, writing a piece for the event brochure for the 50th anniversary, writing answers to an interview for *Starburst* magazine, and writing text commentaries for all 17 episodes of the series for the anniversary Blu-ray re-release (investigating the slightest changes to scripts, model numbers for refrigerators seen on screen for barely a second, and trying to make out the brand name of a pair of pyjamas seen on screen for even less). Whilst I was paid for the last of those tasks, the others have been what I would call a pleasure. Most other people would regard all of that as pointless time wasting.

Then, as I mentioned, there's the internet.

If one hasn't been online for a couple of days it can take hours to wade through all the repetition in the hope that the occasional gem can be found. Sometimes, once in a blue moon, there are posts which make me sit bolt upright. One such instance was the news that someone had an old reel of 8mm footage in the loft. Some emails, calls, a trip down to the South West, and then another to a studio later, the most beautiful footage ever uncovered relating to the Portmeirion shoot in 1966 was on a disc, and later found its way onto the 50th anniversary Blu-ray box set. Then there was a fantastic fan-made reproduction of a poster seen on screen in the background of a scene for just a few seconds, something in which nobody outside of a very small group of people would be remotely interested. The average human being just does not understand the allure of *The Prisoner*.

But among such highlights come annoyances. There are many 'fans' who feel that the Village authorities were in the right all along and that Number Six was some sort of troublemaker. Then there are those who, no matter what evidence you have given them, will always think their idiotic theories are right ("In *Once Upon a Time*, Number Two says, 'See you in the morning, Drake,' thus proving that Number Six is John Drake," is a regular one – he didn't, of course; he says "break"). My wife often asks me why I bother arguing with these people, and defending what McGoohan and others had created half a century before. "Oh that's just another of the things you do if you love *The Prisoner*."

I don't think my love affair / obsession / interest in / fascination with (delete as appropriate) *The Prisoner* will ever end, even though the 50th year since its production has introduced some sort of closure.

At *Fall In*, the 50th anniversary celebration staged by Network in Portmeirion on Friday 29th September 2017, guests gathered on stage, in between 35mm screenings of episodes (probably the last time such screenings will ever take place). Catherine McGoohan spoke, as did actresses Norma West, Jane Merrow and Annette Andre, and actors Derren Nesbitt and Peter Wyngarde, and crew member Seamus Byrne. Nicholas Briggs, executive producer at Big Finish (perhaps better known as the voice of the Daleks in the modern take on *Doctor Who*) stated that Catherine's interview at the event was, "The most inspiring I have ever heard".

Each had their own tale to tell. Some had positive experiences of working on the series, and some less so, but the key part of the event for me was when the guests all said thank you and goodbye, on stage, at the end of the evening.

When Jane Merrow came on stage she was clearly emotional when remarking to Catherine that there was no better person to speak on behalf of her late father. It was like Jane was saying goodbye to Patrick, an actor earlier that day she had referred to as having loved. The 50th anniversary was the last chance for such an event, some might say, and at the end of the celebration it is true to say that the curtain was seen to fall. Surviving cast and crew are few and far between, and the fans who attend events such as this are becoming more aged with each passing get-together. My wife wondered if she was the youngest attendee at *Fall In*... If she wasn't, then she wasn't far off. The 50th anniversary – the last hurrah. Or was it?

As *The Prisoner* enters its fifties, I see my task with *The Unmutual Website* (http://www.theunmutual.co.uk/) not as producing a memorial to a great series, but to use it as a tool for keeping the series alive. Although it engages existing fans through its trivia and factoids, announcements and reviews of new books and other releases, along with news about former cast and crew and changes at Portmeirion, the website also seeks to reach new fans of the series, and in doing so pass the baton of appreciation on to others, much like it had been passed to me all those years ago.

What a waste of time, some people might say. But to mis-quote a rather catchy, yet pretty poor, song from the 1980s, it's My Favourite Waste of Time. Thanks for the trip, bro!

Quiz Answer – "Total Immersion" was the tagline for *Catch My Soul*, the only feature film to have been directed by Patrick McGoohan.

The Champions

1968-1969

David Tulley is a support worker for mental health based in Leeds West Yorkshire, who specialises in Autism. He is a published author and has had many stories and poems in print over the years, in publications like *Just 17*, *Woman's Own*, *Prism Scifi* and many more. He was a winner in the Yorkshire Young Poets Competition, and his story *Down the Wooden Hill* was a prize winner in the Huddersfield Arts Council short story competition. His work has also been broadcast on radio. He co-wrote the first two independent *Blake's 7* original cast audio plays – *The Mark of Kane* and *The Logic of Empire* – and had the satisfaction of watching Paul Darrow break up after saying one of his lines! He has been a fan of ITC shows all his life, with *The Champions* first and foremost, but *Captain Scarlet and the Mysterons*, *The Prisoner* and *Department S* are all high on the list! He has three daughters and is very happily engaged.

Stephen La Rivière is a producer, director and writer currently tangled up in a messy relationship with puppet heroes of the '60s. Stephen was the producer of three new episodes of *Thunderbirds* made to celebrate the 50th anniversary of the classic series which came about as a result of his earlier work on the book *Filmed in Supermarionation* and the documentary of the same name. In the mid 2000s, Stephen worked for a time producing a series of retrospective documentaries on classic television series and films for various DVD releases.

Breakfast of Champions

David Tulley

A man is lying in the snow, face twisted, racked with pain. Flakes adhering to his scalp and the side of his face. He hears a sound and goes for his gun, moving with nightmarish, painful slow motion. His face in its agony is like that of a small child. The small movement hurts him so much that he seems on the verge of tears, but he's being very brave and tries not to show it. An old man is there, looking down at him with infinite compassion. The man passes out.

A man is lying in the snow, so good looking as to be almost unreal, like a grounded Adonis. He comes to, raises himself and shields his eyes against the sun. He smiles soft and slow, then a shadow draws over his face. Memory. He whirls to look for his friends, lying in the wreckage of their crashed airplane.

The Champions is my favourite ITC show. It is so much a part of my life – and has been from the moment that I first saw it, aged six or seven. I loved it so much that I asked my mum to buy me *The Sixth Sense is Death* – the solitary *Champions* novel, written by John Garforth – with my precious pocket money. The book totally mystified me, but at least it had photos of my heroes on the cover! This acquisition was quickly followed by the *Champions* dot-to-dot, puzzle and painting books, the latter of which had an amazing story, much better than the one devised for the *Sixth Sense* novel. I also collected all the gum cards, including the decoder – and all these years later, I have still got them, though I'm in the market for a gum wrapper!

In terms of more recent collectibles, I have an autographed photograph of all three of them – Alexandra Bastedo, Stuart Damon and William Gaunt – with Alexandra's name signed in gold, reminding me of the Champions' scars in *The Beginning*. I also have the soundtrack CDs, issued by Network. I love the music of *The Champions*, from Tony Hatch's soaring theme (my 'phone tone!) to the percussive bass of *The Search*, the swooping combat of *The Experiment*, and the nightmarish tones of *The Invisible Man*. Those soundtrack CDs are amazing; I've played them all to death…

Three people rescued from a crash in the Himalayas. Shades of Shangri La, Lost Horizon.

Dennis Spooner loved that film.

Three people, twisted, wrecked, broken and crushed. Reborn, rescued by a lost, advanced civilisation and augmented, made better, stronger, faster. No bionics, just flesh and blood, but better... Telepathic, with a strange lilting windchime sound as they share each other's minds and sensations... including kisses...

Mmmm, that did wonders for my imagination. I wonder what sex was like for the other two!

Two of the three even look like super humans. Stuart Damon as Craig was incredibly decorative, the greatest James Bond that never was; my daughter Chloe often used the phrase, "As handsome as Craig!" as a description when she was growing up. Alexandra Bastedo simply glowed; beautiful and yet strong and dynamic. William Gaunt was less conventionally handsome, but so graceful, moving like a dancer.

Craig, Sharron, Richard.

Let's get this straight. I *loved* this show as a child. Even today, it delights me when I watch it, and I still feel the old thrill of first discovery. I enjoy the camaraderie between the three central characters of the series, the warmth and affection between them. The opening titles, which take place against the stock footage backdrop of the famous waterspout in Geneva, were a guarantee of a hour well spent (and it's definitely on my bucket list to have my picture taken there, where they're supposed to be!). The little after-titles snatches of heroism and derring-do, showcasing our heroes' special powers – to run, leap, out-think, out hear, out see and outsmart every bad guy and girl – captivated me. The gold scars that fade were their badges of honour, the unseen medals of the Champions.

I played *The Champions* in the playground and I was always Craig. Later, I found Richard to be the more interesting male character. Sharron was a radiant creature, and Alexandra Bastedo was regularly listed amongst the world's most beautiful women. My firstborn daughter was named Alexandra, so she certainly had an effect on me... Ms Bastedo generously wrote to me in the last year of her life. I still have her messages, and the scarf she gave me that she wore in the episode *The Search.*

As a young watcher of the show, I never saw the contradictions within it. The Tibetan shaman puts Richard's hands in a gesture of prayer as he takes his leave, but they were never guilty of pacifism in the subsequent adventures. Later in the same pilot story, they mow down and mangle an entire battalion of Red Chinese for the greater good and the survival of the free world. In *To Trap a Rat*, Richard playfully leaves a drug dealer in a position where he is quite likely to be killed by his own men. In *The Search*, a dastardly henchman ends up being ejected through a high window… and so on.

But I love the little gentle moments of the show, the genuine affection of the characters towards each other, the warmth and fun, the revelling in their new-found awareness, their joy in their new selves. It was palpable.

Consequently, I still remember the sheer horror I felt when I first saw *Autokill*, in which they were pitted against each other in a fight to the death. The sheer frenetic violence of that final fight, in the very last episode, has always stayed with me – Sharron wrenching Richard's head back by his hair, Richard's frenzied clawing for Craig's throat, before Craig knocks him out, blood splattering everywhere, and then embraces him like the brother that he is… Wow!

When the three actors were reunited for the 2006 Network DVD release of the show, there were still sparks to be seen of the old chemistry and magic. I watched enthralled, whilst also missing the presence of the fatherly Tremayne, as played with real authority and false beard by the great Anthony Nicholls, who died in 1977 at the age of 74. Now grey haired, and suffering from bad backs and the like, they were so completely still my heroes.

Similarly, I was greatly moved when William Gaunt turned up at the end of *The Timber*, a recent movie, arriving out of the ice and snow; it was like seeing an old friend from my playground days, my past rushing back.

Thirty episodes – about a third of them really good, a third good, enjoyable stuff, a third frankly slow and plodding – and all of them fun! One episode is truly outstanding, *The Interrogation*. Don't take my word for it, go and watch it. Pinteresque, riveting drama in an ITC show? You'd better believe it. Stock footage to the nth degree but superb, economical writing, and a superlative guest star in Colin Blakely; one of the best pieces of TV ever, up there with *Fall Out* and the last episode of the original *Twin Peaks*. I told Dennis Spooner as much when I met him in Leeds. I like to think he was flattered, but he rather sheepishly told me that the story was written and produced with virtually no budget due to the chronic overspend on another episode (*To Trap A Rat*).

It may have been cheap, an episode born out of production limitations and necessity, *but it was amazing*. From the principal set, a spider-like room, to the genuine sense of panic and claustrophobia, and Craig's desperation as he pulls the door off its hinges to reveal the brick wall behind, the flawless way the reality of the cell melds into the vivid recollection of his past, it is an astonishing hour of television.

Thinking of the episodes where each character shines, *The Interrogation* is obviously my favourite 'Craig episode'. For Sharron, it is *Shadow of the Panther*, the one where the agent dies of fright in the lift and his hair turns white, with a voodoo element and an absurdly young Donald Sutherland. It sports some risqué innuendo: "You should see my pillow…" *(Full of bullet holes.)* "Craig! What are you suggesting…?" There are also some really eerie moments as diplomatic types with machetes stalk the corridors of a hotel, like something out of an old Amicus movie. Finally, for me the series high point for Richard comes in *Happening*, which centres upon an atom bomb test in the Australian outback, and Richard is slap bang in the middle of it, suffering from amnesia due to a parachute jump that he'd made without the essential item… The episode boasts an excellent guest star again (Jack MacGowran), and some lovely dialogue… "Here you lie, poor nameless git. You upped and died when you got bit…" We see Richard getting buried in a shallow grave, before he is resuscitated by an open heart massage from Sharron, who is half a continent away. Michael Gough, simmering, sallow and bitter, with that rat trap mouth, also adds class to this adventure.

These choices closely parallel the stars' own, except that Mr Gaunt has claimed to prefer *The Gilded Cage*, the one with the telepathic kisses… Mmmm. I love *The Beginning*, too; it engendered a lifelong love of flying jackets in me! Mine is just like Richard's.

Other episodes that are worth a special mention include *The Silent Enemy*, with its deadly island, the beaches of which are littered with dead fish, and a submarine with a crew of corpses; *Autokill*, for that breathtaking fight; and *The Experiment* – Sharron's second finest hour – London Bridge is falling down, and we witness Marion Grant (Caroline Blakiston), that super woman, chopping into the neck of her adversary, striking him so hard and sharp.

Yes, *The Champions* was a great show, wonderfully played and joyously unlike the run-of-the-mill, conventional cop shows that proliferated back then. These guys were, to coin a phrase, very different.

They Were The Champions

Stephen La Rivière

"Oh my god..."
"God almighty!"
"Gee whizz!"

As a documentary filmmaker, you never know how these sorts of moments will turn out. You often can't judge how people will react – and worse, you often don't know how everything will register on camera. A happy but muted reaction from an on-screen contributor can look like they are underwhelmed if you're not in the room itself. However, one moment I captured on camera didn't disappoint. It was completely pure – the reaction of three old friends, who hadn't been together for decades. In this moment, The Champions were reunited (and, in case you were wondering, the three quotes above were their very positive reactions).

I can't remember now how the idea for getting Alexandra Bastedo, William Gaunt and Stuart Damon back together again came about. But when Network Distributing was a client of my company back in 2006 I was always trying to find ways of doing something beyond just a series of talking head interviews. Where possible, I wanted to try and create stuff that on a technical level was acceptable for television, but on an editorial level catered directly to the target audience. There were enough superficial documentaries on TV about old shows for a 'casual' audience, after all.

I was 21, extremely naive about the business of making programmes, ambitious to do good work (I'm not sure I always succeeded there!), and I loved old television. And whilst the work was hard and not always especially fun, the chance to meet so many heroes from in front of and behind the camera was the ultimate anorak dream. For a period of a year, various cast and crew members from shows spanning *Upstairs Downstairs* to *Danger UXB*, *The Saint* to *The Persuaders!*, visited us at Pinewood to record new interviews and commentaries.

In 2005, we recorded a series of interviews for *The Champions* in preparation for a forthcoming DVD release. Individually, Alexandra Bastedo and William Gaunt visited us, and in July that year we flew to America, where we interviewed Stuart Damon. Stuart in particular had been a joy. His larger than life personality filled the room – and his sheer love for his co-stars whom he hadn't seen in decades shone through. And it continued to shine through back in England when we viewed the rushes. So often with these programmes there was an element of, 'We had fun making it, but there were all these problems...' That was absent here. All three of them recounted individually stories of their pure joy for several months in the '60s making the show. Their only sadness was that it didn't continue.

...Maybe we could get them back together?

We sounded out the idea. Would they want to be reunited? "YES – of course!" came the response. But – there's always a but – Stuart couldn't leave California as he was a regular on *General Hospital.* The idea had been to fly him to London. Maybe even do an event for the fans. However, that was impossible. And the cost of flying Gaunt and Bastedo to America – first class, plus hotels – was prohibitive. Network put more money into their DVD extras than most companies, but they were still miniscule compared to broadcast budgets. It annoyed me that even though Network was, at that time, a member of the Virgin group of companies, there was no provision to help us get discounted Virgin tickets!

So the project was off – until my business partner mentioned that, as he flew so much for his job, he had a lot of flight miles that he could donate. He could let us have enough to fly Bastedo and Gaunt to America. The project was back on! Telephones start ringing again... and then another spanner in the works. There's only really one week during which it can be done – but William Gaunt is on holiday that week with his wife. Catastrophe. It's definitely never going to happen now, I thought. Then the phone rang again – from William's agent. William and his wife are prepared to move their holiday to California – if we pay for the flights for both of them. The project was back on... once I'd done some grovelling to Network and my business partner for more money and air miles.

The trip to America itself was hell. An absolutely rammed schedule awaited us. We arrived in New York, got off the plane and interviewed Joel Fabiani for a forthcoming *Department S* DVD. Then we immediately got on a plane to Canada where we spent three days shooting *Due South* interviews, followed by an unforgettable trip (read into that what you will) to Las Vegas with Tony Curtis. Finally, we drove to Los Angeles where we filmed interviews for other forthcoming DVDs. And the final day – when we were all broken by tiredness and thoroughly fed up – was the day to reunite The Champions.

The shoot was a logistical nightmare. Not just getting them all into the same country, but getting them into the same room. After all this effort and expense, we didn't want to come away without at least two commentaries from them. So we had to find a recording studio that had both the technical set-up that we wanted, but also the space to sit all three of them down. Eventually, we found a place and all was set. My co-director Tom went off to meet Stuart, and I went off to meet William and Alexandra. We would go with them separately in their cars, recording their thoughts about the impending reunion. The final documentary tells a little white lie in the edit, as in reality it was Stuart who arrived first – and we bundled him into a cupboard whilst we got Bastedo and Gaunt into the building. Then it was time. Stuart entered the recording studio and laid eyes on his co-stars for the first time in decades. "Oh my god!" he exclaimed. The emotion was so pure. A brief glance around the crew saw a mixture of smiles and maybe even a tear. "We're still here, looking down at the grass!" said Stuart. The reunion with his young friends, now old, had reminded him of his mortality.

The following interview was hilarious – as were the commentary recordings. Time was running out, and Stuart desperately needed to get away for a filming commitment, but we managed to fit it all in. Mission accomplished. We returned to England exhausted, but buoyed by how brilliant the three of them had been.

The resulting programme, entitled *We Were the Champions*, was released in 2006 accompanying Network's release of the series. It was a difficult time for me personally as I was desperately overworked doing all this stuff – and indeed, the edit of the programme was made more complex by a severe infection that had robbed me of sight in one eye. And yet, when I rewatched the documentary for this chapter, I wasn't reminded of the difficulties, but the joy of that day in the studio came flooding back.

There's a sad coda to the story. In 2013, after a break of several years, I collaborated with Network again on a documentary called *Filmed in Supermarionation* about the history of Gerry and Sylvia Anderson's '60s puppet shows. During this time the possibility of doing another reunion in London was mooted – a chance for the fans to meet Alexandra, Stuart and William, along with a special screening of some episodes in High Definition. Initial discussions were had, but in 2014 Alexandra Bastedo died aged only 67.

Sadly, we now live in the period where our heroes of yesterday are moving on to Lew Grade's office in the sky. So I'm very grateful that during that period that I, and others working for other companies, were afforded the chance to capture their memories on tape. They may be gone, but their stories live on.

Department S

1969-1970

Mike Kenwood works in the computer industry. In his spare time he has been a tea boy, dogsbody, researcher, production assistant, interview question compiler, and associate producer on assorted DVD extras for BBC / 2|entertain Ltd, StudioCanal, ClearVision and Umbrella Entertainment. He has written features for magazines, CDs and websites and co-authored three books, *Fags, Slags, Blags & Jags: The Sweeney: the Unofficial Companion to the TV Series* (with George Williams), *Sweeney! The Official Companion* and *The Callan File: The Definitive Companion to the Classic Spy Franchise* (both with Robert Fairclough).

A Voice Comes Over Clear

Mike Kenwood

I am 6, I'm sitting in a car, and it's 1972.

As head of Maths in the school that I'll later attend, my Dad's rota of teaching responsibilities has ordained that on this particular Autumn Saturday afternoon, he should support the Sports department by helping oversee 22 boys, much bigger than me, while they play around with a rugby ball, trying to injure each other in a muddy Wiltshire field. On arriving home in Bath afterwards, just as dusk is falling, and noting Mum and my sister (then 3) haven't got back from their own separate (and probably more civilised) Bristol afternoon out, we find a visitor, mooching at the top of our drive. A hungry, lonely young tabby cat that will live with us contentedly for another 18 years.

Later that night, the gist of the conversation went roughly: "Dad, can we keep him?" "Maybe, if no one else has lost him." Mum and sister, arriving home, agree.

"Can we call him Jason?"

It is the only cat name I know: the Siamese from *Blue Peter*, which, like Jon Pertwee's *Doctor Who*, is just entering my radar.

"Of course we can."

I'm passing on this peripheral memory of my first cat, because it's occurred to me since then that maybe my parents weren't just indulging me by going along with this name. 'Jason' was *popular*. Maybe, once my sister and I were bathed, fed and put to bed, Mum and Dad would settle down on their pine green settee, and seek an hour's escapism from the power cuts, the nightly Vietnam / Northern Irish Troubles news, and the task of marking their respective piles of exercise books by watching a certain character's ITV exploits.

I'll never know for sure now, but I'd like to think they did.

***

A decade later, the return from a family holiday coincides with publication of O-level results, and Mum and Dad give me £30 for my grades. With this I buy my own black and white TV. We haven't had black and white since 1974, but I don't mind, a colour set is beyond my finances anyway. From now on, if my choice of programme is different to family consensus, I can watch what I want.

A-levels ramp up, the Physics, Chemistry and Maths combination gets more difficult, and Channel Four ramps up too, showing *Callan*, *The Prisoner* and *The Avengers.* While ineptly discovering girls and alcohol and music, I am riveted by all these shows, observing repeats on my monochrome set.

My school friend George is taping many of these reruns, as, in the words of *The Young Ones,* "Yes, he's got a video!" He edits his own compilation together to run a lunchtime lecture at school – announced by the headmaster as concerning "*The Prisoner*, and what it was supposed to be about." This abstract brings about hilarity from the whole assembly; everyone's been watching and they're clearly just as perplexed by *Fall Out* as those who saw it first time round.

***

1984 sees *Doctor Who – Planet of Fire*, my first real induction to actor Peter Wyngarde, although I have seen him as a Number 2 in *The Prisoner*. By now I'm a hard core *Who* fan, going to local group meetings. I'm fairly dismissive of this story, but I'm impressed by Wyngarde's guest performance as a fervent high priest; it's nuanced, forceful, and ultimately poignant. A fandom rumour is circulating to the effect that, in addition to Peter Davison imminently departing, Anthony Ainley's Master is on his way out too, and in our Saturday afternoon *Who* meeting there is excited speculation that the villain will regenerate by taking over the body of Wyngarde's character in the final episode. Someone remembers him being good in the recent *Flash Gordon* remake, which I haven't seen. So there's some disappointment when our theory turns out to be total rubbish.

***

"You should be working!" I am told, about a month later. Exams are incoming. I'm looking at Diana Rigg instead; I've strategically relocated the monochrome set from the dining room upstairs, into my bedroom. This set would later accompany me to university in Guildford, where further revision dilemmas would occur while repeats of *Randall and Hopkirk (Deceased)* aired during my finals, and to Portsmouth, where I get my first Proper Job.

***

1990. Sunday morning. "I need a drink – I'm sure I've done something terrible to myself." I'm feeling a bit removed from my friends, so I'm frequently popping back to Bath for a weekend catch up. I tend to do one of two things – either a Saturday afternoon trip over to *Forever People* in Bristol, a *Forbidden Planet*-style shop where I can pick up fanzines and books, including precious reference works such as *Time Screen – The Magazine of British Telefantasy*, and *The ITV Encyclopaedia of Adventure* – or a Saturday night out in Swindon, where my friend Darren lives. I met him through *Who* fandom, and my friend Stuart is now in his band. In a cider den called the Beehive, we swap recollections of old shows and bands, discussion about one topic leading to another, forensically trawling our schoolday memories. On this particular morning after, I'm necking coffee and nursing a sore head, before heading back to Bath for a parental Sunday lunch, when Darren has a quick rummage on his shelves… "These one-hour *Danger Mans*, they're good." He hands me three or four tapes. "Oh, and I've got some *Department S*, too somewhere…" Clutching a carrier bag of VHS tapes, I blunder my way off towards Swindon station.

Arriving back in Portsmouth, I switch on the monochrome set, now connected to a chunky, second-hand VHS machine. I hope it doesn't do its usual trick of trying to mangle these tapes.

***

I fast forward to Darren's recommendation, *A Small War of Nerves*. First impressions: an excellent opening hook, with a man who's off his face on a train; having ranked up a few Glastonbury festivals by now, I can identify with this. The *Prisoner*-style surrealism fades, but the hook's enough to draw me into the *story*: a solidly-plotted investigative thriller, with three likeable characters – a methodical female scientist in Annabelle, a forthright male action hero in Stuart, and the flamboyant-but-sharp figure of Jason himself. I'm thinking the set-up is not unlike Pertwee / UNIT *Who*, with Jason disliking authority and working as an unconventional adviser rather than a full-time employee. Suddenly I squint at the black and white screen harder. It can't be… I rewind and check. The scientist is only being played by Anthony Hopkins! Wyngarde and Hopkins deliver a tour-de-force conclusion.

I spin the tape on over the rest of the week, noticing the fourth regular, suave Sir Curtis, there to assign cases; I'm pleased to note the progressive

’60s production team has cast a black actor in this part. Fun is had trying to spot both the guest actors and the join between the second unit location footage and that shot at Elstree; it’s harder in black and white.

I only have the three episodes at this point – *Nerves*, *Hambledown* and *Six Days* – but I am hooked.

***

It’s 1991, the mood is mellow, and there’s music in my ears. Bath and London friends have converged on Portsmouth for the weekend. We’re playing pool in the pub opposite my flat, feeding the eclectic jukebox with as much punk as possible. Amid the playlist, I notice *Is Vic There?* by ‘Department S’. I select it, taking a flyer just because of the name, not letting on that I’ve never heard the track before. To my relief, it’s a belter, Herbage, Lordan, Mizon, Roxy and Toulouse riffing on both Monty Python and Iggy Pop. I’m a convert, immediately. Must find out more. And I will, once I’ve finished my pool grudge match with “Big H”.

***

“Big H” is one of my closest Uni friends, a psychedelic-shirted, argumentative Bowie / Iggy fan who works in a second-hand shop. He’s another collector: visits to him generally involve me arriving at Waterloo on a Friday afternoon, enjoying seeing the approach of the capital city where so much of the television I love was made. No Whitehall briefings though; things usually tend to start in West London instead. The shop known as Number 64 is just the sort of den of countercultural iniquity that Stuart Sullivan would doubtless have made a few enquiries in, before having a proper, old-fashioned, breakable-furniture, sugar-glass, sock-’em-in-the-jaw punch-up. It’s a hive of aggressive hippies, bullshitters, chancers and geezers. The customers *all* haggle. “H” and the other staff are *Black Books* years before *Black Books*, scathingly quaffing their own alcohol stashes behind the counter from noon onwards, probably just to ensure they give as good as they get. Over the course of their lives, some of these staff will run abroad, appear on TV, write bestsellers, become part of Britpop. Others, like “H”, will start their own businesses based on the Number 64 template. Both shops are great, wild places to start the weekend; people-watching, chipping in for a round from the off licence, and periodically wandering off round the aisles to see what interesting second-hand VHS tapes, vinyl, and CDs have come in this week.

Later, I'll try not to leave them behind in whatever pub we inevitably decamp to.

***

London Weekend Television: there's a wave of '90s nostalgia for all things '60s and '70s, as the people who were children in those decades come of age and start media careers, or become consumers. ITC photo postcards have been on sale for a while, but now official VHS tapes are available to buy in the stores, too. Naturally, these percolate through to the second-hand market, and naturally "H" brings some of this stock home with him, ostensibly to "check it's all right." Plus, to misquote – "Yes, he's got a satellite dish!" A portal to the past, via UK Gold and Bravo. Bravo for Bravo, with its reruns of *The Champions*, *Danger Man*, *Joe 90*, *The New Avengers*, *The Prisoner*, *Randall and Hopkirk (Deceased)*, *The Persuaders*, *Space: 1999*, *UFO*, in addition to *Jason King* and *Department S*. Moving into the shared house, amid a heady blur of other off-air recordings and purchases, I suddenly find I now have pretty much all of the Department's adventures.

***

Then there are the spoofs. Harry Enfield's *The Playboys*, starring "Jason Queen", features three camp millionaire heroes, who in the titles indulge in a variety of pre-case-Jason-King-or-*Persuaders!*-style shenanigans: driving, waterskiing, flying a plane. They then usher various sexual partners – including a sheep – out of their bedrooms. Replete with innuendos and bad back projection, it's funny, but the *Comic Strip*'s effort, *Detectives on the Edge of a Nervous Breakdown*, has more room for manoeuvre and it's more affectionate to its sources, teaming up some thinly-disguised detectives from *The Sweeney*, *The Professionals* and *Spender* with a certain "Jason Bentley from Department Z".

It's a little like a *Doctor Who* Anniversary special - you see all these diverse hero characters taken out of their own times and places and thrown together, squabbling, to solve a problem. Jason describes one of his typical cases as follows: "I usually drive the Bentley to a large country house belonging to some mad, rich Colonel. Whereupon I drink a bottle of claret, smoke fifty cigarettes, and have everyone arrested." The *homage* even includes giving the Colonel part to Richard *Hambledown* Vernon. The Bodie, Doyle, Regan and Spender characters are dismissive of Jason's efforts but in the end, he is the elder statesman who solves the case, making further analysis of the "lab reports" before laying out the villain while quaffing a glass of claret.

Naturally, I love it, and can still quote most of it verbatim to this day.

***

It's 1994, the house is a mess, and burglars have been in. Rolling in from the pub, we don't actually notice this for a few minutes. No complex, locked room mystery here – just a child-burglar climbing through a small window, and letting his colleagues in. They steal some hi-fi equipment, and, much more poignantly, jewellery and a watch belonging to H's late parents. My own loss is comparatively minor – my new VHS recorder with a tape of *Sweeney* and *Department S* episodes still inside it. (They leave me with the monochrome set, and the older, tape-chewing machine.) Perversely I can't help wondering whether the burglars watched these episodes, and if so, what they made of *The Bones of Byrom Blain*.

***

It's 2005, and I'm at Memorabilia, Birmingham NEC. Hundreds of fans are ambling around the stalls. The setting is reminiscent of cult film *Repo Man*, with a café called *Food*, and a bar called *Drink*. I'm in *Drink*, reviewing my afternoon's purchases, and meeting up with friends from all over TV and film fandom. Some of them are looking after guests, sitting with them as they sign autographs and have photos taken. There are big queues for George Romero, the cast of *Red Dwarf*, and for Antonio Fargas, who's posing with the *Starsky and Hutch* car.

Peter Wyngarde is amid this scene, sitting behind his trestle table, eccentrically dressed in a Rupert Bear hat with FCUK written on it in biro. I have to see him, but I need to psych myself up first. My spies have told me that he's somewhat disenchanted with his hotel, and I can immediately envisage him saying, 'What a dreadful room. Did you choose it yourself?' Plus, while he has a variety of photographs on sale, the picture of him as General Klytus is the one that's outselling the others. Yes, the one where his face can't be seen! Small wonder if he's looking a little fed up.

Steeling myself, I walk over, and opt to buy a photo of him in a flowery shirt, feeling rather tongue-tied as he signs. He seems to approve of my choice but it's hard to tell. Is there a hint of wind-up humour in his eyes? Maybe. Stammering out a few compliments about his career, I thank him and beat a retreat.

I don't normally get celebrity fear. The only other person it's ever happened with is Tom Baker. So Peter's in good company.

***

It is 2017. Looking back over all these disparate memories, I reflect on how many are related to fandom, and the joy of discovering shows through other people. Through my interest in this and other programmes, I met many of my best friends, including my soulmate, and it started my own modest sideline in writing. Umbrella's 2004 box set still sits proudly on my shelf, and I have recently set out to discover the adventures of Jason & Co all over again. Somewhere, there are missing planes, space-suited burglars, and deserted villages, waiting. Good, clear, simple *storytelling.*

So, here's to the '60s, '70s, *Department S*, and the company that made it happen – ITC. God bless 'em.

Indeedy-deedy.

Randall and Hopkirk (Deceased)

1969-1970

Vanessa Bergman lives in London and works for Public Health England. She was founder of the Randall and Hopkirk (Deceased) Appreciation Society (RAHDAS) and main organiser of *Action '93*, the ITC convention. She attends the annual *Festival of Fantastic Films* at which she gave a presentation about *Randall and Hopkirk (Deceased)* in 1990. She is also passionate about dogs and is a qualified dog training instructor, who has trained her own Shetland Sheepdogs for obedience competitions and breed shows. In 2004 she took up flying lessons but sadly they proved too expensive! More recently, she became a regular worshipper at her local church and enjoys being involved in various church activities. She is in a long term relationship with Dennis whom she met whilst on holiday in Dorset, where he still lives.

Steve O'Brien is a film and TV journalist. In a 20-year career, he has written for *SFX* magazine, *Sci-Fi Now*, *Total Film*, *Horrorville* and *Empire* and is a regular contributor to the official *Doctor Who Magazine*. Steve has also made many appearances in documentaries included on the *Doctor Who* DVD range and the *"Cult of..."* series for BBC Four. He's also the co-author of BBC Books' *Whographica* and a forthcoming book on *Buffy the Vampire Slayer*. He also once watched an episode of *Blake's 7* with '80s porn actress Traci Lords.

Neil Jones has been a spectacular underachiever in life, who is never able to see things through. He has had a modicum of success as the writer and director of micro-budget zombie feature *Stag Night of the Dead* and was the writer / director (and lead) in *Danger Man* fan film *Vendetta for a Dead Friend*. He has produced and directed over a hundred short films and forgettable corporate videos. Obsessed by anything connected to Patrick McGoohan, he can occasionally be seen in his *Prisoner* edition Caterham Seven, spooking local horses around the lanes of Bedfordshire where he lives with his long suffering wife and son. He is also fixated by the original series of *Randall and Hopkirk (Deceased)* and has filmed an (as yet unreleased) new episode entitled *Where a Ghost and A Prince Meet*. At the time of writing Neil is now officially eleven years into his mid life crisis.

How the Spirit Moved Me

Vanessa Bergman

I honestly can't remember when I first fell in love with *Randall and Hopkirk (Deceased)*, whether it was from the first episode they screened or from half way through the series. Fortunately though, it was a series my dad enjoyed, otherwise I might never have got to watch it on its first screening in September 1969 – and probably not until many years later. Dad was the 'breadwinner' and head of the household, so we all fell in line with whatever he wanted to watch on the box, not that there was an awful lot of choice in those days, seeing as there were only three channels in Britain. I can't remember what was on the other two channels on those Sunday evenings – probably religious programmes, something I quite enjoy these days, but back then, no way! It was also not until the mid-Seventies that my dad relented to my brother's and my pleas to get a colour TV, so my first outing into the world of *Randall and Hopkirk* was in glorious black and white! I looked forward each week to see what new case they had to investigate and what embarrassing situation Marty was going to get Jeff into.

It was probably the idea of having a non-spooky, friendly-looking and definitely unconventional ghost around that appealed to me, but as a 14 year old, hot-blooded school girl it was the rugged looking Jeff Randall who I fell madly in love with. My friends were into singing stars such as David Essex and Donny Osmond, but with me it was Jeff Randall.

Two of my prized possessions were a Jeff Randall alarm clock, the one with the two bells on top which would be hit by a small hammer at the time it was set for, and a Jeff Randall sweater, the brown one with stripes round the neck, cuffs and waist band. Mine wasn't quite the same, but it was near enough. As we only had black and white, I didn't know the actual colour until a few years later when the series was repeated on Sunday afternoons and I got to watch it at a friend's house; Jackie's parents were richer than mine and could afford a colour telly. Then I realised that Jeff's sweater was a darker brown than mine, but I never did get one which was identical. Oh well, such is life. At least I got to see my hero in living colour.

In the early '70s it was a popular trend for film stars as well as pop stars to have their own fan clubs. I was already a member of the official fan clubs for handsome American actor Robert Wagner (who was very popular at the time in the 1968 TV series *It Takes A Thief*) and fellow actor Leonard

Nimoy. It wasn't long before I became a member of the Mike Pratt Official Fan Club. I also joined Ken's and Annette's clubs for good measure, but Mike's was the most active, with Joan Hobbs, the club secretary, sending out regular newsletters and organising competitions and club get-togethers. The meetings were always in Hampshire, where she lived, so I never got to go. I had no idea where it was and it may just as well have been on the moon.

However, during 1970 Mike was performing in a season of Shakespeare plays at the Mermaid Theatre in London and Joan arranged for club members to meet him backstage if we came to his performances. Now, I'm no fan of Shakespeare plays, but the pull of meeting my hero Mike Pratt was too much, so I just had to go. I booked for the appointed date which was 30th May 1970. Mike played the part of Edward Poins, gentleman-in-waiting and also partner-in-crime to Prince Henry in *Henry IV, Part I.* Prince Henry, or Hal, was played by Welsh actor Hywel Bennett, who, two years earlier, had appeared with Hayley Mills in Roy Boulting's suspense thriller *Twisted Nerve* and went on to play regular character Shelley in the TV series of the same name.

In case you're thinking, wow, what a brilliant memory I have, you would be wrong. Mike and his fan club meant so much to me that I wrote a detailed account of that day. I still have it and referred to it to get the actual date and the part taken by Mike. Other things I had forgotten I had written were my seat number, which was C23, and the names of the two friends I had made that day, Mary and Kathy, who were in row F. Sadly, I never saw them after that day or kept in touch. What a pity there was no Facebook in those days!

After the play, which according to my account I thoroughly enjoyed, was the bit that I and about thirty other club members had been waiting for. We were ushered through to a small room. It was set out with a beautiful spread of sandwiches, cakes, tea and soft drinks, but I think I was too excited to eat! A short time later in walked our Mike, wearing a black shirt and paisley waist coat.

" 'allo, our lot!" he said.

"Hello!" we all chorused back.

He asked if we had all enjoyed the play and of course we all replied, "Yes!"

I think we were all dumbstruck, so to break the ice he asked where we were all from.

Mary and Kathy were from Clacton. Other places, according to my account, were: "*Bournemouth, Weymouth, Dover and other faraway places –*

even MANCHESTER!" Obviously, as a 14-year-old, anywhere north of Watford was definitely a foreign land!

Unlike guest appearances today, where celebrities charge for autographs and photographs, Mike gave his autograph freely to everyone, signing autograph books, programmes, souvenir postcards, scraps of paper and whatever anyone had to hand. He wrote in my autograph book "*To Vanessa, With every good wish, Mike Pratt*" which I still have!

I had drawn a picture of Mike which my mum insisted I should bring with me to show him. I was ridiculously shy in those days and, although I had shown the picture to Joan Hobbs and Mary and Kathy, I was far too shy to show it to Mike. While he was signing my autograph book, Mary and Kathy, who were standing behind me, whispered loudly, "Show him that picture!" Mike heard and loudly whispered back, "Show him what?" So, I had no choice but to show him my drawing to which his response was, "It looks more like me than I do!" He then added to his signature, "Thanks for the drawing!"

After the autograph session was the Q & A session where most questions were, naturally, about *Randall and Hopkirk*. It was here where I first learned of Mike's accident, in which he broke both legs, and that he was in a real hospital bed in *The Ghost Talks*. Mike recalled, "I was taken to hospital... swearing somewhat!"

Someone asked about his blond hair in *The Champions* (as Raven in *Twelve Hours*). He replied that he was filming for the spy thriller *A Dandy in Aspic* (1968) at the time and had been required to dye his hair for the part.

On being asked if there was going to be another series of *Randall and Hopkirk (Deceased)*, he said he wouldn't be doing a new series and that the company that produced the show was having financial trouble. So, ITC was having financial problems at that time... Interesting!

All too soon, it was time for Mike to get ready for the evening performance, but before then, Mum and Dad had come to pick me up. Dad had brought his cine camera with him. Mike was happy to oblige when Dad asked if he could film him with me, a small, but treasured piece of cine footage, which I converted to video many years ago and have still yet to convert to DVD!

On 8th August 1970 there was another chance for club members to meet Mike after his performance as Stephano in Shakespeare's *The Tempest*, again at the Mermaid Theatre. This time my seat number was O14 and I made two more new friends, Marion and Jackie. I wonder where these people are now?

Mum, Dad and my brother Russell came to pick me up afterwards as we were going straight down to Bournemouth for our family holiday. I don't remember much of the holiday as I was still in awe of meeting Jeff Randall himself once again! I was also being extremely protective of my left forearm as someone had started the trend for Mike to autograph hands, wrists, arms and elbows and obviously, I had no intention of being left out. The sight of everyone gathering round Mike with their arms and elbows extended towards him must have been quite comical, but to all us fans it was a serious matter and when Mike wrote "4 arm – to wrist" in black felt pen on my forearm with an arrow pointing towards my wrist and a scribbled signature, it meant far more to me than anything else in the world! For several days, I was very careful not to wash my left arm and was very upset when the message and signature began to fade of its own accord.

As well as arranging for club members to meet Mike, Joan Hobbs also ran club competitions and one of them was to write an original *Randall and Hopkirk* story. I had a go at this and called it *...And All for Half a Million*, in which the beneficiary of a country estate worth £500,000 (an exorbitant amount of money for such a property at the time!) was murdered. It was probably an amalgamation of several episodes, all rolled into one, and wasn't very good, so I don't recall actually winning the competition. However, the series was quite popular amongst my school friends and my story quickly got passed around the class and even to some of the teachers. Several friends suggested I should re-write it as a script with the idea that it could be performed as an end-of-term play. Dad had dabbled in TV script writing (alas, none were accepted) so he was able to help me with this. I got some friends to help recruit Sixth Formers and teachers to play the characters, but without a drama teacher and without an experienced lighting and special effects engineer, it was not a success and sadly – or perhaps, happily – the play never got off the ground.

However, I had contacted series creator Dennis Spooner to ask if I was permitted to write and produce such a play as I didn't want to breach any copyright laws. He wrote back and told me to go ahead, but he was interested in seeing the script. Wow, I couldn't believe this! Dennis Spooner, creator of my all-time favourite TV show, wanted to read my script!

Unfortunately, a postal strike developed. How was I to send him the script? Mum to the rescue! It was half term and Borehamwood, home of Elstree Studios, was but a short bus ride away, so she came with me to deliver the script personally to Dennis Spooner's office. Of all the luck, he was away that day, but we left it with his secretary. A day or so later I came home from school and there was my script laying on the doormat with a business card attached giving Dennis' phone number. Dennis Spooner had actually returned the script personally to me! I was so grateful to the postal staff for going on strike!

That evening, I spoke to Dennis. What a lovely man. He liked the script (probably it gave him a good laugh) and was interested in coming along to see the play. He also hinted that perhaps Mike and Ken would be interested too. I must have been speechless as I can't quite recall what my response was. I remember feeling bad, though, about having to inform him when we decided the thing had to be cancelled – although, deep down, I think I was secretly relieved!

Dennis began his career writing comedy scripts for Harry Worth and, as my dad was into scriptwriting, I thought he might like to chat to him about it. So Dennis and Dad spoke for quite some time, talking about scripts for various TV shows and comedy shows, and football too, if memory serves me right, sounding as if they had known each other for years. The scriptwriting thing interested me and as Dennis was working on *Jason King*, the spin-off from *Department S*, he sent me a couple of the scripts, for *As Easy as ABC* and *Variations on a Theme*. These inspired me to write my own *Jason King* script, *Shall I Kill You Now?*, which I sent off to Dennis for his comments (by this time the postal strike was over). He returned it a few days later, replying that the script was good but to be accepted for television I would need to write a completely original script, not for an existing series, as they already had their team of writers and would not be interested in any new ones.

With inspiration from Dennis and help from my dad, I was all set for a scriptwriting career. I wrote, or started to write, several detective and mystery scripts. I even wrote a script for a detective with a dog called Cagney – and what appeared on TV shortly afterwards? First, there was *Longstreet*, an American TV series which starred James Franciscus as Mike Longstreet, a blind detective who had a beautiful white German Shepherd guide dog called Pax, who helped him with his cases. This ran from 1971-72, and then ten years later, along came *Cagney and Lacey*. Was someone nicking my ideas?

My scriptwriting career was over before it had a chance to begin. It was hard work and I just got bored and lost interest, something that to this day I deeply regret.

The Mike Pratt Official Fan Club closed down around 1972 and I lost touch with Joan Hobbs, the club secretary. In 1973, I started work at the Kennel Club, the governing body for pedigree dogs, where one of my duties was to check the qualifications for dogs entered for the following year's

Crufts Dog Show. As I was checking the qualifications of a top winning Manchester Terrier, I saw the name of the owner was none other than Joan Hobbs, living at the same address in Hampshire. I could hardly believe it. What a coincidence! The world of pedigree dogs had now become the love of my life and once again, Joan Hobbs shared the same passion! I just had to write to her and tell her where I was working and how I had come across her name and details of her dogs.

In no time at all, we were in regular contact, but this time our letters were all about dogs and dog shows! I did ask her if she had any memorabilia on Mike or *Randall and Hopkirk* but she was not forthcoming and had obviously lost interest in the show and its stars. Dog showing tends to do that – it takes over your life! When I became involved in dog training and showing during the mid-Seventies to mid-Eighties, I too lost some interest in TV, and *Randall and Hopkirk* faded into the dim and distant past. Happily, Joan Hobbs, who is now in her eighties, is still around and still lives at the same address in Hampshire. She no longer keeps or shows dogs, but we still send each other Christmas cards!

It came as a shock when I read about Mike Pratt's death on 10th July 1976, as for a few short years he had been a big part of my life, and I was sorry that my interest in *Randall and Hopkirk (Deceased)*, the show which I adored, had diminished. My interest was not to be rekindled until 1988 when the series was reshown. My love for it then returned and in 1989 I was moved to set up the Randall and Hopkirk (Deceased) Appreciation Society (or RAHDAS for short). The society ran successfully for five years, with regular newsletters issued, fan get-togethers at *Randall and Hopkirk* filming locations, and many great friendships being forged. We even welcomed musician Guy Pratt (Mike's son) to one of our meetings.

During the time I was running the Society, ITC began releasing videos of their shows such *The Saint*, *The Champions*, *The Persuaders!*, *Department S*, and many more titles including *Randall and Hopkirk (Deceased)*. In early 1991, an idea sprang to mind that would not only promote RAHDAS and the other fan societies of the time (Six of One, Fanderson, The Saint Club and The Morning After, among others) but would also be a showcase for ITC related material, including their new video releases. My idea was for an ITC convention that would run over a weekend during which fans could enjoy episodes of their favourite ITC shows – screened continuously throughout the weekend – and meet guest stars who had worked for ITC both in front of and behind the cameras. Sure enough, when the idea was proposed to ITC, they were very enthusiastic.

I set up a small committee with suitable RAHDAS members who were also members of other fan societies, so that between us we represented a proportion of cult classic ITC produced shows. I took on the role of chair person and chose people from Six of One to represent *The Prisoner* and *Danger Man*, Fanderson (*Thunderbirds*, *Stingray* and other Gerry Anderson productions), The Saint Club (*The Saint* and *Return of the Saint*) and The Morning After (*The Persuaders!*). I also chose RAHDAS members to look after registration, the dealers' room, the green room and other stewarding duties. A special mention must go to the late Colin Lench, a RAHDAS member who became a dear and close friend to many of us. Although it was not his profession, Colin was a very talented artist, and he used his wonderful artistic skills to create all our artwork.

One of my tasks was to find a suitable venue and eventually I chose the Shepperton Moat House. The Elstree Moat House (built on the site of the famous Thatched Barn) would have been ideal, of course. It had been my first choice but it proved far too expensive for our small budget.

The convention was booked to take place in March 1993 and after considering a number of possible titles for our event, we eventually settled upon *Action '93*. It was originally to have been called *Action: 1993*, to parody *Space: 1999*, another ITC classic, but it quickly became shortened to *'93* as it was much easier to say!

Action '93 was a huge success. Approximately 200 people had registered for the weekend, and we had a wonderful line up of special guests, including Kenneth Cope, who of course played Marty Hopkirk, Gerry Anderson, Ed Bishop (Straker in *UFO*), Monty Berman (series producer on *Randall and Hopkirk (Deceased)* as well as *The Champions*, *Department S* and *The Adventurer*, to name but a few) and Robert S. Baker, co-producer (with Monty Berman) of *The Saint*, and who went on to produce *The Persuaders!* and *Return of the Saint*. There was also Alan Fennell (best known for writing episodes of *Fireball XL5*, *Stingray* and *Thunderbirds*), Johnny Goodman (executive producer on *The Saint*, *The Baron* and *The Persuaders!*, amongst many other shows) and George Sewell (who, as well as appearing as Eric Jansen in the *Randall and Hopkirk* episode *Vendetta for a Dead Man*, was well known for portraying DCI Alan Craven in *Special Branch* and as Alec Freeman in *UFO*, among countless other roles).

Kenneth Cope was even reunited at the event with Marty Hopkirk's famous red Mini – BAP 245B – that he, Annette and Mike had driven in the series. This special reunion attracted a lot of attention and cameras began firing away like machine guns! Ken took great delight in posing for photos with the car, although he wasn't wearing the white suit!

The event attracted a lot of media attention and I spent a lot of my time giving interviews to various tabloids and also to one or two special interest TV shows. The weekend even got a mention on one or two radio shows, though unfortunately it was mistakenly advertised as a *Thunderbirds* weekend. Consequently, there were families with young children dressed in *Thunderbirds* costumes turning up at the door, and they were disappointed not to see the puppets or FAB 1! Some of the parents even complained about it, but it was the radio programmes which were at fault for giving out incorrect information. On the whole, everyone enjoyed what was on offer.

In fact, RAHDAS itself gained quite a bit of media interest during its years of operation. For instance, in 1990, the society was featured on British Satellite Broadcasting (BSB), the first franchised UK satellite station. It all began on the evening of Thursday 12th April, when I received a telephone call requesting me and approximately fifteen RAHDAS members to be at the BSB Studios in London the following Wednesday to appear on *The Mike Smith Show*. Mike was hosting a series of discussion shows based on people's obsessions, entitled *A Particular Passion*, and his topic for this recording was to be 'fans and fan clubs'. How appropriate that we should be invited!

Fifteen was out of the question, but in a couple of hours I had rounded up five eager members who had been waiting for their chance for stardom, and on Wednesday 18th we duly arrived at our pre-arranged rendezvous and made our way to BSB's Marcopolo House on Chelsea Bridge Road. Panic set in immediately on arrival as the security guards refused to admit us, even on the production of our invitations!

Eventually, we were escorted to our specially reserved seats and shortly afterwards, the show commenced. During the 'warm-up' session, we discovered we were surrounded by Kylie Minogue and Cilla Black fans, not to mention *Crossroads* and Royal Family supporters! At the time, I had various items of merchandise for sale to RAHDAS members, including T-shirts and sweatshirts emblazoned with the *Randall and Hopkirk* logo and the words 'Appreciation Society' underneath. I thought it would look good if we all wore RAHDAS sweatshirts for the show, and happily the rest of the group thought so too! I must admit we all looked quite resplendent as we sat together, showing all those that tuned in how proud we were of our club. The Kylie Minogue Fan Club, whose members sat in front of us, looked rather dull by comparison!

The recording seemed to be bugged by gremlins from start to finish and it took around two hours to complete the 60 minute programme. The show was due to be transmitted on Monday 30th April at 10.30pm on BSB's Now channel. The recording session seemed to be nearing completion when Mike Smith finally introduced the Society, and before I had time to say "Marty Hopkirk", he began to quiz me about RAHDAS. I began to feel the blood drain from me as I realised I was totally unprepared for the questions he asked me – I had been practising the replies to the questions I assumed would be inevitable, but I had assumed wrong and struggled to come up with a reasonable reply in the short time I had to answer, to "What do you actually do in your society?" Anyway, Mike seemed happy with the reply. He nodded his thanks and went on to question the Kylie fans.

The recording session eventually ended, thank goodness – I was dying for a cuppa, and the seats were definitely not designed for comfort. As we sipped what passed for tea and coffee from the vending machine, Mike Smith came into view. Not only did he agree to have his photo taken with the RAHDAS team, but he also seemed genuinely interested in the programme and the Society. He did decline the offer of enrolment though! An interesting day was had by all, and at last RAHDAS had a claim to fame – even if only three people would ultimately glimpse us on the elusive BSB!

Shortly after our TV appearance, I was invited along to a local radio station in Dunstable to talk about the Society to radio host Paul Ross (brother of Jonathan). Unfortunately, it didn't go as well as I hoped it would and I realised Paul was just making fun of the fact that a fan club could exist for such a quirky show. A short while later, I did a telephone interview for another radio station, which went marginally better, but I wasn't comfortable being interviewed about the show or the society and decided against doing any more. I really didn't want either the series or RAHDAS to be ridiculed.

The quirkiness of *Randall and Hopkirk (Deceased)*, and the fact than an appreciation society existed for fans of the show, found its way to a chap called Stephen Jarvis, who, in 1993, compiled a publication called *The Bizarre Leisure Book*. He contacted me one day to ask if RAHDAS could be included in his forthcoming book on obscure fan clubs. I thought this could be good publicity, so I agreed. He visited me one evening and we chatted about the series and about the society, so that he would have an understanding of what both were all about. However, I was rather shocked to discover that RAHDAS was to share the same publication as The Test Card Circle, The Flat Earth Society, trainspotting, brickspotting and The Institute of Totally Useless Skills, to name but a few. The book contains no less than 150 "off-beat leisure pursuits", as Stephen describes them. Happily, I was relieved to discover that Six of One (The Prisoner Appreciation Society), The Saint Club, A Guide to Avengerland and the Land of the

Giants Appreciation Society were also listed amongst the weird and wacky ones like the Sausage Appreciation Society and the Wallpaper History Society. Suddenly, *Randall and Hopkirk (Deceased)* didn't seem so quirky any more!

Several months later, Geoff Tibballs contacted me as he wanted to write a book about *Randall and Hopkirk*, and wanted me to give some feedback. At long last, someone was taking it seriously! The book, called simply *Randall and Hopkirk (Deceased)*, was published in 1994, and sported a foreword by Kenneth Cope. It can still be obtained online and is well worth having if you're a fan.

Although RAHDAS did run successfully for five years, nothing lasts forever, and sadly I was forced to close the club down in 1994 due to personal commitments. Happily, the friends I had made through RAHDAS had no intention of losing touch, and we agreed to continue to meet up two or three times a year to spend a day together having a laugh, enjoying a meal together, and visiting *Randall and Hopkirk* locations, more often than not with our excursions starting out from our spiritual home, 'Merston Manor' (seen in *The House on Haunted Hill* and *Who Killed Cock Robin?*, and otherwise known as The Edgwarebury Hotel, now The Manor Elstree). To this day, we still meet up for fun days out together, though after a quarter of a century we have – for the most part – exhausted the *Randall and Hopkirk* locales and have branched out into other things and series as a focus for our get-togethers.

So strong were our friendships that, when I announced that I was having to close down RAHDAS, they were not going to let me slip away quietly. Instead, they organised a surprise farewell party for me. And what a surprise it was. It started one morning, in March 1994, when I was tricked into going to the Edgwarebury Hotel with my dear friend Colin Lench, and was astonished to find a group of all my RAHDAS friends greeting me as I entered. They had arranged a treasure hunt with 'treasure' hidden in various nearby *Randall and Hopkirk* locations. It was all great fun and most unexpected. But that wasn't all. The next surprise was when, later that same day, Colin again tricked me, this time into going to the Toby Oaklands Hotel in Borehamwood (built on the site where MGM Studios once stood). I was again startled when I opened a door and there they all were! They had decorated the room with banners, balloons and fairy lights. There was a lovely table spread and, right in the centre, was a beautifully decorated cake with the *Randall and Hopkirk* logo. I couldn't believe they had done all this for me and I got quite emotional! As previously mentioned, Colin was an exceptionally gifted artist, and I was presented with a lovely framed picture of Jeff, Marty and Jeannie, which he had drawn especially for me, and which all my lovely friends had signed around the border.

But there was another surprise yet to come. I was completely overwhelmed when, a short while later, a familiar figure entered the room in the form of none other than Jean Hopkirk herself, Annette André, together with her lovely husband Arthur Weingarten (writer and producer on several American TV series including *The Man from U.N.C.L.E.*, *The F.B.I.*, *Ironside*, *Murder She Wrote* and many, many more – not forgetting *Maigret*, which starred Annette, and through which they first met). Annette was always very appreciative of RAHDAS, and made very favourable comments about it and the fact that it was keeping the memories of *Randall and Hopkirk (Deceased)* very much alive. All in all, my incredible RAHDAS friends had given me the most amazing day, even though the reasons behind it were rather sad.

Friends have come and gone over the years and, sadly, we have lost some friends along the way, including the one-time owner of Marty's Mini, but we have also made masses of new friends, lovely people who have now joined our elite RAHDAS Gang. From the bottom of my heart I thank each and every one of them, past and present, for keeping the *Randall and Hopkirk* flag flying!

Deceased, But Not Forgotten

Steve O'Brien

If you were, like me in the mid-1980s, prone to faking – or at least exaggerating – illness in order to secure an afternoon off school then you'd have been naturally quite intimate with the television of the Incorporated Television Company.

So my memories of *Man in a Suitcase*, *The Baron* and *The Protectors* are always mixed in with the joy of having a craftily planned (sometimes unplanned – I wasn't a complete shit) day off from learning. It's difficult to separate Richard Bradford, Steve Forrest and Robert Vaughn from memories of laying on my folks' living room settee, hot water bottle over my sometimes poorly, mostly not, tummy, *Radio Times* on one side of me, *TV Times* on the other.

But the truth is, few of those ITC series, or the ones I saw later, ever truly seduced me. Those episodes of *The Baron* washed over me like episodes of *Farmhouse Kitchen*. *Man in a Suitcase*? Best place for him. *The Saint*? Diet James Bond. *The Protectors*? When's *Take the High Road* on?

But *Randall and Hopkirk (Deceased)* was different. Not only was it proudly fantastical, but it was funny and light-footed in a way its stablemates weren't. And where most of ITC's other shows lurched for a sellable fantasy of transatlantic sophistication, *Randall and Hopkirk* seemed to paint a world that was scuzzier and more recognisably real.

Mike Pratt's casting was central to *Randall and Hopkirk*'s uniqueness. He may have only been 37 when he played Jeff Randall, but he already had the deep-grooved facial lines of someone 20 years older. Thirty-seven-year-olds don't look like Mike Pratt nowadays, certainly not the ones on TV anyway. Jeff Randall seemed to be someone more at home in the messier, fag-stained world of *Public Eye* than a series about a man partnered up with a crime-solving ghost. More ABC than ITC.

Jeff was a bloke who, unlike Craig Stirling, Simon Templar or McGill, lost more fights than he won. A slightly seedy, leather-jacketed gumshoe who can't even afford a decent apartment (though he seemingly had fine taste in music, from the look of his LPs).

Take a look at Monty Berman and Dennis Spooner's initial pitch for the show, and it makes specific mention of *Here Comes Mr Jordan*, *Blithe Spirit* and Hal Roach's *Topper* films as pointers as to the tone of the series. But, as legend goes, Lew Grade was sceptical of the pair's initial outline, and it was left to Ralph Smart to okay the making of the pilot.

Outside of those ghostly touchstones though, everything else about that early version of the show was recognisably on-brand. 'Steven Randall', as he was then, is described in the pair's pitch as "ambitious [and] in his late twenties, early thirties. A direct, blunt, honest man of tall, athletic build."

The eventual Jeff Randall would be at least tall, but ambitious? And athletic? With a fag never out of his mouth and a bottle of scotch never far from his feet, it's a stretch.

It's said that droll Irish comedian Dave Allen was considered for the role of Jeff, before it went to Mike Pratt. Pratt, who'd guested in episodes of *Danger Man* and *The Saint*, and who was probably best known as a songwriter (he co-wrote, with Lionel Bart, the song *Little White Bull*, for which they received a prestigious Ivor Novello award) was once described as having "the weather-beaten features of a mountainside." Despite being under forty, his body-punishing lifestyle gave him a look way in advance of his years.

"He was a very destructive bloke, but brilliant," said director Robert Tronson. "Halfway through the episode I did, Mike got into a fight in a pub and came back with a huge black eye. He was so apologetic about it. But I think he was pissed most of the time."

What really sets *Randall and Hopkirk (Deceased)* from its crime show peers is that it's *funny* and central to its comic character is Kenneth Cope. Not only did Cope have a background on *That Was The Week That Was*, but he was warm in a way that Pratt wasn't. If blokes liked Pratt for being the fag-chewing, whisky-glugging perpetual bachelor, women – and kids – embraced the cuddly and Beatle-mopped Cope.

Spooner's original concept for the show was that there would be as much *Topper* as there was *Bulldog Drummond* in the show's tonal makeup. But there was a constant tug of war between director Cyril Frankel and Berman, who favoured a more rigorously dramatic approach, and Spooner and Cope, who were pushing the series in a more comedic direction.

Cope was reportedly never shy of voicing suggestions as to how the series could be "comedied-up". He once suggested a scene where Marty could be integrated into footage of Bobby Charlton scoring for England to show that it was Marty that blew the ball into the net with his ghostly powers. The idea proved too costly, it appears, and Cope never got his moment of World Cup glory. "Cope was inclined to broaden my concept," Frankel once said. "Then I would have to try and bring him back."

But it was Pratt who became the only cast member to actually pen an episode. It's probably the most comically-flavoured of the run and the only episode Charlie Higson decided to remake for his Noughties reboot. *A Disturbing Case* is certainly *Randall and Hopkirk (Deceased)*'s finest hour (well, 49 minutes) as Jeff finds himself in a mental hospital, being ordered about in a trance by a villainous psychiatrist.

But while it seemed the public took *Randall and Hopkirk (Deceased)* to their bosom, critically it fared about as well as every other ITC series (i.e. not well). "As watchable English entertainment it can go jump in a lake," moaned the ever-moany *Daily Mail*, while *The Evening Standard*, poised with its imaginary cigarette holder, hissed that, "Kenneth Cope wears the perpetual worried look of a soul that realises his purgatory is having to come back and appear in a series like *Randall and Hopkirk*." Ooh, get her.

While *Randall and Hopkirk (Deceased)* no doubt suffers from some sometimes dismal scripts and a slightly mercurial identity, it's the likeability and fallibility of its leads that marks it out in ITC's vast canon. It's often laugh-out-loud funny, and we've got to be thankful to a cast that not only had the talent to perform it but to fight for it too.

"When people remember *Randall and Hopkirk* they talk about the comedy," Cope said a few years ago. "That's what made the show."

It was the humour of *Randall and Hopkirk* that probably appealed to the young Charlie Higson too. But sadly the Vic and Bob-fronted remake suffers from the opposite problem – there's too much comedy. While some of Higson's embellishments deserve applause (he definitely ups the fantasy elements, with many scenes taking place in a Dali-esque limbo-land where Marty is tutored in all things spirit by Tom Baker's white-frocked Wyvern), the tone is often too arch and exaggerated to properly motor the drama.

There were, blessedly, a few Easter Eggs for fans of the original. There's a Cope House and a Spooner Drive in the show, and even Mike Pratt popped up (24 years after his death) for a CGI-assisted cameo. Sadly, Kenneth Cope turned down an invitation to make an appearance. I interviewed him for *SFX* magazine around the time of Higson's remake and he was apoplectic about the "tastelessness" of including Pratt in the new show and insisted he wouldn't be going anywhere near it.

The 1999 *Randall and Hopkirk* couldn't begin to touch the 1969 version. And, nearly fifty years on, that original is still an incredibly special series to me. In fact, going down memory lane like this has made me want to pull out the DVD boxset for a full rewatch.

Hmm, might have to call in sick for work (reaches for phone...).

'Welcome to the Club' *

Neil Jones

For some reason, despite having a very happy childhood, I have very few memories from my early years. However, two images always stuck fast in my mind. The first was of a man trapped in a cave with a huge television screen behind him and the second was of a different man dressed all in white dangling from the rear seat of a car brandishing a machine gun.

Both images were vivid but I was never really sure whether they were something I'd actually seen or simply dreamt. In 1977 the first of these jolted back into my consciousness when ITV re-broadcast the final episode of *The Prisoner*, *Fall Out*, and Number 6 stood trial.

The second was Marty Hopkirk in *Murder Ain't What It Used to Be!*

So why is it almost fifty years later that I'm sat at my desk trying to explain the effect that *Randall and Hopkirk (Deceased)* had on me and just why (given that I'm not prone to writer's block and habitually write scripts) am I continually having to backspace delete my thoughts?

Perhaps I should just admit in public for the first time I wanted a friend like Marty in my life. I wanted someone who only I could see; to possess a superpower to beat any adversary or win any adventure. Even now that I'm the wrong side of fifty I still do.

Rest assured this is not an acute case of nostalgia. I'm not going to witter on that they don't make shows like *Randall and Hopkirk (Deceased)* any more (even though they don't) nor that it was the golden age of escapist TV (even though it was). A retrospective viewing of many shows from this period can be painful, take for example *The Man From U.N.C.L.E.*, which second time around is only just about bearable for the opening and closing titles and theme.

Randall and Hopkirk (Deceased) had and still has something indefinable. A moment in time when the right cast, production team, writers and composer's orbits all came into alignment at precisely the right phase.

I once asked the late great Brian Clemens why TV was so good in this era and mentioned Roy Ward Baker's name. There was a long pause on the telephone line, in fact so long that I thought I had upset him. "They were film makers," he replied.

He was right.

In those days I remember sitting on the sofa with my brother (the days when you'd actually watch TV with somebody else) and we would shout out Dennis Spooner's and Monty Berman's names just before their title cards flashed up on screen. Their names appearing was the precursor to great entertainment.

At its best *Randall and Hopkirk (Deceased)* remains their finest collaboration and therein lies the issue with the show – genre.

Having set up the conventions of Marty's death and after-life-existence brilliantly, the series only consistent element was its inconsistency.

It doesn't matter any more who was responsible for the tone of the show, only that it didn't develop the dark, black comedy that was just crying out to be served up each week.

Take for example the opening to *But What A Sweet Little Room*. The scene of Anne Fenwick beating at the window whilst being gassed, only to see Arthur "Bunny" De Crecy (the wonderful but tragic Michael Goodliffe) digging her grave, is still for me truly disturbing.

This was, for me, the perfect tone for the show – black comedy. Instead the series was a mash up of different genres each week, lurching from slapstick (e.g. the embarrassing fight scenes in *The Ghost Who Saved the Bank at Monte Carlo)* to contrived underworld double-dealings that led to its inevitable cancellation.

Randall and Hopkirk (Deceased) exuded an eeriness that no other TV show could rival. This is exemplified in *For the Girl Who Has Everything* through the stand out character of Mrs Pleasance, who can see Marty, and shows how the parallel of the dead and the living alongside each other could have played out beautifully. What a shame then, that just like Mrs Pleasance, this aura seems to shuffle off its mortal coil in the last act of that episode. By the way, was it just me who was upset when Mrs Pleasance died?

Whilst the erratic tone of the show is up for debate there is no question on the contribution of the two leads. Mike Pratt and Kenneth Cope turn in wonderful performances. Together they transcend the limitations of the cathode ray with a beautifully observed friendship. Okay, so I don't know many private detectives, especially ones that are dead and destined to walk the earth for eternity, but they actually seem like normal blokes.

Pratt's portrayal of hard-boiled Jeff is timeless, like a modern day Philip Marlowe. Cope's gift for comedic timing is the perfect foil, like a Liverpudlian version of Felix from *The Odd Couple*.

Unlike Sean Connery, who by *Thunderball* clearly doesn't want to be James Bond, Pratt and Cope continue to work as hard as they can, even with the weaker scripts, and excel in the ones that do work.

Annette André looks beautiful throughout and does as much as she can with the limitations of her role, but obviously relishes the on set chemistry with Jeff and Marty.

The fourth star of the show is Edwin Astley. Few series have had such a contribution to the show's feel than the theme and incidental score throughout *Randall and Hopkirk (Deceased)*. Even the briefest of Astley's cues is a work of art.

In these pre-VHS or YouTube days you pined for the Chambers and Partners title sequence with Astley's harpsichord because it was the only time you'd hear it.

Additionally, the series basked in the wonderful performances of stalwart actors such as Ivor Dean, the aforementioned Michael Goodliffe, Meredith Edwards, Freddie Jones, Doris Hare, Marjorie Rhodes, Jeremy Young and Ronald Radd. I should also mention that Valerie Leon's appearance in *That's How Murder Snowballs* may well have made a significant contribution to my voice breaking.

It's this chemistry and the craftsmanship of the production team that makes me so obsessive about *Randall and Hopkirk (Deceased), Danger Man* and *The Prisoner.*

When both *Randall and Hopkirk (Deceased)* and *The Prisoner* were green lit to be re-made I was excited. Now to any purist this may seem at odds with what I have claimed to date. The trouble is that an original series is *finite*. Its done, finished and there's only so much recycled behind the scenes anecdotes to feed your hunger for the show you loved. You wrestle with your conscience to even accept a new incarnation. Even sitting down in front of the TV to watch the *reimagining* feels like a betrayal of the original series.

I didn't hate either AMC's *The Prisoner* or the BBC's *Randall & Hopkirk (Deceased)* reincarnations. In fact neither series brought out *any* emotion in me.

Perhaps then, this is the point. Both updated shows were broadcast and passed by barely acknowledged either in the press or publicly – no one talked about them. There was no excitement; the phone lines at ITV didn't light up like a Christmas tree as they did in 1967 when *Fall Out* didn't spoon-feed the audience what they wanted.

And, just for the record, I'm not against remakes. Take *New Captain Scarlet* – I didn't think they could pull it off but Gerry Anderson's CGI series is better than the original *Captain Scarlet and the Mysterons.* I even wrote to Anderson to tell him this. He wrote back to thank me, albeit a broken man, complaining that ITV had cannibalised the series within a sprawling kids Saturday morning show.

So how do you keep the spirit of an original series like *Randall and Hopkirk (Deceased)* alive?

Several years ago I wrote and filmed a new episode of *Danger Man* called *Vendetta for a Dead Friend.* Okay, so it was only a fan film, but it was designed to recapture the soul of the original series and this is how my conversation with Brian Clemens came about, after he had watched it.

"Some parts could stand alongside the original series," he told me which was probably the highlight of my artistic life.

Spurred on, I wrote a new *Randall and Hopkirk (Deceased)* script called *Where a Ghost and a Prince Meet.* The sixty-page script almost wrote itself as I could hear Jeff and Marty's dialogue / feuding in my head.

4. INT. R&H OFFICE DAY

JEFF RANDALL IS SAT AT HIS DESK, DEJECTED. HE FLICKS THROUGH A STACK OF RED BILLS MARKED "OVERDUE" AND "PAY IMMEDIATELY". AFTER A FEW MOMENTS HIS DEMEANOUR CHANGES AND DEJECTION TURNS TO INSPIRATION. HE FISHES OUT THE LAST SURVIVING FIVE-POUND NOTE FROM HIS WALLET AND FLICKS THROUGH THE SPORTS PAGES OF THE MORNING PAPER TO SCAN THE HORSE RACING ODDS. WITHIN A FEW SECONDS HE HAS FOUND A SURE-FIRE WINNER BUT AT THAT PRECISE MOMENT THE NEWSPAPER AND BILLS ARE SENT SPIRALLING INTO THE AIR BY A SUDDEN GUST OF WIND. HE TRIES TO SNATCH THEM MID-AIR BUT FAILS... THEN GRIMACES.

JEFF: Marty.

MARTY MATERIALISES ON THE OPPOSITE SIDE OF THE DESK - HANDS ON HIPS IN INDIGNATION.

<u>MARTY:</u> This is no way to run a business, Jeff.

<u>JEFF:</u> Thanks Marty. Perhaps you'd like to chip in a few quid to help pay some bills...

JEFF DROPS DOWN ON ALL FOURS TO CLEAN UP THE AFTERMATH.

<u>MARTY:</u> Never would have come to this in my day...

JEFF STANDS UP, FACING MARTY.

<u>JEFF:</u> Yes, well, what would a ghost know about the cost of living?

I was pretty pleased with the script, especially when one of the editors of this book, Alan Hayes, wrote back saying that it could have been the 27th episode.

We went into production (again as a fan film) and planned to shoot the episode soon after.

Everything was scheduled and we hired a grand country house for the shoot. All the elements were there. The crew had worked together on numerous productions and we were a close-knit team. The story was true to the series, set in a haunted house with a feuding family (complete with evil twins) and the plot centred on the plot of *Hamlet* to bring out the Gothic black comedy. Even the weather was on our side.

It was a tough shoot. As with most low budget productions, time means money, and we shot the entire episode on location in two days.

That was four years ago and the edit is still on my Mac as I write this. Not because I haven't had the time to finish it, indeed the effects are better than the original series; the locations are stunning and there's nothing technically wrong with it.

The problem is it doesn't work.

The chemistry isn't there and there's no special effects, slick editing or production design that can gloss over the fact that it doesn't have the *magic.*

And that's why it won't be finding it's way onto YouTube any day soon, because it's not a fitting *Randall and Hopkirk (Deceased)* tribute.

But there is one thing about the episode (spoiler alert) that will drive me to finally complete it – Jeff and Marty come out winners at the end.

* Marty to Jeff from *But What A Sweet Little Room*

Strange Report

1969-1970

Richard McGinlay writes for *The Avengers Declassified* (http://www.declassified.hiddentigerbooks.co.uk/) and *Sci-Fi Online* (http://www.sci-fi-online.com/), when he's not busy editing children's titles for an illustrated book publisher. He is the author of *Two Against the Underworld* (with Alan and Alys Hayes), *Dr Brent's Casebook* (with Alan Hayes) and four titles in the *My First Encyclopedia* series. He also provided liner notes for Big Finish's *The Avengers: The Lost Episodes* range. Richard is obsessed with missing episodes, so if you happen to have any lost recordings of *The Avengers, Doctor Who, Public Eye* or *Ace of Wands* in your attic, please let him know...

<u>REPORT 2016</u> ODDITY
'A most peculiar crime series'

Richard McGinlay

You may find it strange of me to report, in a book all about ITC shows, that I haven't actually seen all that many ITC shows. In fact, I have seen only two of them in their entirety: *The Prisoner* (1967-1968) and *Strange Report* (1969-1970).

The first ITC programme that I can recall seeing is *Return of the Saint* on its first transmission in 1978-1979. I would have been aged eight to nine at the time, and I didn't see much of the live action, but I enjoyed seeing the animated stick man in the opening titles, having all sorts of exciting adventures. I would typically watch that bit of the programme and then it was time for me to go to bed. (It was the same with the *Pink Panther* films – I would watch the cartoon characters in the title sequence and then be off up the wooden hill.)

I did once see a later part of an episode of *Return of the Saint* for some reason. This I now realise was *Yesterday's Hero* (1978), in which Simon Templar (Ian Ogilvy) tries to help a character called Roy Gates. I distinctly remember Templar calling out Gates' first name as the latter ran away from him. The reason this sticks in my mind is because my father's name is Roy and I found the coincidence memorable. Little did I realise until I came to write this essay that Roy Gates was played by Ian Hendry, an actor whose work has figured prominently in my life in recent years (more on that later).

Fast forward to 1983-1984, when Channel 4 followed up the success of its repeat screenings of filmed episodes of *The Avengers* by rerunning *The Prisoner*. I was 13 at the time, and quite intrigued by the trailers for the series, but I somehow managed not to catch the exploits of Number 6 (Patrick McGoohan) until the penultimate episode, *Once Upon a Time*, by which point there was a considerable buzz surrounding this remarkable show. I think most readers of this book would agree that *The Prisoner* is one of ITC's most cerebral and idiosyncratic shows, and that the penultimate episode is not the best place to jump on board!

After the precedent set by Channel 4's screenings of *The Avengers* and *The Prisoner*, reruns of other vintage film series followed on this and other UK channels in subsequent years – though a great many of them, I'm ashamed to say, passed me by. *The Baron*, *The Champions*, *Randall and Hopkirk (Deceased)*, *The Persuaders!*, *The Protectors*... I didn't see any of them!

I did catch bits of *Man in a Suitcase*, thanks to the influence of a friend, Jeff. The episode *Brainwash* particularly stands out, owing to the repeated refrain, "I'm going to shoot you, McGill." In fact, for me this was even more of a repeated refrain than usual, because Jeff sampled the phrase and used it in an audio-visual compilation (Jeff was an early adopter of recording and editing technology). Perhaps another reason why *Brainwash* is so memorable is because its scenes of mental torture, full of weird sounds and strobe lighting, are reminiscent of *The Prisoner*.

During my first year of higher education (1990-1991) at Bretton Hall, Wakefield (then a College of Leeds University), I had another chance to see *The Prisoner*, and, as with *Man in a Suitcase*, it was all down to the influence of a friend. This time the friend in question was Laurence (or Lol for short), a drama student who lived in the same hall of residence as me on campus (in the student Village, you might say). He impressed me by revealing that he had the whole series on VHS tape, courtesy of Channel 5 Video. At just 17 episodes, *The Prisoner* was not a long-lived show, but across nine videotapes it made for an impressively substantial collection. I borrowed them from Lol a tape at a time - two episodes per tape, apart from the odd (in both senses of the word) one, *Fall Out*, at the end.

Thanks to Lol, I learned some interesting behind-the-scenes information about *The Prisoner*, such as the fact that *Once Upon a Time* was filmed several months before *Fall Out*, during which time guest star Leo McKern had become considerably less hirsute, and so a shave and a haircut for his character (Number 2) were written into *Fall Out* as part of the bizarre process of reviving him. I also learned that some fans believed that Number 6 was supposed to be the same character that Patrick McGoohan had previously played in *Danger Man* (though Lol didn't agree) and that the reason why Number 6 swaps bodies to be played by Nigel Stock in *Do Not Forsake Me Oh My Darling* is because McGoohan had toddled off to America to appear in the film *Ice Station Zebra*.

During my second year (1991-1992), the enthusiasm for *The Prisoner* that Lol had instilled in me was in turn passed on to others. By this time, I had moved off campus and was sharing a house with two other students, Dave and Rob. I was studying English and Social Studies, whereas Dave and Rob had a different 'side order', studying English and Inter-Arts. Short of interesting things to watch, Dave one day decided that he would buy something on video, and he asked his housemates for recommendations. I suggested *The Prisoner*, and as a household we worked our way through the series. Along the way, I passed on the knowledge I had inherited from Lol, including the trivia about *Do Not Forsake Me Oh My Darling* and *Ice Station Zebra*.

This became something of an in-joke for us, because as part of his coursework Rob produced several video projects. He also starred in them, as did Dave, and I was in a couple of them, too.

Of the two that I was in, the first was a *Doctor Who* episode. Part drama, part pastiche, part clip-show documentary, it starred Rob as a newly regenerated Doctor, with Dave as a beardless guise of his arch enemy the Master, and featured me in a cameo appearance at the beginning as the previous Doctor. I was supposed to be the then most recent Doctor, the Seventh, as played by Sylvester McCoy, who was lured to his demise by the Master. However, high winds and feeble microphones meant that many of my lines were barely audible, necessitating an explanatory voice-over to be added by the new Doctor. The episode explored the Doctor's character, through the device of Rob's incarnation suffering from post-regenerative amnesia, which the evil Master tried to use to his advantage to mislead the hero about his true nature. Though clearly inspired by Sylvester McCoy's first *Doctor Who* story, *Time and the Rani* (1987), in which another evil Time Lord (the Rani) caused the Doctor to regenerate and then took advantage of his memory loss, in some ways our 1992 amateur production uncannily predicted the plot of the 1996 *Doctor Who* TV movie, in which a new, beardless Master lured Sylvester McCoy's Doctor to his death, the new Doctor (Paul McGann) forgot who he was, and McGann recorded some additional explanatory narration for the opening scenes. The Bradford-born Rob also gave us a northern-accented Doctor more than a decade before Christopher Eccleston came along!

Our next co-venture was an entirely original (and decidedly strange) story entitled *Near Smiling*. In this, Rob was the mysteriously nameless hero, the Man in Black, who for reasons none of us could quite explain eventually came face to face with an equal-and-opposite doppelgänger, the Man in White (shades of *The Schizoid Man*). Dave was his amoral and unwilling sidekick Graves, while I, sporting wild hair inspired by David Lynch's *Eraserhead*, was Ways, a man who liked to collect brains (as you do).

The trouble is, Dave had a habit of popping off to another county to visit his girlfriend, Claudia (or Claude for very slightly shorter), and on more than one occasion Rob had to make do without one of his leading performers, having been left a note that read something along the lines of: "Hi guys. Gone to see Claude for a few days. Try and carry on as best you can without me." As a result, some planned *Doctor Who* scenes involving Rob's Doctor and Dave's Master were replaced by direct-to-camera talking head material of the Doctor in the college's video-editing suite (standing in for the TARDIS interior) and the episode ended on a cliffhanger rather than resolving the clash between the rival Time Lords. Similarly, Graves mysteriously vanished towards the end of *Near Smiling*, rather than having a conventional resolution to his character arc.

Rob and I used to joke about Patrick McGoohan leaving a similar note for the *Prisoner* production team in his absence: "Hi guys. Gone to make *Ice Station Zebra*. Try and carry on as best you can without me."

Other influential shared viewing experiences during my student days and the house-sharing years that followed graduation include *Star Trek: The Next Generation*, *Doctor Who*, *Red Dwarf* (my memories of Dave's real note and McGoohan's imaginary one are also inextricably intermingled with the tone of the note left for Rimmer when his crewmates attempt to sneak off and go fishing without him in the episode *Dimension Jump*: "We tried to wake you but couldn't. See you in three weeks.") and *Men Behaving Badly*... but no ITC shows.

Fast forward to the present day, and once again I have found myself watching an ITC programme because of the influence of a friend. The friend on this occasion is Alan Hayes, the co-editor of this esteemed volume and my co-author in recent years on the subjects of *The Avengers* (primarily the mostly missing first series starring Ian Hendry) and its short-lived predecessor *Police Surgeon* (also mostly missing and also starring Ian Hendry). The ITC show in this instance is *Strange Report*.

In the intervening years, I had developed a taste for vintage videotaped productions, in particular those that suffer from lost episodes. This arose from my love of the partially missing *Doctor Who* and led to me revisiting *The Avengers* (at which point I made Alan's acquaintance), which in turn led to me being introduced to other series of a similar vintage: *A for Andromeda*, *Redcap*, *Public Eye*, *Callan*, *Ace of Wands*... but no ITC shows.

So when Alan and co-editor Rick Davy began to commission essays for *Playboys, Spies and Private Eyes*, we faced a problem in terms of what I could write about. My first choice was *The Prisoner*, but several other writers had already bagsied that highly regarded subject. (I've written about *The Prisoner* anyway, as you will no doubt have noticed!) Alan suggested that I should write about *Strange Report* instead, a series that he felt sure would appeal to me.

Prior to that point, I had never seen *Strange Report* – indeed, I had barely heard of it – though it does have a couple of things in common with

The Prisoner. Like *The Prisoner*, it did not last for very long. It had an even shorter run, at just 16 episodes. And like *The Prisoner*, *Strange Report* is hardly what you would call standard ITC fare.

In contrast to the typical youthful action heroes of filmed adventure series, the main character of *Strange Report*, criminologist Adam Strange (Anthony Quayle), is a more mature, professorial figure, not unlike the Doctor in contemporary *Doctor Who*. Like the Doctor, he is accompanied by a couple of younger assistants, forensic pathologist Hamlyn Gynt (Kaz Garas) and artist Evelyn McLean (Anneke Wills – who had been a *Doctor Who* companion in her previous role as Polly Wright). Ham takes care of most of the fisticuffs and other physical action in the show, though both of them need rescuing by their friends from time to time, and both of them provide sex appeal and a sassy attitude. Ham is an American, from Minnesota, no doubt with the aim of appealing to the American market.

Ham is often a reluctant participant in Strange's cases and tends to need a bit of gentle cajoling in order to get him on board, but inevitably Strange's powers of persuasion win him over in the end – just as Alan's powers of persuasion won me over when I was initially hesitant about tackling this unfamiliar series!

Strange is a very calm, quiet, laid-back hero, and Alan had correctly predicted that this would appeal to me as a fan of *Public Eye* and of the doctors played by Ian Hendry in *Police Surgeon* and *The Avengers*. Barring one aberrant moment near the beginning of *REPORT 4407 HEART 'No choice for the donor'* (the first episode to be filmed), in which he almost clobbers a visitor in an instinctive act of self-defence, Strange eschews violence, preferring to reason his way out of conflicts. This is demonstrated best of all in *REPORT 2475 REVENGE 'When a man hates'*, in which the unarmed Strange approaches a mentally disturbed killer (played by Julian Glover) and manages to convince him to give himself up to the police.

The series manages the impressive feat of being glossy yet low-key at the same time. The closest it comes to traditional ITC glamour is *REPORT 3906 COVER GIRLS 'Last year's model'*, an episode that revolves around the fashion industry, but even here the razzle-dazzle is offset by humour, with eccentric characters including the temperamental fashion designer Madeleine (Lisa Daniely) and an enthusiastic sewing machine specialist (Ron Pember). "There's a lot, of course, of other various matters in this world that I know nothing of," the latter informs Strange, in a scene that would not seem out of place in one of the wackier episodes of *The Avengers*. "Music for one… and football for another. I can't tolerate the silly game, so of course I've no interest in it. But, er, without being boastful, sir, I must say that as far as sewing machines go, sir, well, I am something of a master in that particular field." Just as I imagine that *Public Eye*'s Frank Marker would do, Strange expresses reluctance to take on a case about stolen dresses, feeling out of place in such a setting – a subtle acknowledgement that this is not the show's usual territory.

A few episodes have an international flavour. In *REPORT 7931 SNIPER 'When is your cousin not?'*, Strange is lured to an Eastern European country in order to solve the murder of a student protester. In *REPORT 4977 SWINDLE 'Square root of evil'*, a large amount of foreign currency is stolen and taken out of the country. In *REPORT 2641 HOSTAGE 'If you won't learn, die'*, a Chinese diplomat is kidnapped and held to ransom. However, even these are decidedly low-key and unglamorous. The foreign setting of *SNIPER* is a grim communist state. The showdown at the end of *SWINDLE* takes place under grey skies on the North Sea. *HOSTAGE* resembles *Callan* (and also the brainwashing aspects of *The Prisoner* and *Man in a Suitcase*) in its disturbing scenes of mental and physical torture, with sleep-depriving noises and strobe lighting.

In other stories, the subject matter is downright gritty. The topic under discussion in *REPORT 1553 RACIST 'A most dangerous proposal'* is obvious from its title. Both this episode (in which a bigoted politician stirs up hatred) and *REPORT 3424 EPIDEMIC 'A most curious crime'* (in which desperate illegal immigrants run the risk of death at the hands of ruthless people smugglers) still have a lot to say about that the political situation today, more's the pity. Meanwhile, *REPORT 2475 REVENGE 'When a man hates'* is a hard-nosed police procedural featuring Jack Regan himself, John Thaw – though at this point in television history he looks more like his Sergeant Mann character from *Redcap*.

Talking of guest stars, among other familiar faces (including Keith Barron, Ed Bishop, Robert Hardy, John Laurie, Rosemary Leach, Bernard Lee, Ray McAnally, Zienia Merton, Ian Ogilvy, Richard O'Sullivan, Louise Pajo, Martin Shaw and Sylvia Syms), Frank Gatliff appears in the episode *RACIST* as a plain-clothes police inspector called Matthews – just as he did in a now missing episode of *Police Surgeon*. Almost as appealing to me is the fact that both *The Avengers* and *Strange Report* have an episode about illegal currency entitled *Square Root of Evil*!

Another thing I enjoy about *Strange Report* is the way in which the opening titles are played into each episode. The live action of the opening teaser builds to a dramatic high, at which point the picture freezes and the series title caption appears, in the style of a rubber stamp on a dossier. Simultaneously, Roger Webb's distinctive main theme is cued in, beginning with a sensational "DUUUN DUN DUUUUN!", and then we are carried into the title sequence. I do love a good segue into titles, and this is no exception. It is at its most effective at the beginning of REPORT 1021 *SHRAPNEL 'The wish in the dream'*, where it immediately follows a shocking explosion. However, it sits rather oddly against a few of the more low-key teasers, such as that at the beginning of *COVER GIRLS* – a rather underwhelming "Oh, no!" from Lisa Daniely.

If I had to single out my favourite episodes, I would have to say *SHRAPNEL* (a gripping psychodrama that is marred only by the fact that the guest star credits near the start of the programme give the viewer a big hint that a certain supposedly dead character is still alive), *REVENGE*, REPORT 4821 *X-RAY 'Who weeps for the doctor?'* (a storyline that really keeps you guessing as to whodunnit), *HOSTAGE*, REPORT 8944 *HAND 'A matter of witchcraft'* (every series needs at least one supernatural episode, and this is *Strange Report*'s) and *COVER GIRLS*, in that order.

One thing that *Strange Report* doesn't give me – as a viewer with a fascination for lost material – is any missing episodes. In contrast with many non-ITC shows from the same period, all the episodes produced of *Strange Report* still exist today, though there are only 16 of them. However, you could say that some episodes are absent by reason of not having been produced in the first place. The series was intended to have a longer run. As a UK/US co-production with NBC's Arena Productions, the idea was that after the initial batch of episodes had been filmed at Pinewood Studios and around London, the production (and Strange) would move to the States. This idea fell through because Anthony Quayle and Anneke Wills did not want to relocate for such a lengthy period.

We can only imagine what shape the series would have taken if it had run to a full season or more. I like that kind of imagining. Would the move to America have been prompted by Ham returning home for some reason and then needing his friends by his side? That seems a fairly likely option. Or would the UK and US episodes have been interleaved in a more alternating fashion (the episodes that were made were transmitted in a quite different sequence to the order in which they were produced), making it more of a globetrotting series? We may never know.

What I do know is that I have, not for the first time, been introduced to a vintage television show that is precisely my cup of tea.

Jason King

1971-1972

Alan Hayes runs the *Randall and Hopkirk (Declassified)* website with John Holburn and Vince Cox, and has co-written a series of books about *The Avengers* and one about its progenitor, *Police Surgeon*, for Hidden Tiger. He has designed *The Prisoner: The Essential Guide*, written by Rick Davy, and the *Prisoner* audiobook *Everyman*, both for Quoit Media. Alan has also designed print materials for the theatre group Dyad Productions, many of which have been displayed and distributed at the Edinburgh Fringe Festival. He lives in Hertfordshire, is very happily married, and both he and his wife are in servitude to a phenomenally bolshie cat called Zoe.

Three Jason Kings Too Many

Alan Hayes

My feelings regarding the *Jason King* series are somewhat dichotomous. I am inordinately fond of it, of Peter Wyngarde's wonderfully languid central performance as Jason, of Laurie Johnson's theme and incidental score, of the distinctive title sequence, of the humorous bent of many of the episodes, and yet I know full well that it marks the point at which ITC began to lose the plot. When viewed as a whole, *Jason King* can only be seen as a disappointment in the light of its forebear, the inventive, enjoyable and clever *Department S*. The stories in *Jason King* are, by comparison, often pedestrian, and rely for their entertainment value on glitzy overseas location work and Wyngarde's hugely enjoyable presence.

Those overseas locations undoubtedly added value to the series, an innovation which had begun in the 1950s when second-unit camera crews had doubles stand in for star actors and staged car chases in exotic places. The cameras would, of course, then cut to shots of Simon Templar, John Drake or the Champions playing out the main thrust of the action on the studio backlots or against back-projection screens. It was quaint, but rather transparent. It's an element of the ITC shows that I have a particular nostalgia for today, but with British broadcasters upgrading from 405-line to 625-line screens in 1969, such camera tricks were quickly becoming all too obvious to viewers – though I'm sure it was fairly obvious even on those 405-line receivers! Consequently, starting with *The Persuaders!* in 1970, all future ITC action series would properly explore Europe, though, with the notable exception of *Shirley's World*, the wider world was, it seems, too big an ask!

Several episodes of *The Persuaders!* were filmed in foreign locales, and it would be the same with *Jason King*. Unfortunately, the series would move away from the superior 35mm film – which was being used on *The Persuaders!* and had been the norm for all previous ITC film series – to the lower resolution, and much cheaper, 16mm alternative. The result was a show that ought have looked colourful and opulent (as indeed *The Persuaders!* does, particularly now that it has been beautifully restored and issued on Blu-ray) instead looking little better than 8mm home movies. Had *Jason King* have been one of those series set in the grimy, dangerous underworld of Europe's big cities, then 16mm film could have played to its artistic intentions, but the show was quite the opposite and did not benefit from grainy, desaturated, low resolution, grainy film stock. It looked cheap.

My first encounter with *Jason King* did not come until the late Eighties and then only via a single episode that I had managed to track down from unofficial sources. This episode was *The Constance Missal*, an episode that remains my favourite of the whole series due to its comedic tone and Peter Wyngarde's thoroughly amusing performance as Jason masquerades as an expert in ancient manuscripts.

I would encounter further episodes through channels of greater legitimacy: with videos of a small number of episodes from ITC Home Video in 1992 and DVD releases from Carlton and later Umbrella and Network in subsequent years. This is where I really became acquainted with the series, but my most significant brush with *Jason King* came in 1989, a time when my sole experience of the show was that episode, *The Constance Missal*...

At around this time, several ITC shows were being repeated in afternoon slots on Thames Television, my local ITV region, including *Man in a Suitcase, The Champions* and *Randall and Hopkirk (Deceased).* Several friends and I were becoming increasingly taken with the adventures of McGill, Craig Stirling, Sharron Macready, Richard Barrett, Jeff Randall and Marty Hopkirk courtesy of these screenings.

We'd all previously been entranced by the surrealist, imaginative exploits of *The Prisoner* on Channel 4 and I had been a big fan of *The Persuaders!* and *Return of the Saint* back in the Seventies, the days of my youth.

Now – and this is the point at which this chapter becomes seriously embarrassing for me – our little group had started doing 'comedy skits' at *Doctor Who* and telefantasy conventions as the Gotham City Rejects (the name came from our then obsession with the Sixties *Batman* series starring Adam West). Probably the best thing we ever did was in fact *Batman – The Last Rip-Off*, performed live at the *Elydore* convention in March 1989. People actually laughed in the right places, and somehow I came away with best actor award for playing the Joker with an unintentional Welsh accent! Stage fright has so much to answer for...

Generally, though, our productions, be they performed before audiences at conventions or recorded on videotape, were diabolically bad. You think of the worst video production you've ever seen... No, we were worse than that. The only way in which we broke new ground was to plumb depths that no other fan production had ever descended to. We'd started off on video in December 1988 and January 1989 with a *Doctor Who* skit, *Cardboard*

Nemesis, which was loosely based on the Sylvester McCoy story *Silver Nemesis*, and witnessed a cardboard Cyberman terrorising shoppers on the high street at Woolwich, South East London. Watching the footage today, I'm staggered that we weren't arrested for filming without permission, not to mention having a chap going around with what might, from a distance, be confused with a real gun. Maybe the silly Cyberhead allayed people's fears! Despite having written it (maybe "written" is too strong a word), I was so camera shy that throughout its 20-minute running time I put on an excruciatingly bad American accent, as if that would improve things or render me somehow invisible…

The *Batman* production was next up, and then we turned to ITC for our next thing to spoof in *The Men from ITC*, subtitled *Why Don't the Dead Stay Dead?* Goodness knows what ITC had done to deserve the talentless tribute film that we together conspired to produce.

We drew on the small number of series that we knew about from the Channel 4 and Thames repeats, and threw a few other characters into the mix that we knew of but hadn't seen a great deal of. As a consequence, the central characters were going to be McGill from *Man in a Suitcase*, Danny Wilde from *The Persuaders!*, a certain Jason King (who we'd *all* seen in *The Constance Missal*), Jeff Randall and Marty Hopkirk, and John Drake from Danger Man (though the final character was effectively Number 6, even down to the costume and protestations of, "You won't get it!"). There was also a series of additional characters of our own invention (not that we should ever have owned up to creating them) such as Jason's au pair Prunella Goodthighs and a painfully stereotypical hay-chewing yokel.

For my sins – as I was co-writer of the project – I was cast as McGill (back when I needed make-up to make my hair appear grey – in some scenes my hairline is fringed with very obvious talcum powder!) while my fellow scriptwriter, a mate called Steve, would be my partner-in-detection Danny Wilde. Of the remaining major characters, Jeff and Marty were to be played by other friends Martin and David, and Danger Man would be portrayed by a chap called Daniel. Finally, Jason King was to be brought to vivid life, Zapata moustache and all, by our wonderfully theatrical chum Philip. Surnames, before you ask, have been withheld to protect the guilty! In the fullness of time, though, Philip's participation would prove not to be *quite* as regular as we were hoping it might be…

The script was stupidly overblown and ambitious, which is perhaps unsurprising considering the number of writers, all of whom were playing major roles in the production and wanted something meaty for their characters to do. What should have been a small-scale production with the emphasis on laughs became an ensemble piece, which was pulled in too many directions as Steve and I tried to keep all contributors happy and actively involved. The sentiment was laudable, but with our meagre resources – and acting talents – it was doomed to failure from that point on.

We were also determined to incorporate visits to memorable locations, thus putting as much of our pathetic budget up on the screen as possible. Therefore, we planned our filming days to take in locations in and around London, as well as at Brighton and Portmeirion, where the most ambitious scenes would be recorded. The Brighton location, as specified in the script, was intended to be filmed on the cliff-top there. We hadn't done our homework; there are no cliffs as such at Brighton... It was that sort of production, but we continued with the sort of enthusiasm reserved for the terminally idiotic, totally oblivious of this salient fact.

We plotted out a shooting schedule (the plan meant that we would be shooting every weekend for about four months!), made trips to charity shops to get a set of costumes together, and enticed friends to play some of the smaller roles, often against their better judgement.

The plot, such as it was, witnessed Roger Moore (in his dual guises of Simon Templar and Brett Sinclair) attempting to eliminate his ITC rivals. Having stolen McGill's trusty suitcase, he'd placed the ITC contracts of his fellow stars within, and left it in Jason King's apartment. This action was intended to draw the other stars out into the open so that he could dispose of them and be guaranteed the top role in ITC's next film series.

I don't think we ever really considered that the now sadly missed Roger Moore was a gentle, caring fellow, not exactly known for a disposition towards knocking people off. It was very much a "that'll do for now" idea, a bit like a working title that you'd change for a better one later. However, we were so anxious to get outdoors with the video camera that "that'll do" was as far as just about anything ever got with the script.

One by one, the good guys got knocked off – and this led to Jeff Randall becoming a ghost alongside Marty Hopkirk.

Martin, playing Jeff, made a major impression in the role, but for all the wrong reasons. For starters, we discovered that he couldn't deliver dialogue while he had a cigarette in his mouth; every line that he spoke was immediately preceded with him having to take the (fake) fag out of his mush! We only picked the very best... However, this was a small indiscretion compared to what can only be described as an ill-judged mix of method acting, exhibitionism and gross stupidity.

Although we tracked down a white suit for David to wear as Marty, Martin, even in those days a big chap, was not as easy to costume in this fashion. We eventually decided that it might be amusing if Jeff was to blip into existence in a white towelling dressing gown, since the delivery of his white suit had been delayed due to a backlog in the spirit world's laundry section. Martin, always game, agreed to this, and we told him that as he would be filmed sitting in the back seat of a car, it didn't matter what he wore on his lower half, as only his head and shoulders would be in shot. We filmed the sequences in the street outside my parents' house in Shooters Hill – trying to keep our faces straight as Martin struggled with the cigarette prop – and then he exited the car. We heard a loud, piercing scream as he did so. David's partner Jane was the source, and the reason for her outburst was that Martin was wearing no trousers or undergarments beneath the dressing gown. We had noted the former, but certainly not the latter.

David tried to calm Jane down. Someone helpfully suggested that she might find a bucket useful, while I remonstrated with Martin and asked what the hell he was doing with an uncovered undercarriage.

"I didn't have any white underwear and I thought it wouldn't be true to the part to wear another colour," was his considered answer. Martin was clearly taking Stanislavski's techniques several steps too far.

Meanwhile, David was trying to convince Jane that it had all been a terrible hallucination. Hyperventilating like someone who had just bitten into and swallowed a Naga Viper chilli, she screamed that it had indeed been terrible. She wasn't wrong.

Back to the plot, before someone sues…

Danny gets himself killed by a poisoned olive that Roger Moore had placed in his Creole Scream cocktail. McGill, pretty much the last man standing, then comes a cropper, too, having taste checked the poisoned olive – but not before he had downed a succession of household detergents, hoping to purge his system à la Number 6 in *The Girl Who Was Death*! Everything then led to the big finale on the annoyingly non-existent cliffs, where the ghosts of the Men from ITC were to put Roger Moore on trial for his crimes.

If this all seems incredibly misogynistic, with its predominantly male cast, there was a very good reason. Those of us who actually had girlfriends or female friends couldn't convince any of them to become involved in the production (they were far too sensible and discerning!). As a result, the likes of Sharron Macready would only appear in the finished article in stock footage from the original programmes themselves, overdubbed with silly voices courtesy of me and Steve. Well, it seemed funny at the time…

Once filming had commenced with some location work featuring Daniel as Number 6, we began a series of weekly get-togethers in and around

Shooters Hill and Golders Green, which was Daniel's neck of the woods. Over the next few weeks, we shot scenes at Daniel's parents' place with Jason King (Philip) munching lasciviously on a jam-covered crumpet and almost completely failing to deliver a coherent sentence without bursting into convulsions of laughter. We shot McGill arriving by parachute (stock footage of a skydiver jumping from a plane after which we cut to me jumping off a step ladder with a bedsheet tied to me!), and skateboarding down a very steep hill (no stuntmen required!). We even staged scenes in a park depicting Roger Moore shooting an informer under McGill's very eyes. Moore had a crewcut hairstyle and wild, bright orange eyebrows for this scene, something I honestly cannot think of a justifiable reason for!

Before long, the demanding schedule and the stresses of working with god-awful material began to take its toll. We set up a big scene for Jason King and our friend Philip failed to show. This, in actuality, was not a huge surprise; Philip was reliable only in being unreliable. If you agreed to meet him somewhere, four times out of five he'd forget the rendezvous completely and not show. On that fifth time, you'd have a whale of a time and forgive him completely for the other four. Philip is one of life's eccentrics, and you have to take him as he comes. The trouble with *The Men from ITC* was that we couldn't take him as he came because he simply stopped coming!

"Where's Jason?" we kept asking. Jason King was proving to be a problem. We were having as much trouble pinning him down as his publisher Nicola Harvester had done in the television series! Where possible, we filmed other sequences on days when Philip chose to stay in bed, or watch a film, or just be enigmatic and mysterious in his local branch of WHSmith's. Peter Wyngarde would have been proud.

We did at least manage to get Philip along to one of the soundtrack sessions much later on, so some of the sequences that he missed filming were at least covered with an in-character voiceover written especially for the session.

Eventually, though, we had to shoot something with the character, even without our resident bohemian. We had pages and pages of script for Philip to perform, comprising scenes of Jason as his fictional alter-ego Mark Caine in fantastical surroundings (almost certainly unfilmable for budgetary reasons anyway!), and others as Jason in more mundane locales. Very little of this material was ultimately filmed, though Daniel agreed to fill Jason's lurid, paisley-styled costume for some stunt work and driving scenes. Since this was to be shot after dark, we thought we could get away with the substitution, but on looking at the rushes, we realised that it was incredibly obvious – and actually quite amusing. We made no effort to reshoot earlier scenes so that Jason would be played consistently by one actor. We were sure that we could 'fix it in the edit' – how wonderfully naïve we were. Unwittingly, though, we had referenced the ITC practice of using 'doubles' who often bore little resemblance to the stars they were standing in for!

Oddly enough, the Roger Moore character also morphed during production from one friend in vision (another David) to someone Daniel knew who called himself Chesham (we never knew his real name – Chesham was where he lived) in voiceover, and finally to me (also in voice only) when he too dropped out of the filming. We should have called the thing *Fall Out*, because most of us did at one time or other.

We were making Ed Wood's notoriously calamitous *Plan Nine from Outer Space* look like *Citizen Kane* by comparison…

And then it all fell apart. The relentless pace of working five days a week in our regular jobs and then filming on the other two was resulting in fractious relationships within the group. Marty Hopkirk didn't like working with Danger Man; Jeff Randall complained that if Marty could have a white suit then why couldn't he; Danny Wilde complained that unless the production stumped up for a Ferrari Dino, he was off; McGill got beaten to within an inch of his life, just like in every episode of *Man in a Suitcase*; and Jason King… well, he was away skiing or having a slap-up meal at Maxim's or something. He certainly wasn't anywhere near our cameras.

The production ground to a halt with less than half of *The Men from ITC* having been committed to videotape. We'd bitten off far more than we could chew, and we called a halt to filming in order to preserve our friendships – and patch them up, too, where necessary.

For months afterwards, Steve and I tried to work out ways to finish off our unwieldy epic. We shot some brief scenes which featured our two characters, with shots composed in such a way that you'd only see our hands on desks, meaning that we didn't have to scout out, hire and trek off to places to film, and chose to intercut stock footage from various television shows that we had on tape. Yes, we were desperate, but we really wanted to finish *The Men from ITC* off – somehow. Anyhow!

We knew, though, that some scenes – with at least two members of the cast no longer on speaking terms! – would prove pretty much impossible to stage, and so we considered our options. Eventually, we decided that the only way we could complete the film simply was to engage a narrator, who would explain the missing scenes and bridge the narrative. We drafted in Martin (Jeff Randall) to do the honours. We told him that we intended to dress him up in a number of silly costumes to stop it being boring. "That's fine," said Martin. What we didn't tell him to begin with was that he would be playing an ant narrator. Yes, you read that correctly. An ant.

One of the little in-jokes that cropped up during filming was that if someone slipped or tripped during a take, they had come unstuck because they'd trodden on a poor, unfortunate ant which was always in the wrong place at the wrong time. I'd run into shot, slip up and we'd have to reshoot: "If it wasn't for Slippery Ant that would have gone perfectly," we'd curse. We found it all very amusing. (But then, we were very easily amused.)

And so, Slippery Ant became our narrator. How we got from "We need a narrator," to "and it has to be an ant," is anyone's guess. There was obviously a *terribly good reason*, but right now, decades later, it completely eludes me. I'd like to say it was the result of a 'lost weekend', but we were definitely sober and just let our weird, nutty ideas have free reign. Oh, for a voice of reason!

When we came up with the idea, we were splitting our sides laughing – in the moment it was *supremely, blissfully* funny, but of course we should have dismissed it out of hand. It would have been far more sensible for Martin to deliver the narration in character as Jeff Randall. But we didn't do sensible. I don't think we even knew what the word meant...

However, it must be said that the day we filmed Martin as Slippery Ant has to go down as one of the funniest, most laughter-filled days of my life. We painted his face bright green, stuck small half-footballs over his eyes, and had him stick his head up through a gap between two tables (the sort used for wallpaper pasting) which we had dressed to look like a street scene, complete with a brick wall backdrop. His head was positioned in front of a model of an ant's body, made in papier-mâché over a wire frame, complete with spindly legs. It looked wonderfully surreal.

We adorned Martin's protruding head in a variety of 'costumes' – mainly hats and other accoutrements – and, because he couldn't see what he looked like, we had to tell him what he was wearing and suggest a character for each 'look'.

It was barking mad, and Martin was an incredibly good sport – even when it became obvious that the green paint would take days to wash out...

Thanks to him, Steve and I were finally able to compile a finished programme, even though it was far removed from the one that we had both envisaged at the scripting stage. We added incidental music, which was composed and played by Steve on his El Cheapo analogue keyboard and drum machine. I even recorded a song for the end titles as 'MC McGill', spoofing *U Can't Touch This* by MC Hammer. It was called *My Suitcase (Where Is It?)*.

Once completed in the summer of 1990, more than a year after the project had commenced, *The Men from ITC* was shown to members of the group, copies were made, and then we all vowed that it was far too embarrassing to ever show to anyone else. Our Jason King had clearly realised this far earlier than we did, and had very justifiably made his tactical retreat...

Coda – The 27 Years Later Affair

Until I came to write this chapter for *Playboys, Spies and Private Eyes*, I had rarely thought of our unfinished 'monsterpiece'. Although it was a resounding failure which was responsible for fragmenting a previously tightly-knit group of friends, I now look back on the project with a great warmth. We may not have had the resources or the talent to pay proper tribute to the ITC shows that we loved so much, but we had at least channelled our appreciation in a creative fashion.

It took me by surprise to realise that I remained proud of *The Men from ITC*, even though I was under no illusion that it was not fit to be shown to an audience, even of likeminded people. And so I set about working out how I could perhaps change that.

Suddenly, the creativity that had inspired the project in 1989 was bubbling up in me afresh, a whole 27 years later in 2016. I quickly realised that a good deal of the film's problems had been introduced by Steve and myself in 1990 when we had desperately tried to complete an ensemble production with only a handful of the original cast willing to be involved. The *Slippery Ant Edit* had a lot to answer for.

Although the original Video 8 camera tapes are long lost, I had kept the VHS master edit of the *Slippery Ant Edit*, and this – by pure luck – had all the music and effects on one audio track and the original, unmessed with sound on the other. With the realisation it would be feasible to create a whole new edit, complete with a brand new music score, I set about working out how the project might be finally – and properly – completed.

Fortuitously, I had kept a copy of the original 1989 script, which I had retained with an eye to one day adapting as a novel, mostly for my own pleasure. Checking through the materials I had to hand, it quickly became abundantly clear that the 'Ant narrative' had to go, along with all the in-jokes (several of which concerned *Doctor Who* and not ITC programmes at all). I also realised that rather than attempt to film the missing scenes, I would have to write new ones which bridged the gaps in the narrative and could be filmed quickly on a budget of next to nothing. With Steve back on board to help with the scripting and my wife Alys offering sage advice (boy, did we need that in 1990!), we proceeded to work on these new scenes. Indeed, we even changed to ending to give the production a twist in the tail.

Also, since this wouldn't go to the original scripted, unfilmed scenes for anything much more than a line or two of dialogue, we decided to give it a new episode title. Besides, *Ghost of a Chance* sounds much more ITC than *Why Don't the Dead Stay Dead?* to me...

Of course, we had a problem since we would be shooting scenes 27 years after the original filming, and this necessitated a plot device that explained why McGill, Danny and Jeff (we got Martin back on board, too) were older, fatter and more bald than they were in the 1989 scenes. The time difference was such that there was no 'getting away with it'. Indeed, when I saw myself go through a door on location aged 24 and the scene cut to a 2016 interior, complete with me at 51, any idea that I had aged well quickly proved to be a complete delusion!

With this in mind, we decided to go hell for leather to make *The Men from ITC* the world record holder for the greatest number of continuity errors in a video production... and this led to us giving McGill a crazy grey wig, as well as casting a third Jason King, who would be played by another of the tribe of Davids that we know. Three Jason Kings? We hoped that viewers would just follow the moustache!

To see if this was more than just another mad idea a la Slippery Ant, we wrote a short scene for David as Jason, designed to go directly after the opening title sequence. If we had fun filming that, we could maybe take the whole thing the rest of the way? Written in the style of the "one of The Champions" introductions seen in each episode of that series, we plonked Jason and *Department S* colleague Annabelle Hurst (Alys) in a 1972 MGB and took to the country lanes of 'Avengerland', with the car seen passing through Letchmore Heath (seen in many ITC shows) before it pulls up with a flat tyre opposite Deeves Hall Farm barn (another ITC locale).

The weather on the filming day in March 2016 was poor, with a persistent fine rain threatening to postpone our filming. As our Jason had driven some seventy miles to be with us, we decided that not going ahead wasn't an option. We guessed that if we could get through an afternoon's filming in dismal conditions like these – and enjoy it – then we could probably cope with anything. Remarkably, the shoot went well, David was superb, and quickly we were thinking of how and when to film further bridging sequences.

Between April and July, we staged a further three filming sessions in locations as exotic as Steve's house in Essex and the row of garages behind ours at St Albans, shooting very much on the cheap – the biggest financial outlay being for the takeaway pizza at the end of each filming day.

However, we soon realised that one vital setting we'd envisioned was too grand to be filmed either at our place or at Steve's, and so we ended up hiring a former country mansion, the Grade II listed Shrewsbury House on Shooters Hill. Built in 1923 in a grand style complete with Ionic portico, Shrewsbury House is today an independently run community centre, and for me it abounds with memories. Then under the aegis of Greenwich Borough Council, it was where I attended nursery school, it housed my local library, and I was a member of art and film making groups there in my teenage years. It proved an ideal filming location with its wood-panelled interiors and ornate fireplaces, and for purely personal reasons, when the opportunity arose, I made sure that we filmed at least one scene in the former library (it sadly closed in 1990 due to cuts in government funding). We visited the House on three Saturday afternoons in June and July, shooting scenes which even included a séance!

The April to July filming involved six performers: myself as McGill and Roger Moore (I wasn't cast because of any similarity to Roger, it must be said!), Steve as Danny Wilde, Martin as Jeff Randall, David as Jason King and an office clerk, and Alys as an over-the-top fashion designer in the style of Dame Zandra Rhodes.

However, Alys had also become our fourth Jason King – yes, underneath the big wig, Zapata moustache and mutton chops was Alys, entering into the whole madcap spirit of the thing when, due to his distance from the filming location, David had proven understandably unavailable for an after dark shoot. Alys was brilliant, too.

But that's five cast members, you say… The sixth was another gender-bending recast, with my mother Rita doubling for McGill when I was on screen playing a different role during the séance scene. She was filmed from behind, looks nothing like me, and is at least a foot shorter than I am, so that was another ITC box ticked, just as it had been during the original 1989 filming for *The Men from ITC*.

With just a couple of pick-up shots outstanding (one of which would finally see the originally planned Portmeirion visit, but for a brief, newly written scene to end the programme after the closing titles), the production wrapped on 30th July 2016, more than 27 years after the filming of its early scenes had taken place. The final edit was completed exactly one month later. Our ludicrously overlong production schedule must qualify as some sort of record – and I'm pretty confident that we're the only film to have not one but four Jason Kings! You can never have too many Jasons!

Now that *The Men from ITC* is finally completed, albeit in a different form to how it was originally envisaged, the question was would I consider showing it to a general audience? Would people enjoy it, despite the terrible acting, awful script and atrocious continuity gaffes? My answer was still no.

I contacted Steve, and asked him to arrange a premiere for us. By this, I had in mind a gathering round his gaff for those involved, with maybe a couple of other friends who we knew would see the funny side.

Steve had bigger ideas than that, not that he told me, and consequently we gathered – against the better judgment of most of the cast – at The White Bus Cinema in Southend for a private screening on Saturday 17th September 2017. We'd invited friends and colleagues along; tickets were free (do you really think we'd have the nerve to charge for this???) and somehow we ended up with an audience of about thirty.

It was both exciting and terrifying. Even Steve was beginning to worry at the reaction. The rest of us – Alys, David and Martin, and very definitely me – were physically quaking in our boots, our hearts palpitating madly.

We'd covered the walls with fake reviews ("It's tragic that the cast lived to complete this debacle." … "*The Men from ITC* changed my life. I am now in therapy." … "I didn't support euthanasia until I saw *The Men from ITC*."), the idea being that by lowering expectations, we might get away with it. Steve and I also delivered an impromptu introduction speech, with much the same objectives. And then the moment arrived…

I sat at the back next to Alys – and the exit! The lights dimmed. I could barely breathe. The first scene played out. Silence. Then the opening titles. Hush. The Jason King 'teaser'. Suddenly… laughter! And then more. In the right places, too, not just at us looking ridiculous. None of us could really believe it, but *The Men from ITC* was *being enjoyed*!

What a result. People enjoyed it. We weren't lynched. They even asked for DVDs of *The Men from ITC*. We were stunned. We were all one hundred per cent unprepared for a positive reaction, but you couldn't wipe the smiles from our faces for weeks.

In closing, I am sorry to announce that it has come to my attention that some copies of the *Slippery Ant Edit* have regrettably leaked out beyond our little circle of shame-faced friends. If you've ever been subjected to it, then I apologise profusely for the suffering that you've been put through.

If, however, after reading this chapter you are determined to somehow view *The Men from ITC* in either of its variations, then before you do, my advice would definitely be to put the Samaritans on speed-dial.

The Persuaders!

1971-1972

Jaz Wiseman is an old-school print designer who started writing about ITC nearly thirty years ago and has spent an equally long time involved in designing and producing a wealth of material for companies all over the world related to *The Persuaders!* and many other ITC series. His passions are punk rock music, Rickenbacker bass guitars and playing the aforementioned music very loudly on the said make of electric instrument. He has been a strict vegetarian for 35 years and is an active animal rights and environmental campaigner. He lives in Dorset with his wife and children, spends lots of his spare time growing fruit and vegetables and loves getting his hands dirty.

Alys Hayes has long been involved in television fandom, notably attending the first ever *Doctor Who* convention in 1977 – something which came back to haunt her when she was interviewed about the event forty years on. She has co-produced tele-snap reconstructions of fourteen missing Series 1 episodes of *The Avengers* for licensed DVD releases and has co-written a book about that mysterious first year of the series. An ITC fan since childhood, Alys remains active in its fandom, particularly as an honorary member of the defunct-but-somehow-still-going *Randall and Hopkirk (Deceased) Appreciation Society* (RAHDAS).

Chain of Events

Jaz Wiseman

For me, *The Persuaders!* represents the jewel in the crown in ITC's film series output. I love the location filming; the episodes in the South of France in particular look so vibrant but I also think the autumnal episodes shot around the English countryside looked beautiful. The guest stars are great, notably Terry Thomas, and the equally talented leading ladies are beautiful, especially Juliet Harmer, Catherine Schell and Viviane Ventura. Brett's Aston Martin DBS and Danny's Dino are like regulars in the supporting cast and the episodes are fun, but the most important part for me is the casting of Roger Moore and Tony Curtis and their on-screen chemistry, which I find to be electric.

Having older siblings has had quite an influence on the person I am today; my older brother, born four years before me, had the briefest flirtation with punk rock music in 1977 while I spent every spare moment of the day kicking a football around re-enacting my beloved Liverpool FC winning matches and trophies. I approached my 10th birthday, my memory of him playing the Sex Pistols controversial single *God Save The Queen* in our shared bedroom is of me being somewhat dumbfounded as he said to me, "If you tell mum I'll kill you." His interest in the band rapidly dwindled as he discovered motorbikes, rock music and that a mix of the two was a hit with teenage girls of the time. The three or four punk records he bought remained hidden under his bed for a year or so until I began to take an interest in punk rock myself and they quickly became part of my record collection and acted as a springboard for my love of playing in my own band.

My eldest sister was born in 1957 and without knowing it, she is the reason I discovered British TV series of the '60s and '70s. We grew up in pubs until I was eight. My parents were always incredibly busy, which meant that my sister ended up baby-sitting the rest of us and I think it made her life a lot easier if the television was on, especially as there were three of us wanting her attention. I don't really have any vivid memories of watching any ITC shows in the early '70s but my brothers and sisters do and they inform me I was glued to the spot and transfixed when *Captain Scarlet and the Mysterons* was on-screen. I suppose they must have been right in some ways as throughout the '70s I would regularly question my mum as to,

"Why did Captain Scarlet shoot Captain Blue?" It wasn't until HTV repeated the series in 1985 that I learned that this was a plot-point in the episode *Special Assignment* and that my memory was right (although Scarlet didn't actually kill Blue as I had originally believed).

Captain Scarlet was very much present in my house in the Dinky SPV, MSV and SPC toys I had, the 1972 and 1973 *Countdown* Annuals, the *TV21* Annual of 1969 (he was on the front and more importantly he and Captain Black, in his Spectrum uniform, was on the back) and John Theydon's paperback. Even though I couldn't remember very much about the series then I was a bit obsessed by it.

Like most boys of my age growing up in '70s Britain, I played "James Bond" at school and although my parents took me to see *The Man With The Golden Gun* at the cinema, it was *The Spy Who Loved Me* that really excited my friends and me. I got the Corgi models of the Lotus Esprite and Stromberg's helicopter when they were first issued and decided to keep them safe in their window boxes after playing with them. I was somewhat disappointed that the model Lotus refused to fire any missiles from my murky bath water as I tried to recreate the scene in the film where Bond, accompanied by Agent XXX, drives the car into the sea, converts it into a submarine and fires a missile to destroy the helicopter that has been chasing them. However, I was now hooked on spy films, secret agents and Bond, and later that year, MB Games' *Spy Ring* became a firm favourite and fed my appetite for some time.

I really enjoyed *Return of The Saint* and thought Ian Ogilvy was great. Certain episodes have stuck in my mind since they were first broadcast, particularly *Duel in Venice* and *Signal Stop* but the rest of my family kept talking about Roger Moore being *the* Saint. This slightly confused me as I would say things like, "but he's James Bond so he can't be The Saint," so this led to my mum and sister telling all about his time as our haloed hero – and how I wished I could have seen an episode of that series.

In 1981, HTV – one of the three local ITV regions I could pick up (handy living on the boundaries) –showed repeats of *Thunderbirds* and the 50 minute episodes of *Danger Man*, a series that I was unaware of but one that quickly became a firm favourite.

Then in 1982 it happened. ITV ran a 'Best of British' season of classic series and included in the selection were the *Saint* episode *The Queen's Ransom*, which although being made in colour was shown in black and white (not that I had any idea of this mistake at the time), and *Greensleeves*, an episode of *The Persuaders!* I really liked *The Saint* but I loved *The Persuaders!* – what was this series that in the space of an hour had made such an impression on me? I knew nothing about it and it was impossible to discover anything more about it; I hadn't even twigged that all these great programmes that I was enjoying were made by the same company, ITC Entertainment Limited. By chance, I found our old copies of the *Countdown* 1973 Annual and the 1974 *TV Action* Annual lying around in a cupboard at home – and both of these contained comic strips for *The Persuaders!* – and in my parents' record collection there was a copy of Geoff Love's *Your Top TV Themes*, an album my mum had bought for me as it contained the *Match of the Day* theme but there they were, Danny and Brett gracing the front cover – time to listen to this again!

So there was I, in the middle of my teenage years, a hardcore punk rocker liking what I thought was probably the most un-punk rock TV shows and thinking I was probably the only person who had these shared interests as my mates then didn't care for these series. Finding information on these programmes back in the early '80s wasn't easy, particularly in rural Dorset and although I enjoyed them I kind of kept it to myself. However, most people who had known me for some time knew of my love of spy films and the like.

It wasn't until Roger Moore quit as James Bond after his last outing in *A View To A Kill* in 1985 that I began to start being more public in punk rock circles about my liking for spy films and TV series. A summer trip to Bristol that year, where I chanced upon a shop called Forever People in Park Street, suddenly made me realise that there were other people interested in old TV series, predominantly Gerry Anderson shows, but other ITC series were getting mentioned in magazines like *S.I.G.* that I found in the shop. It was also in 1985 that HTV were screening *The Champions*, a series that a factory colleague said to me, "You'll like that because you like all that spy stuff!", so I took a chance and set the video recorder to capture an episode that turned out to be *The Experiment* and from there on in, that video machine and HTV started bringing a lot of ITC series to me in a very short time.

In 1986, Channel 5 (the video company, not the TV channel!) started releasing ITC videos, albeit compilation episodes, but still very much welcomed; *The Fiction Makers*, *Vendetta For The Saint*, *The Saint and the Brave Goose* and *The Persuaders!* 'movies' *London Conspiracy* and *Sporting Chance*. Perhaps it was that *London Conspiracy* included the episode *Greensleeves*, the one I'd enjoyed so much four years previously, that really got me hooked on the series. I don't remember how but I came across a fellow fan who lived in Yorkshire and had all 24 episodes that had been taped from Australian transmissions and was happy to copy them for me if I paid for the tapes. That was it. Tapes were purchased and less than a week later they started arriving back at my house and I devoured them with relish.

Now I wanted to know anything and everything about the series and tried to locate information from books and libraries but found very little to satisfy my hunger. It seemed that no-one else was particularly interested in *The Persuaders!* – Gerry Anderson series, *The Prisoner* and possibly *Randall and Hopkirk (Deceased)*, yes, but the series I loved wasn't even getting a mention. It felt like I had no option but to write about it myself and the beginnings of *The Morning After* fanzine were formed in 1988 when I put out an eight page tester that was mainly made up of photocopies of the cover of the three UK paperback books and a list of episodes. I think I made about ten copies and I can't remember where they went or who had them but they were pretty poor and those that did get them must have thought I was either mad or illiterate.

At the same time I wrote to ITC's Service Division asking if it would be possible to buy stills or episodes of ITC series on video but I was disappointed by their reply which was very polite but informing me they no longer offered such services.

It took me some time to regain my confidence and have another go. I think this was partly down to attending Fanderson 90, where I found two original *Persuaders!* scripts (*Someone Like Me* and *To the Death, Baby*) and the original ITC publicity brochure in the dealers' room for the grand total of £30 and chatted about the series to a few people who spoke of it with great fondness. I have no idea who these people were but their shared enthusiasm made me rethink my plans and I thought I'd give it another go on the writing front. I should also mention Vanessa Bergman of the late Randall And Hopkirk (Deceased) Appreciation Society (RAHDAS), who also encouraged me to go for it and kindly passed on ITC's address and the name of Don Mead to me.

I started working on issue one of *The Morning After* (*TMA*) in late 1990, publishing it in late February '91. With some trepidation, I sent off a copy to the ITC address supplied by Vanessa. To be honest, I feared the worst, thinking why would they think this photocopied 16-page fanzine was any good, especially compared to their glossy programmes and classy publicity materials. I was very surprised to receive a phone call the following day from Don Mead, who in turn passed me on to his colleague Jon Keeble, an enthusiastic man who thought I had shown a lot of initiative, energy and desire for ITC programmes. He invited me to their Perivale office at the earliest convenient date to discuss future issues of the 'zine.

A week or so later I set off from the wilds of deepest, darkest Dorset, took the train to London and a Central line tube to Perivale, where I met Don and Jon, who were so incredibly kind and supportive. Jon had arranged for a huge amount of material relating to *The Persuaders!* to be sent up from the archive for me to look at and much to my surprise he gave me what was literally a wheelbarrow full of stuff to keep – my 'reward' as he put it, for doing something off my own back.

With *TMA* now having 'official' status with ITC, it was time for me to start getting serious in what I was publishing and at least for the second issue (July '91) I was able to reproduce some previously unseen photos from *The Persuaders!* I was around this time I learnt that my copies that had been taped from Australia had about six minutes cut from each episode which was hugely frustrating and made me want to urgently see them in their uncut form. Fortunately, I wouldn't have to wait long as ITC phoned me a few months later, asked me to select the first ten episodes and write the sleeve notes for their official VHS release due in early 1992.

As the magazine grew, so did my confidence and address book, and before long I was lucky enough to be interviewing numerous members of the cast and crew who were incredibly supportive of what I was doing. It was these early days in writing the magazine that really gave me the chance to push and promote *The Persuaders!* within like-minded circles and I got to know some very kind and supportive people outside of the programme and they have become life-long friends.

Since 1991 I have managed to publish 31 magazines on *The Persuaders!* (and other ITC series), three books, organised an exhibition of memorabilia, held ten location day tours including an exclusive one at Pinewood Studios with the series location manager Malcolm Christopher as the guest tour guide, celebrated the 30th anniversary of the series with a party featuring nine cast and crew members and a hundred TMA subscribers, spent hundreds of hours in the vaults looking at rare material and found my favourite ever outtake (Roger saying, "And I hate the fucking Germans," during the foreign language promos for the series), worked on a large range of products from calendars to Corgi diecasts, books, videos, DVDs and Blu-rays, been interviewed on national TV and appeared in documentaries and featurettes – I know that I have been incredibly lucky but as Johnny Goodman (Executive in Charge of Production on *The Persuaders!*) once said to me, "You make your own luck in life, and you deserve everything that comes your way because you got off your backside and did something."

Talking of Johnny, I was so very fortunate to meet him and series producer Bob Baker relatively early in the days of *TMA* and I couldn't have asked for a more supportive pair, considerate, good-humoured and ever-willing to partake in my events and work-related career. I was so thrilled that both of them gave me an open invite to call or visit them at any time and I always enjoyed spending time with either or both of them.

Tony Curtis was always a little distant from acknowledging *TMA*. He did write me a very short note once and signed an issue but always seemed reluctant in the 1990s to recognise that Danny Wilde was a fabulous television character and that the series was hugely loved.

On the other hand, I consider myself lucky to have been able to work with Roger Moore on numerous projects over the years since *TMA* started, including *The Saint* calendar, DVD commentaries for *The Saint* and *The Persuaders!*, the Barbican celebration of his work and many more events. He was always so kind, funny, supportive and often joked with me when he got the latest issue about how he was young once and that they were such happy times. He was always generous with his time and gave me answers to all my questions and was kind enough to write me the foreword for my book on the series that I'm hoping will see the light of day in the near future (only twenty years in the writing!).

Friendly Persuasion on Ice Cream Sundays

Alys Hayes

Sunday afternoon ennui. Lunchtime was just over and the pleasure of melted Wall's ice cream in a bowl, swirled into a thick, porridge-like goo, had passed. Dad was having his regular-as-clockwork afternoon snooze in the armchair, whilst I contemplated how to avoid the inevitable boredom that finished the weekend prior to school on Monday (this was England in the early 1970s, a time when pretty much everything was shut on Sundays).

But this particular Sunday in September 1972 heralded the start of the first repeat run of Roger Moore's latest series – *The Persuaders!* – on London Weekend Television. As far as I was concerned it was like a first showing, as I'd not seen the original Friday evening transmissions a year earlier; my family tended to stick to watching BBC1 on Friday nights, as Dad liked to get his regular dose of *The Virginian*.

Anyway, I'd been looking forward to this series as I'd enjoyed the ITC shows I had seen in the previous few years in this weekend afternoon slot – shows like *Department S*, *Jason King* and *Randall and Hopkirk (Deceased)*. All of them had been fun. They were quirky adventure series that I, as a reasonably bright kid, had no problem understanding. Series like these made me realise that 'adult' programmes didn't have to be dour and straight-laced like the seafaring BBC drama series *The Onedin Line* (which was then my mother's current favourite). I was aware of Roger Moore from the occasional episode of *The Saint* that I'd seen, but Tony Curtis – the other lead actor in *The Persuaders!* – was someone I was not so familiar with. I think I'd only seen him in *The Vikings* (1958) – a rather hokey Hollywood epic in which he co-starred with Kirk Douglas. I may also have known that Roger had at around this time been announced as the new James Bond, but I've no recall of this fact.

The family colour TV had been installed in early 1972 and, after a short while of it being a big thing (and it was – a lot of my friends still had black-and-white sets), it soon became commonplace to me. And yet, as soon as that first episode of *The Persuaders!* started, I remember being very taken with the red and blue, and then lurid pink and purple colour scheme of the opening titles. Few television title sequences were this striking, with bold colours, and consequently these really leapt out at me. The series also looked more expensive than the previous ITC shows. I was impressed with how genuine photos of the actors had been woven into potted biographies via a collage of newspaper articles, to explain the characters' backgrounds. Also apparent to me was that both actors had greater status than usual, evidenced by the "Curtis + Moore" caption in the opening titles. These people were obviously so famous that surnames were all we needed to know who they were. But the best bit was the music, the harpsichord and synth waltz of John Barry's theme – it really grabbed me. It was quite different from the usual orchestral signature tunes of other programmes on TV back then and felt more contemporary. However, it struck me, even on this first listen, that it was a little sad sounding, almost like a lament. Many years later, I realised that this was because it was played in a minor key, and although it remains one of my favourite television theme tunes, I have to wonder why it was composed in that way, since the vibe of the programme was predominantly light-hearted. Maybe Barry had not seen any footage when he composed the track.

Once into the episode, I spotted how the usual trope of grainy stock footage being used to establish foreign locales, seen in most ITC programmes, had largely been ditched. Instead, it was clear that in *The Persuaders!* the actors really were on the French Riviera, and not shivering on some home counties film backlot sporting strategically placed palm trees. The cars were fabulous too. I was – and still am – a keen collector of Corgi and Dinky die-cast car models and wished that I could find Brett's Aston Martin and the Ferrari Dino that Danny favoured. I'd have to wait some years for the Aston but still have no Dino model in my collection.

As the weeks went by I made sure we always tuned in to the Sunday showings of *The Persuaders!* and it became one of my favourites, second only to *Doctor Who* in my affections. I loved the apparently easy camaraderie of Brett and Danny and the obvious good humour present in most of the episodes. The whole style of the series felt bang up to date, what with Roger Moore's longer golden hair, the latest sports cars, the 1970s fashions (some of which were designed by Moore himself, if the end credits are to be believed), and more besides. Brett Sinclair appeared to be an extension of the laid-back style of Roger Moore's own character – even more witty, charming and sophisticatedly comedic than he had proven to be in *The Saint*. I loved the way he drawled "Daniel…" when the American was getting excitedly carried away with another mystery.

Tony Curtis seemed a very different character to what I expected; a wise-cracking and sometimes worldly-wise character but also impulsive, not the matinée idol type I'd seen before in feature films. Danny seemed to be someone with boundless energy, always eager to see what was around the next corner and sometimes getting into more trouble than necessary by trying to be in the forefront of an adventure. Both lead actors seemed to be having a lot of fun and my only gripe was in how the female characters were generally not much more than window dressing. But this was still the early 1970s and Women's Lib had yet to make huge inroads into popular culture.

My favourite episode turned out to be *A Death in the Family* with Roger Moore demonstrating his talent for comedy in portraying several ill-fated members of the Sinclair family (both male and female). At this time I hadn't seen *Kind Hearts and Coronets* so I had no idea that the episode was pretty much a re-working of that film. Even now, with that knowledge, the episode remains a complete joy. I was also impressed that Tony Curtis quite clearly performed a lot of his own stunts, rather than having the usual unconvincing stunt doubles take over. This was especially evident in *The Gold Napoleon* in which he climbed up drainpipes and jumped onto a moving lorry – surely unimaginable in today's health and safety obsessed world!

Another great episode for me was *Angie... Angie* - where Danny met up with a childhood friend from their days in the New York Bronx. This instalment showcased Tony Curtis to the full and I got a real sense of what a great actor he could be when given the chance. Milton Gelman's script looked in more depth into Danny's character and upbringing, giving the viewer the opportunity to discover how Danny's deprived background had given him the drive to get himself out of the gutter and make his fortune. The sadness that Danny displays when he realises what sort of person Angie has become is something that touched me as a young child. I understand that Tony Curtis knew the actor playing Angie (Larry Storch) from their time together in the US Navy and perhaps it was this connection that gave the relationship between Danny and Angie such a genuine feel.

The ways in which the two central characters of Brett and Danny approached life so differently was often a subject for humour. For instance in *Chain of Events* Danny sees camping out in the open as a chance to reconnect with nature and has brought with him little in the way of creature comforts, wanting to make the experience "real". Brett's tent, however, contains everything he might possibly need, including a kitchen sink and freezer – he favoured glamping, well before the term was invented. If only my camping holidays with the Girl Guides had been half as comfortable as Brett's woodland stay! To my mind, it is this underlying humorous tone, plus the series' innate style and élan, that has always set it above the other ITC series in my affections.

Whenever I could, I went on to see the series again on subsequent repeat runs over the years, but I didn't really get to view it properly again until the DVD and Blu-ray releases were issued in recent years. Seeing the restored versions in High Definition made me appreciate the series all the more – you can really see how much work went into the production of the show, even if the occasional back projection shots still look as unconvincing as ever, if not glaringly more so (though they are definitely a part of the fun of watching ITC shows). I've never been more sure – *The Persuaders!* is definitely one of the crown jewels in the ITC catalogue.

Whilst writing this little essay I heard the sad news of Sir Roger Moore's death. Another cherished piece of my childhood has slipped away, but I was so pleased with how the media coverage highlighted the love that so many felt for him – both those who knew and worked with him and fans like myself, mourning the passing of another icon – and a very special one at that. Obviously, the main character that journalists identified him with was James Bond, and while I do enjoy many of his Bond films (especially *Live and Let Die*), for me his role as Brett Sinclair in *The Persuaders!* is the one that I love and value most.

Let's raise a toast with a Creole Scream to the great Persuader himself and imagine that, somewhere in another dimension, Brett and Danny are having a good-natured argument about whether the cocktail should be topped off with one or two olives!

The Adventurer

1972-1973

Chris Dale first visited the ITC universe in 1991 when *Thunderbirds* was repeated on BBC2, and he has remained there ever since. When occasionally forced back into the real world he has worked as a writer and voice artiste on several ranges for Big Finish Productions, including *Terrahawks*, *Captain Scarlet and the Mysterons* and *Doctor Who*. He has reviewed all 26 episodes of *The Adventurer* on his website (http://www.chrisdale.org), occasionally makes silly videos on his YouTube channel (http://www.youtube.com/chrisdalek), and is also deliriously happy to be Vice President of the Official Chase Masterson Fan Club.

Alan Hayes runs the *Randall and Hopkirk (Declassified)* website with John Holburn and Vince Cox, and has co-written a series of books about *The Avengers* and one about its progenitor, *Police Surgeon*, for Hidden Tiger. He has designed *The Prisoner: The Essential Guide*, written by Rick Davy, and the *Prisoner* audiobook *Everyman*, both for Quoit Media. Alan has also designed print materials for the theatre group Dyad Productions, many of which have been displayed and distributed at the Edinburgh Fringe Festival. He lives in Hertfordshire, is very happily married, and both he and his wife are in servitude to a phenomenally bolshie cat called Zoe.

Bottom-of-the-Barrel Bliss

Chris Dale

It's hard to believe that it's over ten years now since the launch of ITV4, and even harder to believe that when the channel first started a substantial part of its daily output was made up of pretty much all the major ITC action series. These days the only one that ever makes an appearance is *The Saint*, but from 2005 until the end of 2009 it was a very different story, and it wasn't unusual to find two- or even three-hour blocks of ITC goodness every single weekday.

Unfortunately, it wasn't all smooth sailing. The shows were often edited to make room for adverts, with the channel having a particular knack for cutting out scenes then were directly referenced in a later scene (see the ITV4 version of the *Space: 1999* episode *The Mark of Archanon,* where Alan Carter looks insane for giving an alien a football as a parting gift because the scene where they played with said football was cut out). That, coupled with an announcer who could make Eeyore look positively chipper but who clearly rather fancied himself something of a comedian ("Jason King gets used as bait to hook a double agent now... Ouch!") sometimes gave the impression that the station wasn't so much an official ITV channel but rather just a disgruntled former employee illegally transmitting from a disused fallout shelter somewhere in the Channel Islands. ITV4 was never the perfect home for these shows, but it still deserves recognition for providing what may well prove to be the last regular home the ITC series will ever see on British television. They certainly hadn't received so much exposure since the glory days of Bravo nearly twenty years earlier, even if they were mostly used as cheap filler material that could be easily dropped whenever it was felt a lot of overpaid men chasing a ball around a field could pull in a higher audience than Sir Roger of Moore.

I can still remember the thrill of the initial announcement and seeing the names of all those different series in the upcoming TV listings. Many of them were already available on DVD, but plenty were yet to be released (in the UK, anyway), and tucked away in the list of familiar names was a series that I had never even heard of, *The Adventurer*. It turned out I was not alone; even the most dedicated ITC fans were at a loss to provide any information on the series, and those few who did remember it only had the vaguest recollections of catching the occasional rainy Sunday afternoon repeat in the early Seventies. All our questions were to be answered soon enough however, as at last the big day came when *The Adventurer* finally returned to British television after many years in the wilderness. All across the nation the great British public huddled around their television sets eager to watch the action of *The Good Book* unfold, and when it was concluded they rose up and said in one voice, "What the hell was that supposed to be?"

Right from the very first scene *The Adventurer* is like a masterclass in how *not* to produce a television series. It wasn't just that we were thrown in at the deep end with no idea who any of these characters were because that was par for the course with many of the ITC series, and you always knew that it would all begin to fall into place over the course of a few more episodes. In the case of *The Adventurer* they *never* ever got around to explaining the premise of the show, and while you can sort-of piece together the idea that the main character is an actor who is also a spy on the side – or was it the other way around? – the utter lack of any explanation regarding who any of these people are or what they're supposed to be doing is truly astonishing. For those who are still utterly baffled by the premise of the series despite having sat through the entire thing I recommend seeking out *The Adventurer* novelisation by Robert Miall; it probably won't answer all your questions but at least he *tried* to explain the premise of the series, which is more than the series itself ever did.

For those who have never seen the series or have blotted it out of their minds, *The Adventurer* chronicles the exploits of one Gene Bradley (Gene Barry) as he undertakes various missions for Mr Parminter (Barry Morse), the possible head of some possible secret service department, possibly. Joining him on his 'adventures' are fellow agents Diane Marsh (Catherine Schell) and Gavin Taylor (Garrick Hagon), while back in London Gene can also count on the support of his semi-permanently drunk butler Brandon (Dennis Price). Created by Monty Berman and Dennis Spooner, the show was commissioned by Lew Grade to provide one half of an ITC-produced 'action hour' for U.S. television, with Gerry Anderson being pretty much ordered to provide the other half hour in the form of *The Protectors*. It's strange to think that of the two it was Anderson and his team – relatively inexperienced when it came to making live action series – who successfully produced a confident and fast-paced action series (successful enough to become one of the few ITC series to get a second season) while the usually reliable team of Berman and Spooner were left floundering with an unworkable premise and a notoriously unhappy cast and crew. It's no secret that production of the series was a nightmare for all concerned, and most of these problems seem to stem from the show's leading man, Mr Gene Barry himself.

Despite being one of the biggest American names that ITC had managed to hire up to that point, Barry's star was very definitely beginning to wane by the beginning of the Seventies, and certainly he was utterly miscast as a debonair man of action that all the girls go crazy for. If anything it's almost disturbing to watch him sucking face with actresses young enough to be his granddaughters, but it's also interesting to look at any of the earliest-produced episodes and then skip to one of the last-produced; across the twenty-six episodes he visibly ages about ten years.

Barry is a perfect example of ITC and Lew Grade's insistence that each of these action series needed to be fronted by an American star name backfiring horribly. While it wasn't an uncommon problem for these American actors to struggle in an unfamiliar working environment, Gene Barry evidently arrived in England with numerous other insecurities all of his own. Most notable of these concerned his height, which meant the firing of Stuart 'Too Tall' Damon as Gene's sidekick and the hiring of Garrick 'Short Enough' Hagon as a replacement, before he too (and Catherine Schell) was also let go due to Gene's reluctance to share the screen with pretty much anybody. He also had script approval, which may go some way towards explaining many of the problems the show had in structuring its stories. This, compounded with Gene's difficulties remembering his lines, and his near total lack of charm or charisma, hardly conspired to make audiences want to tune in to the show on a weekly basis.

All this explains why I've always felt justified in poking fun at the guy in a way I might not do about any other actor; whatever negative comments I could ever make about him simply do not compare to his documented on-set behaviour. Among the extras on the DVD set there are interviews with Barry Morse, Catherine Schell and Stuart Damon; three different actors interviewed separately on three different continents, yet all three were unanimously critical of Barry and had not one good thing to say about him. Damon in particular clearly has every reason to look back on this period of his life with sadness since it effectively meant the end of his acting career in England, and there's surely many more stories yet to be shared by other actors who worked on the series (pick up Eunice Gayson's autobiography for a similarly bizarre story involving Gene's concerns about the length of her fingers).

Even if the friendliest, most likable, easy-going actor in the world had been cast in the lead role it would only have gone a little way toward hiding the fact that Gene Bradley as written is an awful, awful character. Much like the actor who played him he's an expert on practically everything, and what little he doesn't know he can usually master within the space of a few days. Not only is he the world's greatest actor, with thousands of young female fans turning up everywhere he goes (unless it's inconvenient to the plot to have them there), he's also an international superspy, a master of disguise, a genius businessman and an all-round sportsman and athlete depending on whatever the story requires him to be that week. All this despite the fact that he dances like a drowsy toddler in a man's body, he invariably struggles to complete a single coherent sentence without a running start, and the clothes he wears are clearly made from discarded curtains and picnic blankets (his trousers alone are the stuff of legend). We don't want this guy to succeed because he already has everything. We don't care when he gets into trouble because it's largely his own fault anyway. There's nothing to admire or to respect about the character, and instead the only satisfaction to be found comes from watching him make a complete fool of himself. On that front the show continually delivers, but I doubt that was the kind of satisfaction they were hoping we'd get out of it.

The Adventurer isn't a complete disaster, mind you. Despite Gene Barry not exactly lighting the world on fire with his charm, two other Barrys seemed to be working overtime to do the best job they possibly could. First, let's talk about John Barry and that theme tune. That wonderful, glorious theme tune. Much like his theme for *The Persuaders!*, Barry's take on *The Adventurer* seems to have written for a different series entirely. It's a theme tune far in excess of what the show deserved, and you almost feel like traveling back in time to the period when Barry was composing the theme, taking him to one side and saying, "John, don't try so hard. It's *The Adventurer*. We'd understand if you don't feel like giving it your all. It's okay. Really. Save your hard work for something that actually deserves it." Then shaking his hand, because good lord did that guy have a serious talent for his music.

I also need to mention Barry Morse, perhaps the show's real hero, both in front of and behind the camera. As Gene's 'boss' Mr Parminter, Morse seems to have been fully aware of the shortcomings of both the series he was appearing in and its 'star', and quickly learned that the best way to deal with Gene was to butter him up with compliments as frequently as possible. In early episodes the Parminter character was there simply to provide exposition then to vanish for the rest of the story, but as production dragged on and it became clear that Morse was the only one capable of getting along with Barry, Parminter's role became more important to the show, with Morse even stepping in to direct several episodes.

Indeed, if there is one singularly damning indictment of Gene Barry's shortcomings (no pun intended) as a leading man it's the fact that the very best episodes the series produced were all made while he was on holiday. His absence allowed not only the Parminter character to take centre stage (with Barry Morse gleefully re-inventing the character from a bland stock civil servant into a bumbling buffoon), but also the return of Catherine Schell and Garrick Hagon after they were fired for the heinous crime of existing. When Morse passed away in 2008, *The Guardian* mentioned *The Adventurer* in his obituary, noting that he "seemed to be acting in a different show entirely". It's most likely these episodes that inspired that claim, as while they're not going to win any awards, the three or four stories produced during this period are a genuine breath of fresh air. There's a wonderful dynamic between Morse, Schell and Hagon that makes you ache for the series this *could* have been, and whenever Gene phones in to remind the audience that he's still technically the star of the show it's just an irritation. They don't need him. They never needed him. This is what the show should have been from the start; Barry Morse blundering around Europe while his two top agents try their hardest to keep him from causing international incidents. That's it. That's all you need. Those four episodes show just how rewarding a formula that could have been, and what a great team the three of them made.

Alas Gene Barry came back and things took yet another nosedive as they approached the end of the series, producing several of the show's worst episodes. These included *The Case of the Poisoned Pawn*, which tries to pass off a game of chess as a gripping action sequence, and *Icons are Forever*, which may just the single worst episode of anything ITC ever produced, except for that *Protectors* episodes about the kidnapped dog. Eventually, finally, *The Adventurer* stumbled wheezing over the finish line, the episodes were aired with a minimum of fanfare, and the show was quickly and quietly forgotten.

By most people, anyway.

The really tragic thing about this whole mess is that despite the casting of the main character the show *could* still have worked had ITC been willing to take a long hard look at its output and admit that the days of the millionaire playboy troubleshooter were drawing to a close. Instead of producing yet another series in that style it might have been worthwhile to subvert expectations and instead try to spoof the genre that they helped create. Indeed one early episode, *Return to Sender*, features a fight scene that hints at what might have been, with an overly dramatic silent movie soundtrack and an absolutely classic moment where Gene's stunt double leaps up to grab a curtain rail which promptly breaks under his weight and leaves 'our hero' landing flat on his backside. It's *glorious*. While ITC had trod the comedy path around that time with series like *Shirley's World* and *From a Bird's Eye View* (I'll leave it up to you to decide the extent to which they succeeded or failed there) it's highly doubtful that Gene Barry would have gone along with this – but if he had refused, there were plenty of other actors out there who might have been willing to give it a go. William Shatner was one name considered for the lead role in *The Protectors*, and if any actor would have been capable of making that tongue-in-cheek approach work I think it would have been him. Go on – William Shatner as *The Adventurer*. You know you want to see that show.

As it is, we'll never know what we might have had – but what we do have remains endlessly fascinating to me in so many ways. I tend to assume that the order the episodes appear in on the 2006 DVD set from Network is more-or-less the production order, and if that is the case then the series handily breaks down into four distinct phases:

> **Phase 1 – Episodes 1-8:** Gene and company in Europe, where convoluted plots are hatched by agents of unnamed foreign countries and extended chase sequences rule supreme.
>
> **Phase 2 – Episodes 9-15:** Gene largely solo, mostly in London.
>
> **Phase 3 – Episodes 16-20:** A now-braindead Parminter takes the lead while Gene is away on holiday and Diane and Gavin return.
>
> **Phase 4 – Episodes 21-26:** *For the love of god, let's just film anything to get this nightmare over and done with.*

Phases 2 and 3 range from solid if unremarkable ITC fare to being really rather entertaining, largely due to Barry Morse's antics, while Phases 1 and 4 are where most of the problems lie. The early episodes have a bizarre habit of dumping so much information on the audience within the first minute or so that it's almost comedic, as if each instalment should come with its own instruction manual to remind you exactly what's supposed to be going on. Adding greater comedy value are some of the wacky schemes hatched by both the goodies and baddies in order to ensure the success of their mission – such schemes as 'let's put Morse code in piano music', 'let's do a *Wacky*

Races-style ambulance chase' or 'let's sneak behind enemy lines in a glider'. Just as amusingly, the later episodes have almost the exact opposite problem, with vital information being withheld from the audience until literally the last thirty seconds and Gene strutting around in a self-satisfied funk because he knows something we don't.

Occasionally, and despite all odds, some genuine, quality moments occur. *Double Exposure* features a rather exciting car chase in Amsterdam, while *I'll Get There Sometime* has another rather inventive chase atop a cable car in Wuppertal, and both of these sequences are genuinely impressive and creative. Sadly, moments like these are few and far between, but that's okay because whenever the wheels fall off this show they fall off *spectacularly*. The chase scene that serves as the climax to the first episode, *The Good Book*, is edited so badly as to make it seem like every character involved is in a completely different country and/or time period to everybody else, while a later episode – *Target!* – sees Gene and Parminter meeting on a ferris wheel. The first time I saw this scene I was almost praying for the back-projection to go wrong, and I was not disappointed. Go take a look and you'll see what I mean. It truly is a wondrous gift. Fight scenes are also good for a laugh too, with scores of stuntmen falling over if Gene so much as waves one of those big beefy fists of his in their general direction, and it truly is impossible to ever forget those clothes.

Despite this unintentional hilarity, *The Adventurer* is doomed to be forever remembered as one of the greatest failures in the ITC canon – and that's why I find it so impossible to dislike the thing. It's bad, sure, and not always entertainingly so, but it's never less than *interestingly* bad. The half hour running time, while surely one of the reasons the show is structurally such a mess, especially in the early episodes, ensures that it never really has a chance to get boring (if these episodes were 50 minutes long I would certainly not be talking about them). It's also a show where the story unfolding on the screen is nowhere near as fascinating as what was going on off-screen, tales which I suspect could fill several volumes. I spent a substantial amount of time about ten years ago re-watching and chronicling the series and producing an online episode guide (still available at http://chrisdale.org/features/the-adventurer/), but even that feels like it's only just scratching the surface. If you're a fan of the worst that Seventies TV had to offer, then *The Adventurer* really is a gift that keeps on giving.

My connection to the show also runs deeper than that though, because *The Adventurer* is one of the most inspirational television series I have ever seen. It truly is. In some of my darkest moments, when I despair of ever achieving any kind of success in any creative field, *this* is the show I look to for inspiration. I remind myself that *The Adventurer* was not only made but actually shown all around the world. Gene Barry proudly wore *those* trousers in public, not caring what anybody thought of him. The fight scene in *Make It a Million* was filmed by intelligent reasoning adults and then broadcast across the nation. Somebody actually edited together that chase scene in *The Good Book* and *didn't* get fired for it.

For those who fear failure in their creative endeavours *The Adventurer*'s true legacy is of actually being something of a call to arms; if they could do it, *I* can do it. Who cares if your idea is crap or your premise is unworkable, just carry on regardless! You do what *you* want to do and to hell with those who would see you fail – and if you do fail, then make sure you fail *spectacularly*. Fail so hard and so memorably that people are still talking about it nearly half a century later. Fail like Gene Barry.

That way, you'll never fail at all.

Marathon Man

Alan Hayes

I have a confession to make. *The Adventurer* is not my favourite ITC series. In fact, thinking about it, it's not even my favourite television series of that name (there is a rather good Richard Carpenter series which goes by the same moniker but omits the definite article).

It's one of those shows that anyone who considers themselves an ITC completist *must* have in his or her collection, but every now and then, when you glance at the DVD shelf and run your eyes lovingly past the official releases of *The Prisoner, Man in a Suitcase, Randall and Hopkirk (Deceased), The Persuaders!* and their like, *The Adventurer* trundles into view, a rough-hewn lump of malformed rock amongst diamonds… and you ask the question posed in *The General* by Number 6 – *why?*

It's a mighty fine question, it must be said. Why do I have *The Adventurer* on DVD, particularly considering that it's hardly one of ITC's greatest accomplishments? I don't have a nostalgic association with it as I never caught the series as a child, or if I did, I don't recall having seen it and it certainly didn't make the impression on me that, for instance, *Return of the Saint, Space: 1999* or *The Persuaders!* did.

I first saw *The Adventurer* as an afternoon filler repeat on Thames Television in the Eighties, and I didn't exactly consider it appointment viewing, though I do recall finding it strangely hypnotic, for all the wrong reasons. There are plenty of series that are better than *The Adventurer* which don't appeal to me, that I wouldn't go out of my way to see, but somehow I can't help but harbour a certain degree of affection for the adventures of Gene Bradley, that clumsy, charmless fashion disaster who is, without a shadow of doubt, the least convincing babe magnet in the history of television.

Despite all its problems, *The Adventurer* is a series that I keep going back to every few years, giving it fresh chances to impress me. Each time, it almost completely fails to do so, but ironically it's a series that I simply wouldn't be without. It's like ITC's equivalent of *Plan 9 from Outer Space*; something so hugely, gloriously inept that it somehow transcends its low standards and becomes strangely compelling. It's the one ITC series that fails on so many levels – in its acting, writing, direction, even its very premise. It boasts a main actor who is so bad that you catch yourself musing that there must have been some terrible mix-up during pre-production which led to the wooden stunt double ending up in the starring role and the big Hollywood celebrity reduced to doing second unit stand-in work. Were that not bad enough, *The Adventurer* spins its yarns in a weird, often garbled fashion, and singularly fails to establish even the basics of who Gene Bradley is and exactly what his backstory comprises (it seems to change wildly from week to week, depending on the focus of each episode). But for some reason, I come back to it more often than I do to series that are palpably superior. Perhaps that says more about me than it does about *The Adventurer*!

I recently gave *The Adventurer* yet another outing – a sort of 'Gene Bradley Marathon', having set myself the target of watching all 26 episodes within a single day. Yes, that's right. I'm an out and out masochist. It's a fair cop!

Early on that Saturday morning in May 2016, I dusted off my trusty Network DVD set, and began my whistle-stop reappraisal of Dennis Spooner and Monty Berman's greatest folly. As *The Good Book* began to unravel before me (and unravel is exactly what it does!) I took in some sustenance: a bowl of muesli, a slice of toast and marmalade, and a frothy coffee. Within a matter of minutes, I was seriously considering putting something stronger in the coffee. If the episode was designed as a proper introduction to the series, it absolutely fails to introduce anything. By its conclusion I was musing on the idea that really there were 27 episodes of *The Adventurer*, and the first – *Dead Wood*, as I dubbed it, the one in which we find out who Gene Bradley is, who Parminter is and who he works for, and how the two men were brought together and began to work as allies – was destroyed in a head-on collision with Gene Barry's ego before it could be transmitted.

The Good Book and several other early episodes are constructed and edited such an outlandish, schizophrenic fashion – with important story and character details revealed in info-dump-crammed flashbacks – that I struggle to comprehend the fact that they were put together by people like Cyril Frankel, who were so well versed in the production of ITC film series – experienced, trusted hands. It doesn't make sense. How did it suddenly go so wrong?

As my Saturday progressed, I quickly came to question the sanity of my self-inflicted marathon challenge. It was a nice day outside; surely I would be better off out of doors, strolling in the park, popping into my local for a pint or two of bitter, rather than be stuck in my lounge watching a washed-up, American one-time-star-actor-turned-zombie who moved with the grace and poise of a blind, three-legged bull? However, I'd made my choice – I was committed, or probably should have been – and at least the on-screen settings were distracting: Nice in *The Good Book*, Beaulieu-sur-Mer in *Return to Sender*, and Amsterdam in *Double Exposure* (which also treated me to a cool car chase – the only disappointment being that Gene didn't end up consumed in the waters of the canal). The latter episode also treated me to a rare view of the swimming pool at the much-mourned Thatched Barn in Borehamwood, but again the directorial choices flummoxed me; why were the dramatic sequences left unscored while others in which nothing was going were slathered in muzak. Weird!

Initial impressions were otherwise not positive, it must be said. Aside from Gene Barry's lumpen central performance and the dismal direction, I wondered why I'd got to the end of the third episode (just three miles into my marathon, as it were) and aside from Gene and Parminter, I couldn't remember the names of the supporting characters played by Garrick Hagon and Catherine Schell. Hagon I recognised from the *Doctor Who* story *The Mutants* (Jon Pertwee era), while Ms Schell will forever be Maya of *Space: 1999* to me… but who the heck were they playing here? I suddenly realised that they were barely referred to by name on screen and were otherwise criminally underdeveloped. Was this due to Gene Barry's infamous vendetta against his co-stars, I wonder? (For those of you still confused after more than forty years, Hagon played Gavin Taylor and Schell was Diane Marsh, names that haven't exactly permeated the cultural consciousness like other ITC characters have done.) Typically, it was not to be until Hagon and Schell were drafted in to cover Gene Barry's absence in *I'll Get There Sometime* (presumably he took a holiday, or perhaps he needed to go off for a fresh application of embalming fluid) that both characters were given some time in the sun alongside the delightful Barry Morse as Parminter. It's telling that those are by far the most entertaining episodes of *The Adventurer*.

My Bradley Saturday continued to stagger towards the afternoon as, comfort breaks aside, I worked my way through four hours of episodes, ending with *Love Always, Magda*, a borderline competent episode with a decent guest cast (but no Hagon or Schell). I broke for lunch, rustling up a bit of cheese on toast as I set another coffee on the go. This may well not have been the healthiest of midday snacks, but watching nine consecutive episodes of *The Adventurer* had sapped my energy to such an extent that junk food seemed immensely appealing. Maybe I was subconsciously hoping that I'd slip into a coma mid-afternoon and in so doing skip a few episodes as they played to a horizontal, unconscious audience of one.

Back to the grindstone. *Nearly the End of the Picture* (it really wasn't – this series was mocking me...), *Has Anyone Here Seen Kelly?*, *Deadlock*, *Skeleton in the Cupboard*... It was 4.00pm and I'd reached the halfway point in the series. There was light at the end of the tunnel, or was that just Gene Barry's charisma lighting up my life? Nope. Of course it wasn't.

Let's stop off here and take a look at the – ahem – 'star' of this series, Gene Barry. First off, you have to wonder whether Monty Berman and Dennis Spooner had based their decision to hire Gene on things he had done a decade earlier, like the international hit American television series *Burke's Law*. Imagine their surprise and disappointment when it suddenly became apparent that in reality they had signed up Gene's ageing, out of touch grandfather...

After watching thirteen episodes back-to-back, I was trying to work out just what it must have been about Gene Barry that had Berman and Spooner scrambling for the man's signature on a contract. There's so little by way of characterisation or anything unique on display on screen that I have to conclude that the reason he got the gig was simply because he was an American name actor; someone whose presence would lead to domestic and international sales of the series. This was of course nothing alien to ITC, who had long championed the inclusion of American stars for this very reason, but the difference compared with their past exploits was that Gene was not fit to follow in the footsteps of the likes of Steve Forrest (handsome, assured, charismatic, sophisticated), Richard Bradford (energetic, vital and unpredictable, a magnetic screen presence), Stuart Damon (quick-witted, creative and likable) and Tony Curtis (inventive, quirky, a brilliant comic performer who could also handle the action; arguably the only true 'American star actor' that ITC ever hired). After working my way to the halfway point in the series, I'd honestly struggle to apply a single one of the qualities listed above to Gene Barry. It's a damning indictment of Gene's star quality, but bluntly, by the time he signed up to *The Adventurer*, he was running on empty.

Bradford and Damon were young American actors on the rise (though ultimately neither would fully deliver on their promise). Barry was a getting-on-in-years import whose star had already sunk midway through the previous decade. By 1972, he possessed all the sex appeal of a burst mattress and sported the looks to match. Had Stuart Damon been cast in the lead role, rather than as a supporting character (who was ditched from the production at Gene's behest for having the gall to be taller than the leading man), then the scenes of young women fawning over and chasing Gene Bradley, the great film star, would have been eminently more convincing. As it stands, the scenes, complete with 'Our Gene', are at best ludicrous, at worst creepy. They would almost certainly be improved by the introduction of a laugh track (to accompany that supplied spontaneously by the audiences at home).

Such an innovation would also have helped cover the crimes committed in the costume department. Gene Bradley's outfits seem to be there to make up for the lack of magnetism of the supposed-star actor. Not even colour co-ordinated on black and white sets, they have you yearning for *The Adventurer* to have been devised for the radio rather than for television. It goes without saying that those crazy jackets and trousers must have looked incredibly hip for ten minutes in 1972, but today, they are just laughable, particularly on Gene Barry, who looks like an over-the-hill Lothario trying desperately to keep up (and fraternise) with the kids – and failing. These sartorial excesses fortunately calm down over the course of the series, but when they're gone, you actually miss them and the mirth they inspire.

And so, the marathon continued. In true *Mastermind* style, I'd started, so I'd finish. I had to. I'd lick this series within 24 hours if it killed me – and I did wonder for a while if it might. I could see the headlines: "MAN DIES OF TEDIUM WATCHING FORGOTTEN TV SERIES" or "GENE BARRY'S REVENGE: ALAN WAS TOO TALL TO LIVE". But then something surprising happened.

At getting on for 5.30pm I finished the next episode, Brian Clemens' *Action!*, one of the shows directed by Barry Morse. Filmed in Edinburgh and at Knebworth House and Wall Hall College, Aldenham, it depicted Gene Bradley being gassed and subjected to mental conditioning. This treatment caused him to stumble around in a daze and be generally comatose. Finally, a compelling episode, in which Our Gene comes into his own in a stupor. You couldn't make it up!

And then – *bliss!* – two episodes which were made while Gene Barry was away doing something less damaging to my psyche than appearing in *The Adventurer*, namely *I'll Get There Sometime* and *The Solid Gold Hearse*. Both episodes sport stunning location work in European cities rarely visited by ITC cameras (Wuppertal in the former, and another German city, Düsseldorf, in the latter, along with a trip to Antwerp, Belgium), both are headed up by Barry Morse as Parminter, the character being reinvented somewhat for comic effect (and wonderfully so), and both feature the welcome return from exile of Catherine Schell and Garrick Hagon (both of whom had by this time fallen victim to the sack because they were guilty of a heinous crime – daring to appear on screen with Gene Barry, who considered he could do it all far better on his own).

I'll Get There Sometime's filming in Wuppertal is particularly memorable, thanks to sequences filmed on and around the city's remarkable monorail (the Wuppertal Suspension Railway). A little bit of trivia, fact fans: the train used in the episode was the Kaiserwagen (Emperor's car), which was first used by Emperor Wilhelm II during a test ride on 24th October 1900. It is still operated on scheduled excursion services, special occasions and for charter events, if you ever fancy a location trip!

The episode places Gene Bradley far from the action, travelling back from Sydney, Australia. Problems on the way prompt him to regularly contact Parminter to reassure him that "I'll get there sometime." With Parminter, Diane and Gavin therefore having the episode practically to themselves, and it being such a joy, there is little doubt that viewers were saying, "There's no hurry, Gene. Take your time, chum." It's like seeing a much better series; what *The Adventurer* might have been without Gene Barry. It would have been a fun show, shot in fascinating places, complete with a trio of characters who work well together. You'd want to see that series, but you know that it'd be smothered at birth. Even in those two delightful episodes, Gene Barry keeps popping in to remind you of the bad old days. It's telling that *I'll Get There Sometime*'s title is focused on the Gene Bradley aspect of the story, rather than on the events unfolding in Wuppertal. It's like Gene's saying, "I may be away seeking the elixir of youth, guys, but I'm still the damned star, and don't you dare forget!"

To the Lowest Bidder saw the much-unwanted return of Gene Barry, but is at least boosted by outstanding location work around the Atomium Park in Heysel, Belgium, and the beautiful Grand-Place in Brussels' city centre. Not a bad episode, but by this point in my marathon (18 miles and within sight of the finishing line) I was beginning to think of my stomach. A break was called for. There was a pizza to be cooked, and more importantly, devoured. This culinary challenge met, I sat down once again, munching on my American Hot as John Barry's fabulous theme to *The Adventurer* played out for the nineteenth time that day. It was just before eight o'clock and my day's 'entertainment' had reached *Full Fathom Five*.

I suspect that this episode was actually filmed before *To the Lowest Bidder*, since in common with *I'll Get There Sometime* and *The Solid Gold Hearse*, it features very little 'Gene Action', and plenty of Barry Morse's ever-amusing Parminter. Again, the location work sparkles (as much as it is possible to do so on grotty 16mm transfers from the Eighties!), with the crew taking in Antwerp's cathedral and port, as well as Tongerlo Abbey (situated to the east of the Belgian city).

As the sun began to set on that May evening, I selected the next episode, the twentieth, *Going, Going...*, a reasonably diverting instalment which set Gene in competition with Parminter, and the night-time hours witnessed me slowly progressing to the end of the series. Some of these later episodes are actually the toughest to get through, as I discovered (and not for the first time), with the exotic locales mostly forgotten, set aside as if they were some sort of aberration, and cheaper London and Borehamwood settings supplanting them. Episodes such as *The Case of the Poisoned Pawn* and *Icons are Forever* really tested the strength of my desire to complete the course. The only thing in their favour was that they were over in less than half an hour each. Small mercies...

A couple of hours later, just before midnight, it was all over. Gene Bradley had negotiated his final mission in *Somebody Doesn't Like Me*, and I'd completed my own, to negotiate the most unloved ITC action series within a single day. The fact that I had managed to complete it, all 26 episodes across 15 hours with the occasional break, left me with a feeling of achievement. I had done something fundamentally daft – watched a series that I *knew* was an artistic disaster, suffered befuddlement, boredom and disappointment, though these feelings were mixed with fascination for the foreign location shoots, joy at a handful of standout episodes, the fun of guest star- and stunt double-spotting, and open-mouthed disbelief at some of Gene's godawful fashion choices. For the most part, it had actually been enjoyable, though quite often not for the reasons intended by the writers, directors and actors involved.

So, as *The Adventurer*'s self-appointed marathon man, here's my final word, not on the series itself, but on the effect it has had on me since I first saw it about thirty years ago. It has a draw for me that I don't quite understand. I *know* that it is bad, but that hasn't stopped me developing an affection for it over the years. I *know* that Gene Barry would most likely be voted ITC's least effective American lead, but that doesn't stop me finding his performances entertaining (though not for the reasons he would have wanted). I *know* that there was a better series in there, struggling to get out, but if it had been Parminter-Diane-Gavin centred, would it still hold the lurid fascination for me that it does as Gene Barry's vehicle? Almost certainly not. I *know* that *The Protectors*, for instance, is a much better series, but it has never captivated me in the way that *The Adventurer* has. Perhaps this means that I have irredeemably bad taste, but the truth of the matter is that there's something completely spellbinding about *The Adventurer*, something that will *always* draw me in, and that something is the question "how did they get it so wrong?" – how did a company with such a glorious track record as ITC, and producers, writers and directors with a wealth of experience, make such a monumental mess of a project as they did with *The Adventurer*? Even though what appeared on screen was often sub-standard, even dull to watch, the behind-the-scenes tale of how a series could fall apart right from the outset and yet somehow stay the course, *and* end up available to buy on DVD many decades later, is something I find endlessly fascinating.

There will always be a place on my shelf for *The Adventurer*, ITC's greatest ever mistake, the last hurrah of Gene Barry's career as an international star, because sometimes I don't want perfection – or even competence. Sometimes I just want to spend twenty-five minutes in the company of a lumbering, full-of-himself fashion nightmare with the acting range of a light switch. In this respect, *The Adventurer* has no equal.

The Protectors

1972-1974

Gabriel Hershman is the author of *Send in the Clowns – The Yo Yo Life of Ian Hendry* and *Strolling Player – The Life and Career of Albert Finney*, published respectively by Lulu.com and The History Press. His most recent work is a biography of the late Nicol Williamson, to be published again by The History Press in January 2018. In each of his biographies, he hopes to illuminate the craft of acting and shed light on the work of great, sometimes criminally underrated, performers in theatre, film and television.

When Harry Ruled My World

Gabriel Hershman

I once saw Robert Vaughn moving briskly and purposefully around Waterstones in Piccadilly, circa 2006, probably while he was filming *Hustle* in London. Still very much Mr Cool, looking just like his on-screen incarnations, dressed in a dark suit, self-possessed, looking effortlessly superior, hair well-greased back. You'd never catch him wearing jeans and a T-shirt in public.

A besotted fan was about to approach him. Perhaps you're thinking I'd be eager to talk to him about *The Magnificent Seven*. Even a decade ago Mr Vaughn was, after all, last man standing. What was it like working with Steve McQueen on *Seven* and *Bullitt*? Or would *you* have mentioned *The Man from U.N.C.L.E.*? Actually – and understand I only had a few seconds to ponder my opening gambit – I was set on a novel approach. I'd flatter him by discussing his treatise on the McCarthyite era, *Only Victims*. Or even broach his opposition to the Vietnam War.

That was just to show that I was not your run-of-the-mill fan but a real aficionado. And actually I did know a bit more about Mr Vaughn than most. *But*... what I really wanted to talk to him about was a series that most people would classify as hokum. But it is the quality of the hokum that I would fiercely defend.

It's 1973, the year of Gary Glitter, Slade and our 'Enry splashing it on all over – and British entry into something called the Common Market. I'm in my divorced father's dull flat in Bayswater on a Saturday / Sunday afternoon. He's getting depressed as he ponders a lonely evening, staring forlornly at the flock wallpaper. But *I'm* very excited. I'm waiting to start jumping up and down when the theme from my favourite show, *The Protectors*, plays out.

The thing is – you never quite knew when that moment would come. The intro to each episode lasted anything up to two-and-a-half minutes, usually featuring dynamics from our hero Harry Rule and then a ridiculous counter-attack from some very smart-looking villains. And then... the fun truly starts with the tune *Avenues and Alleyways*, first banged out to the backdrop of imaginative opening credits. Crooner Tony Christie belts out the lyrics at the end.

And it's the opening and closing theme that gripped me, rather more than the impenetrable storylines which somehow managed to scramble towards their resolutions in the intervening 25 minutes. The opening shots, impeccably edited, always set my heart pounding. Nothing is more iconic of London than Big Ben. But it gets better. Harry appears to sleep with his dog – who likes to share his cornflakes – indicating he's a bit of a softie at heart. He lives in a very modern home. That's obligatory for all super sleuths, of course. But he's also a dab-hand in the kitchen. Not only can he make scrambled eggs but he can effortlessly crush an egg with *one* hand. I was very puzzled by that – literally *never* having seen any male perform such a feat. I asked my father whether he'd ever seen this before. He shook his head. *Never*!

So our hero is clearly a self-sufficient modern man. And our heroine the Contessa is the delectable Nyree Dawn Porter who makes underwater scuba diving infinitely sexy but whose career – it has to be said – probably didn't advance much thanks to this series. But she seemed to have a different dress and hairstyle in each scene. You can understand the attraction for Vaughn – he had the lead role and he said he wanted to get out of America for a bit. But Nyree? And then there's baby-faced Tony Anholt (as the group's gadget man and researcher, Paul Buchet) to whom the wife of the late Glyn Owen once said I bore an uncanny resemblance.

The plots were a bit dubious but the credits – particularly with the Contessa seen against the backdrop of Rome – promised us some international entertainment away from a dull early evening in Bayswater.

Now, the wicked rumour mill has it that the series wasn't up to scratch. A book on adventure series I once bought said that "with apologies to the show's fans, it was dreadful". I'd like the writer to say that to Harry's face! Granted, the format didn't leave much time for profundities. Better to just sit back, and enjoy the heady mix of flared trousers, pukka ties, flowering shirts and exotic locations – much better than heading out to some retro bar.

Robert Vaughn exudes intelligence which isn't necessarily true of heroes in other shows. He comes across as real Ivy League privileged, the kind of guy who would be spouting lines from *Hamlet* at an early age (Vaughn's autobiography is full of earnest pronouncements about acting and politics with *The Protectors* only getting a passing mention). And an extra dimension is thrown in by the presence of numerous side-burned guest stars, usually those who never quite made the front rank of screen stardom but should have done – stalwarts like Ian Hendry, Tom Bell and Ed Bishop.

It certainly compared very favourably to the other half-hour show doing the rounds at the same time, *The Adventurer*, whose hero Gene Barry also cultivated an air of superiority but somehow just wasn't so likeable. *The Protectors* may not be for intellectuals but it certainly had panache. Watch it again to catch the spirit of the early Seventies – a time when a roughhouse roustabout left not so much as a blemish on anyone.

Sadly, I never had that chat with Mr Vaughn. Rather like the show itself, he proved too quick for me. I gather from some of his interviews that he never really understood some of the plots. But then neither did I. Did the other stars understand them? Sadly, there's no one else left to ask; Tony Anholt and Nyree Dawn Porter died young. Fortunately, the episodes moved so quickly that you never really had time to understand that you didn't understand – if you get my drift.

The Protectors was a bit of froth but classy and enjoyable for all that. And when I breezed into my little school on a Monday morning we'd all start singing the theme song. Just like the series itself, we didn't know the meaning of the lyrics but it sure was fun. I wanted to be Harry Rule. Occasionally I've fantasised about being another fictional character – but Harry was the original and the progenitor. But I'm still trying to crack an egg like he did.

The Zoo Gang

1974

Alys Hayes has long been involved in television fandom, notably attending the first ever *Doctor Who* convention in 1977 – something which came back to haunt her when she was interviewed about the event forty years on. She has co-produced tele-snap reconstructions of fourteen missing Series 1 episodes of *The Avengers* for licensed DVD releases and has co-written a book about that mysterious first year of the series. An ITC fan since childhood, Alys remains active in its fandom, particularly as an honorary member of the defunct-but-somehow-still-going *Randall and Hopkirk (Deceased) Appreciation Society* (RAHDAS).

New Tricks on the Riviera

Alys Hayes

Take four well-known but slightly older actors, put them in an ensemble piece about one-time French resistance fighters, then let them have fun dressing up and chasing villains in the south of France. This is the general premise of *The Zoo Gang*, one of those series that I remember fondly from the early 1970s. Being a BBC-orientated family meant that we didn't see the original evening showings of this series. However, we were regular viewers of the repeat runs of ITC series, which tended to be shown on Saturday mornings and Sunday lunchtimes (according to my fading memory). I recall seeing *Thunderbirds* and then *Department S*, *Jason King*, *Randall and Hopkirk (Deceased)* (to mention a few) with my parents, as we ate our Sunday roast dinner, but my favourite up until this point was *The Persuaders!* with its witty duo of Roger Moore and Tony Curtis. I also watched *The Adventurer*, but we'll gloss over that! So when *The Zoo Gang* came along I was something of an ITC connoisseur and looked forward to enjoying a new programme whilst guzzling my Walls ice cream dessert. The fact that the stars of this particular series were nearer pension age than usual didn't bother me. Maybe it's because my own parents were of an older generation than normal (my mother was in her early forties when I was born), but I had no problem connecting with these characters.

The series was based on the novel by Paul Gallico, which I have only recently got around to reading. It is fascinating to know how much ITC had revised the concept. Whereas Gallico's Zoo Gang were five French men, the TV series recast the group as only four – English ex-commando Thomas Devon (John Mills) known as 'The Elephant', Canadian mechanical genius Alec Marlowe ('The Tiger' – Barry Morse), American antiques dealer Steve Halliday ('The Fox' – Brian Keith), and French café owner Manouche Roget ('The Leopard' – Lilli Palmer). Obviously this reflected not only the British production but ITC's usual eye on attracting programme buyers in the international and, particularly, transatlantic markets. In addition, the TV Gang were made much less brutal in their methods – unlike their literary counterparts they did not go as far as executing certain criminal undesirables, preferring instead to leave justice to the police and criminal courts.

The Zoo Gang also leads on in production terms from *The Persuaders!* in some ways. Most outside footage is genuinely shot on location around Nice, Cannes and other parts of the French Riviera (no stock footage with place name captions on this series). Both main and supporting cast are present at these locations so it obviously wasn't a cheap series to make. Ken Thorne's incidental music is another link to *The Persuaders!*, although ITC chose Paul McCartney and Wings to compose and perform the main theme. I remember thinking how 'cool' it was at the time to have a pop group (and one connected to The Beatles) performing the theme. The overall effect seems to make the series say "...these guys may be older but they're just as capable as the younger generation...". Years later I bought the CD version of the Wings album *Venus and Mars*, partly because it had *The Zoo Gang* theme as a bonus track.

Over the course of the six episodes the gang manage to finally trap an old French collaborator, whose betrayal of a fifth Zoo Gang member, Claude – the husband of Manouche Roget – led to Claude's death and Manouche's desire for revenge. The collaborator, a Monsieur Boucher, now operates as an art thief and the Zoo Gang manage to 'frame' him (no pun intended!) for the theft of a Rembrandt self-portrait, using tricks they first developed during the war. One of their signature devices is a smoke-bomb in a cigarette packet – a device that Manouche's son Georges recognises, which could make things difficult for them as Georges is now a local police detective. However, all ends well for the gang and they receive part of a reward for the return of stolen artworks, which they decide to put towards the building of a new hospital facility in Claude's memory. This aim of raising money drives most of their endeavours – one time resulting in Alec being caught by the police after getting involved with conning a gold-smuggling ring by paying with counterfeit money. The Zoo Gang are not averse to bending the law if it raises cash for the hospital.

The series also allows for a little light comedy which often seems to involve John Mills in a variety of disguises, including one where he seems to have more than a passing resemblance to Colonel Sanders of Kentucky Fried Chicken fame, albeit without the Colonel's Southern drawl. This would seem to hark back to Mills' early professional life, when he was known as a song-and-dance man as well as a comic actor rather than the war hero and establishment types that he ultimately became known for. Another episode sees him as a tramp – possibly referencing the role in *Ryan's Daughter* for which he had recently won an Oscar.

Mills and Barry Morse were the actors that I recognised – whereas I did not recall seeing Lilli Palmer or Brian Keith in any other shows. It was my mother who explained their backgrounds and I have since spotted Palmer in various films from the 1940s and 1950s – but Brian Keith remains something of an unknown to me. Indeed, considering the fact the he was the youngest of the *Zoo Gang* cast, he seems to me somewhat older and emotionally removed in his portrayal compared to the other leads. But it was Mills and Morse whose portrayals I revelled in the most, these gentlemen teaching me an important life lesson – that it was possible to grow older without losing the playfulness of youth. Perhaps the way in which their characters behaved provided me with a counterpoint to the relationships that I had with my own parents (both of whom were of similar ages to the *Zoo Gang* cast), who did not tend to indulge in what I considered fun and usually cited their ages as an excuse for not doing so.

Guest cast members in *The Zoo Gang* were often familiar to me, and included Peter Cushing and Jacqueline Pearce, portraying a somewhat unlikely married couple, considering the sort of roles for which they were known, in *Counterfeit Trap*. Cushing was an actor I was already learning to look out for in film and television roles and he even had a link to my all-time favourite series *Doctor Who*, having played the lead role in two mid-Sixties cinematic excursions for the character. Roger Delgado was another guest star I was really pleased to see – again there was a connection to *Doctor Who*, with his electrifying portrayal of The Master then being so recent. He features as a kidnapped South American revolutionary in *Lion Hunt* – a story filmed not long before his tragic death in 1973. Ingrid Pitt turns up as a movie star in *Mindless Murder* and Kieron Moore, a regular guest in so many film series, appears in *African Misfire* – another art theft story, but this time with a twist.

Of course, since the series was set in France, most of the characters involved were French and the audience is generally supposed to assume that pretty much everyone is speaking French most of the time. Obviously the non-French members of the Zoo Gang would be fluent – considering their wartime roles but the lead actors tended not to lay on the accent too much. However, some of the guest stars did go over the top a little – step forward Ed Devereaux in *Lion Hunt*! This, coupled with printed English language headlines in featured editions of the *Nice-Matin* newspaper, does jar a little when watched with a modern sensibility but the practice was not uncommon at the time when making a series aimed at English-speaking audiences. After all, this was the era when Caucasian actors were still often blacked-up or given oriental eye make-up in order to play other nationalities.

The Zoo Gang does get overlooked in comparison to other series from the ITC stable. This is possibly because, being only six episodes long, it didn't generate the same amounts of sales worldwide as many of the other programmes. Apparently a series needed around sixteen episodes to qualify for syndication, so the episode count of *The Zoo Gang* fell rather short. This is a real shame and an opportunity missed, I feel, as I would like to have seen more and think that the series would be better remembered if it had had more time to bed in and find a regular audience. Within a short space of time, Barry Morse and John Mills each went on to play roles in two other series that became favourites of mine – *Space: 1999* and *Quatermass* respectively – both were productions which showcased older leads or supporting cast. This is something not seen so often today as the cult of youth generally prevails in popular culture – indeed, at the moment there are few dramas and cult shows where the leads are over forty (with *Doctor Who* being an exception at present).

I know it may be because I am now older myself, but I do feel that broadcasters are missing a trick by focussing so tightly on the younger actors on television and in the cinema. A few more series in the *Zoo Gang* mould would not go amiss and it would help people to see those with a bit of grey hair as more than just hospital patients or victims. The only recent programme that treats older characters in a similar way to *The Zoo Gang* is *New Tricks*, but even that has been pensioned off now. Meanwhile, if you have not seen *The Zoo Gang* then I can recommend it. To me it's an underrated little gem - short but sweet and proof that older can be better.

Return of the Saint

1978-1979

Rick Davy is a researcher from Wales (originally from London) and is owner of The Unmutual Prisoner and Portmeirion Website. In 2017 he wrote *The Prisoner – The Essential Guide*, and in 2014 the biographical content of the book *George Markstein and The Prisoner*. Rick was also involved in the 50th anniversary Blu-ray / DVD special edition released by Network, contributing text commentaries for all 17 episodes in addition to other content. An aficionado of several ITC shows, he also co-ran the *Randall and Hopkirk (Deceased)* fan club Faithful Unto Death.

Ian Dickerson discovered *Return of the Saint* as a child. He's not been the same since: the Saint on TV led to the Saint books, radio shows and comics and yes, even the Saint films. Amidst the education he struck up a friendship with the Saint's creator, Leslie Charteris, and his family. With their permission he excavated and studied the Leslie Charteris collection at Boston University and went on to write, direct and produce documentaries on the making of *The Saint* and *Return of the Saint*. He oversaw the recent reprints of the original Saint books in both the US and UK and was a co-producer on the 2016 TV movie *The Saint*. For the sake of what little sanity he has, Ian has also written about a wide range of subjects, none of which come with a halo, including talking mashed potatoes, Lord Grade and satellite links. Ian lives in Hampshire with his wife and two children. And an awful lot of books by Leslie Charteris.

All Kids Need A Hero

Rick Davy

Picture the scene. It is March 2014, and a man in his early forties is as excited as he has ever been. He is sat in the front passenger seat of a car, being driven at high speed down a deserted North Wales bypass, while a CD of cult television theme tunes (track 42 of disc two, to be precise) blasts out of the stereo. The car is a white Jaguar XJS. The bonnet has an unusual decal, the sun visors have autographs on them, and the boot contains two replica number plates which bear the digits 'ST 1'.

Picture also this scene. It is the late 1970s, and a boy, aged around seven, wearing grey shorts and a white Fred Perry t-shirt, is as excited as he has ever been. He is sat on a red and orange patterned carpet in the front room of a terraced house in the heart of East London, while the theme tune of a cult television show blasts out of a large colour television set. He has with him a small Corgi model car. The car is a white Jaguar XJS. The bonnet has an unusual decal, and the car's number plates bear the digits 'ST 1'.

The man in his forties and the young boy are both me. The car is owned by a pal of mine, who I shall refer to only as Mr S. The series in which it appeared only ran for one season of 24 episodes, and its star now lives in Los Angeles. The car is that which was driven by Ian Ogilvy, as Simon Templar, my childhood hero, and the TV series in which they appeared was *Return of the Saint*.

Return of the Saint is the only television programme which I can recall totally immersing myself in as a child. I didn't just live for the programme, I *lived* the programme. Whilst it was on screen, and I don't even know if it was the original run or repeats that I was watching (the passage of time has not etched the finer details and dates into my mind as much as the memories of enjoyment and escapism have been), I was savouring and absorbing the action. I was watching the coolest guy I had ever seen, saving the day in the most fantastic and unusual locations and situations that I had encountered, and every single one of these situations was carefully remembered and re-enacted over the next seven days, until the next instalment was televised.

Toy soldiers would double as villains, toppling down from the banister as easily as the dummies had done from cliff-tops on screen (not that I knew they were dummies at the time. Oh, to be that age again, when even the most obviously-faked of stunts looked as real as anything). The Corgi XJS would fly off the top of our stairs, always catching up with whatever other Whizz-wheels, or Matchbox cars were fleeing it. There I'd be, in my own little world at least, knocking out the villain, and saving the day in my little white Jag.

The only line I drew in my re-enactments was not wasting time trying to impress girls (that would come many years later). I was only about seven after all, and I don't think my Mum would have appreciated playing the role of a Russian heiress being locked in the wine cellar. Not that we had a wine cellar, other than in my mind. The back of the sideboard doubled for it. So, a German stormtrooper with a snapped off rifle (doubling for an Italian heavy) would take orders from a Saxon horseman (doubling for an unscrupulous politician), while Darth Vader (doubling for an imprisoned innocent) lay in the corner, just behind the wine glasses and Marshall Ward catalogues which always seemed to fill the furniture and that I dare not move. Perfect!

Without sounding like the sort of bitter 'things were nowt like this in my day, lad' old man that I always promised myself I wouldn't turn into, us kids from the Seventies didn't have what kids have now. Other than a Binatone tennis game (where the only real excitement came from a 'double beep' if you managed to deflect the ball from your bat to the top wall), we didn't have computers or games consoles. There were no elaborate fancy dress costumes for a couple of quid in the supermarket like there are now, so a towel round the head made an effective Dracula, or Batman. Being the youngest of three boys I had a plethora of handed down toys, for which I was always grateful, but I wasn't sure what to do with most of them as they either didn't work, or were for 12 or 17 year olds (there being five years between the three of us). So more often than not, until life afforded us a little more cash as the Seventies moved into Eighties, and we moved to Essex, my imagination was my favourite toy.

I was too young to appreciate punk or popular music, and much of what was on television at the time, but the year after The Stranglers sang "whatever happened to the heroes?" I had found my very first one. Simon Templar. Cue halo music.

But why was this series, out of all the fantastic content that the ITC stable created, the one that particularly caught my imagination? Watching it now, the action sequences aren't great, much of the acting is pretty poor, the writing very formulaic, the locations don't resonate with anything remotely inhabiting reality as I knew it, and the car I spent all my time playing with hardly appears in most of the episodes.

But what *Return of the Saint* does, which not many other ITC series did, is give us an out-and-out hero. Someone a kid in the East End of London could daydream of being. I wanted to *be* Ian Ogilvy. Okay, I wanted to be Trevor Brooking as well, and when the sun was shining that's who I was in the garden pretending to be with my home-made football goal (built more to protect my Mum's battered plants than to help with my shooting skills). But when the sun went down, and I came inside for my tea, I was The Saint. Simon Templar. Ian Ogilvy. In his little white Jag. Not that Mr Templar would have eaten beefburgers that had little bits of onion already in them, accompanied by chips cooked in a death-trap deep fat fryer, with a United biscuit (whatever happened to those?) for pudding.

Watching the series now, with my wife, who is seeing the episodes for the first time, on DVD, Ogilvy is still the suave action hero I remember him as, and some of the episodes are great fun, and are not as dated as one would expect. Other episodes are maybe not so good, but Ogilvy is a great leading man even through the weaker stories, and there are some superb guest turns (most memorably from Joss Ackland in *The Nightmare Man*, which is probably my favourite episode, Maurice Denham in *The Village that Sold its Soul*, and Ian Hendry in *Yesterday's Hero*, to give just three examples), and more than enough action to keep one entertained.

That, pretty much to me, as a kid, was what I wanted. Entertainment! My tastes and appreciation of TV series and films has changed as I have gone through young adulthood into middle age, but all I wanted back then was *fun*, and Ian Ogilvy delivered this in spades! It also, like so many ITC shows, has a great title sequence (the stick man used to give me something of the heebie-jeebies at the time, though) and a memorable theme tune (famously in more recent times celebrated by Alan Partridge). Track 42, CD two, you will recall. The 7" vinyl version I still own to this day; it was one of the first records I ever owned. Not *the* first. That dubious honour belongs to Althia and Donna's *Uptown Top Ranking*. As well as the 7" vinyl, I pestered the parents for the two hardback annuals which were produced, and every time a rather poorly drawn version of my hero was appearing in *Look-in* magazine I'd make sure it came through the letterbox, delivered from the local newsagent along with my Dad's copy of *Railway Modeller*. And, my pride and joy, the little white Jag that flew down from the top of our stairs.

Ogilvy would have made a better James Bond than most who subsequently took that famous role, and I'm not at all embarrassed when I mention that he was my childhood hero. His portrayal of Templar did everything in a decent way, he was only ever underhand in the same way that the television versions of *Dick Turpin* or *Robin Hood* were. His Templar was never over-violent, always doing things in a suave, cunning and intelligent way. Unlike many leading male characters of the late 1970s and early 1980s, he was a believable (yet unreachable) and decent hero.

Outside of children's television in the afternoons, and the Saturday evening *Doctor Who* slot, there wasn't much for kids to watch during that era, I seem to recall. It was an era of great television drama, but most of it was made for an adult audience. Whether it was period classics such as *Lillie* or *Pennies from Heaven*, or darker-in-tone offerings like *Gangsters*, which finished the year *Return of the Saint* began, or *Boys from the Blackstuff*, which began as *Return of the Saint* finished, the shows of the time were not made for a young boy who wanted to watch something fun, harmless, and action-packed. The bleakness of Britain in 1978 seemed to transfer from real life to the supposed-escapism that what we were watching on our screens. *Return of the Saint* was the exception.

The exotic locations therefore certainly played their part in the series' success, places like Tuscany or the French Riviera were the opposite of the unkempt dark streets of the East End, but yet the episodes based in London are perhaps the ones which I now feel have the most merit (and were probably less expensive to make, and money was reputedly the reason Lew Grade cancelled the series, despite its immense popularity). And then, of course, there was that little white Jag, the coolest car on television (yes, even cooler than *The Dukes of Hazzard*'s General Lee Dodge Charger).

The Prisoner is probably the ITC series which resonated with me most as a teenager, and also now as an adult, and the series that I have invested most time in, both in terms of re-watching the series and in terms of fan and event involvement. It's rightly referred to as a tour-de-force of television, and a masterpiece, but Number 6's situation and behaviour and persona was never one that a primary school child would want to swap his own life for. He wasn't exactly a bundle of laughs, that Six fellow.

UFO is another great ITC show, and what kid doesn't like wacky low-budget science fiction, but all the characters spent most of their time being rather miserable (or at least that's how it seemed to me as a lad). Well, apart from Colonel Foster. So okay, yes, I admit, there may have been a time when the little white Corgi Jag would fly off the top of our stairs with a Plasticine nose stuck on the front as it became an Interceptor, flying after a UFO (well, more likely a plastic lemon squeezer doubling as a flying saucer) that was heading for Cornwall. Or the hallway, to give Cornwall its proper name.

Randall and Hopkirk (Deceased) is another fine series, one which I came across on ITV during an afternoon off school in the mid 1980s, which I appreciated more and more as I got older, but what kid wants to be a destitute private eye, or worse still, a dead one? *The Persuaders!* is yet another favourite ITC series of adult me, but what kid understands what being a playboy or an oil tycoon is all about?

All kids need a TV hero, and it was always Ian Ogilvy for me. As I got older, these thoughts morphed into wanting to be Michael Praed, he of HTV's *Robin of Sherwood,* but that was only for a short time. When I was aged 12 or 13 I think, I thought that hanging around in a forest with Ray Winstone and Clive Mantle, with Judi Trott in tow, would be great way to spend my time.

But they weren't heroes. They were a passing fancy. I didn't sit on our stairs for hours racing Robin Hood around after villains, singing Clannad's theme as I did so. I didn't run round the garden shouting "I am not a number," or 'Only you can see me, Jeff!' Well, maybe once or twice in my twenties. But what I *did* do was spend all week beating up villains and flying off the stairs in my little white Jag, waiting for the following Sunday when my hero would be on the large screen again and there would be new plots to learn and re-enact.

Was it actually a Sunday? It always felt like one. Sunday evening TV was never made with kids like me in mind before or after that. *Songs of Praise* signalled tea time, and the closing titles of *That's Life* signalled bed time. What happened in between was a conveyor belt of shows for my mum and dad, and adult me (*Last of the Summer Wine*, *Shoestring*, etc).

Roger Moore's version of *The Saint*, appreciated by me now, was unseen by me at that time, Patrick McGoohan's John Drake character in *Danger Man* was also not encountered until many years later, since I was born some years after the heady ITC-laden schedules of the 1960s. But even if I had seen those series, I'm not sure I'd have dashed into the playground to chat about those characters with my pals, as I did with *Return of the Saint*.

Nowadays, more than thirty years on, I no longer want to be Simon Templar. But the memories of having a hero to aspire to, however silly and unrealistic that aspiration may have been, will always be there and will never be denied. It's just that life has evolved. The ability to take a trip in the car I watched on screen is now only a phone call away. My childhood hero is now on social media, posting snippets of what he watched on TV the night before (or rather what his good lady wife did), and I don't have to wait a week for the next 48 minutes of action, as all the episodes now sit on a shelf in my office, on shiny discs.

But what of the little Corgi car, with the unusual decal and number plates that bear the digits 'ST 1', that each day kept me occupied by chasing and catching all manner of thieves and villains in their matchbox cars, on the red and orange patterned carpet? It now resides in my youngest son's car box, a little more battered than it was – alongside Lightning McQueen, Captain America's car, and Postman Pat's van – alongside all of *his* heroes. Yesterday, I heard one fly off the top of our stairs.

Being Hoppy Uniatz

Ian Dickerson

Watching TV can get you into trouble.

September 1978: I'd celebrated my ninth birthday just three months prior and spent most of my free time either cycling around the neighbourhood getting into mischief, watching TV or reading. Those latter two in particular I did without restraint; a typical Saturday involved a morning glued to either *Swap Shop* or *Tiswas*, followed by a visit to the library which I'd eventually leave taking a fair chunk of their stock with me. But when ITV started running trailers for a new show that was debuting on Sunday evenings, called *Return of the Saint*, I was in trouble. It had everything my simplistic nine year old self wanted out of life; action, guns, fast cars and some rather lovely ladies. I watched the first episode and was hooked, ensuring a spot was reserved on the sofa for future Sunday evenings.

I got into even more trouble when I discovered that one of my brothers had a couple of books about the Saint; they quickly found their way from his bookshelf to mine (I got out of trouble for that misdemeanour when I gave him a complete set of the recent British reprints).

And when I discovered that there were even more *Saint* books, lots more *Saint* books, I spent the next few years in a very much pre-internet age, spending as much pocket money as possible tracking down and buying every single *Saint* book. It wasn't unusual for me to cycle eight or nine miles over the Malvern Hills to visit my favourite second-hand bookshop in the hope they had a *Saint* book I'd not yet discovered. The Saint and Leslie Charteris did wonders for my fitness…

In the back of one of those books was a page about The Saint Club with an address inviting you to write off and join. This was all well and good but my parents thought I was mad, for that book was even then a good twenty years old; even if the Club was still alive and kicking what were the chances of them being at the same address?

Very good, as it turned out, for a couple of weeks later I got a letter from the Honorary Secretary of the organisation, a retired policeman by the name of Norman Turner. I never met Norman but he kindly, patiently and tolerantly answered all of my letters promptly and informatively. And he kept sending me the Club's Christmas letters, which were written by

Charteris himself, and were thus guaranteed to ensure my long term membership.

Over the next few years, as the literary *Saint* was effectively retired and I completed my book collection, the Club became the only source of *Saint* news and goodies. I bought large quantities of *Saint* notepaper and wrote copious letters on it, including one or two to certain *Doctor Who* related organisations, which much to my surprise ensured my reputation was made at the singular *Doctor Who* convention I've attended.

Fast forward a few more years and I'd blundered my way into college where I was studying how to build a TV studio amongst other things. As internet ubiquity was still a few years off I made a regular trip to the college library every Friday to study the latest edition of *Broadcast* magazine, the trade paper that conveniently included a lot of job adverts in the back. But in one edition, and rather sadly I can recall it as being the one dated Friday 13th January 1989, the job ads held no interest for within the first few pages was an article entitled "LWT spends £7.5m on new series of *The Saint*".

I was in trouble. Again.

College held no interest for me for the rest of that day. Shortly after that I wrote a letter to Norman Turner, pointing out that with a new series on the horizon it was time to sing and shout and tell the world how wonderful the Saint and The Saint Club was. Well, I thought so anyway.

Unbeknownst to me Norman had passed away and the gentleman who had taken on the Club wasn't overly enthusiastic. He did, however, helpfully pass my letter on to Leslie Charteris, who then promptly rang me up. Once I'd picked my jaw up off the ground we had a long chat and he kindly invited me to lunch the following week.

We dined at the Four Seasons restaurant in Mayfair and somehow a friendship was born. I've often pondered why it worked; he was a successful if retired novelist and I was a horribly naïve teenager and very much a Fan. Sure, I was very much in awe for the first couple of times we met, but I quickly grew up. And Leslie, although a loving father, wasn't known for his tolerance towards children and teenagers, a residue from his own eventful childhood, I suspect. I was probably just in the right place at the right time – lucky, really.

From then on we spoke at least once a week and dined generally once a month. Early on in our friendship I vividly remember calling him on a Saturday evening, after every episode of the 1989 series of *The Saint* had aired, and hearing his brutally honest reaction to the films. I remember sitting in his study enjoying a post-prandial coffee as he answered my questions and told dirty jokes. And I remember my reaction when he asked me to help write a book...

He was kind enough to open up his address book for me. It wasn't that he wanted to, but I'd started asking lots of questions about the TV incarnations of *The Saint* and he didn't have the knowledge to answer them. So he told me to call a friend of his, Robert S. Baker.

Uh-oh, more trouble.

I did call Mr Baker. He told all his friends to call him Bob but I never could; I'd spent a chunk of my formative years looking at his name on end credits of films and TV shows, I had far too much respect for him to do that. He invited me out to lunch with him and his lovely wife Alma. And he kindly answered my questions. And when he moved out of Elstree Studios he was generous enough to ask if I wanted to come and get some spare bits and pieces that he had lying around.

~~Mr Baker~~ *Bob* was also kind enough to open up his address book and through him I got to meet writers like John Goldsmith and Terry Feely, production folk like Malcolm Christopher, Johnny Goodman and Lord Grade. And some chap called Moore.

Shortly after the 1989 TV series had stuttered to its early grave Leslie began teasing me about some big *Saint* project that was under discussion. I didn't let him tease me for long. When he told me that Paramount wanted *The Saint* I was sanguine, but when he told me he was writing an outline for them my gob was well and truly smacked.

It was around that time that ITC got in touch with me. Well, ITC Home Video to be exact. They were looking to launch much of their library content on VHS and wanted some help picking the best of *The Saint* and *Return of the Saint*. Was I interested? Was I ever...

When Leslie died in April 1993 he had read some of the scripts for what became the 1997 movie. He wasn't enthused and offered guidance for some of the more minor problems and some serious words when they tried to break terms of the contract and kill off Simon Templar (to have him replaced by his son in case you were wondering). Ultimately, the film staggered through a seven year development period, which might perhaps explain the less than Saintly final results. Those of us who knew Leslie were glad he wasn't around to see the final product; his widow was so unhappy with the final version of the script that she insisted Paramount remove his name from the film.

With the internet evolving fast many folks were adopting online pseudonyms and identities for a wide variety of reasons. When it came to choosing one for myself I was determined not to go for anything obvious, so opted to hide behind the name of Hoppy Uniatz, the name of the Saint's intellectually challenged sidekick with an unhealthy fondness for whiskey. Can't think why I picked that.

With Leslie's passing my friendship with his widow Audrey got a lot closer. They'd never been terribly keen on the spotlight and with Leslie gone, her social circle shrank over the following years. But interest in *The Saint* remained and I quickly grew to appreciate her contract negotiation skills as I found myself talking with people at Fremantle, who'd taken an option on the TV rights to the character. They hired scriptwriter Stephen Nathan to work on a pilot script but it never quite came together and when, with their option up for renewal they proposed, allegedly with the backing of the ABC network in the States, casting Liz Hurley as Simone Templar, I discovered just how varied a vocabulary a long-retired former movie actress had.

More Saintly mischief headed my way when Steve Bailie, a friend and literary agent turned scriptwriter, suggested a contemporary twist on a period *Saint* adventure. He penned a short sample script illustrating the concept which was met with enthusiasm by key folk such as Sir Roger Moore. But it wasn't to be, with further progress being hampered by an unfounded but well reported rumour that Val Kilmer would return to the role.

To everyone's gratitude that rumour quickly bit the dust when Bill MacDonald approached the Estate. Bill had been involved in the Paramount film but the project had been taken away from him and his partner Robert Evans long before Val Kilmer got involved. He was keen to do *The Saint* on TV properly. So was Geoffrey Moore, Roger's eldest son. They teamed up and so began years of lengthy phone calls, meetings, writing and plans.

I just couldn't help but get involved since Audrey, then in her late 80s, didn't use the internet or even fax machines. Indeed sometimes it was enough of a challenge getting her to answer the phone since she did enjoy her peace and quiet (and as I get older I begin to understand that).

Thing is, it's *The Saint* and for years I've espoused that whilst I'd dearly love to see a *Saint* TV show set at the time of the original stories, I also firmly believe there's a place for someone with the Saint's philosophies, attitudes and skillset in the 21st century. So when people start talking to you about it and seem to be on the same page as you creatively, there's bound to be more trouble ahead.

That trouble took the form of meetings, numerous Skype calls, contract discussions, script reading, occasional script rewriting, all sorts of things over the next few years as the project slowly progressed one step forward, two steps back and then, eventually stuttered to a halt.

In 2005 more trouble arrived, courtesy of Ian Ogilvy. He was over in the UK doing some promotional work for his children's books and I managed to persuade him to come down to our local school. I should perhaps provide some context and point out that at the time we lived in a small village on the outskirts of the New Forest and the school had around a hundred and forty pupils, and yes, one of them did share my surname. But Ian came down, did a lovely talk, signed and sold a lot of books and generally seemed to enjoy himself. At lunch he mentioned to me that he'd just been interviewed about his role in *Upstairs, Downstairs* for a documentary on the making of the show. But what really stood out for him was that the producer was a 21 year old, Stephen La Rivière.

Before I knew it I was working with Stephen on a documentary about the making of the Roger Moore series of *The Saint*; two documentaries in fact, one for the black and white episodes and one for the colour episodes. And since timing, and a sense of humour, is everything, we got Ian Ogilvy to narrate them. A short while later, with Stephen having gone on to bigger and better things – just look at those marvellous *Thunderbirds* episodes he's produced – I got to work on a documentary about the making of *Return of the Saint*. And we managed to persuade Roger to return the favour and narrate that programme…

The return of *The Saint* on TV stuttered along for many years; at one stage I even persuaded possible Saint – or at least he was very much favoured at the time – James Purefoy to write an introduction for my first book, unoriginally entitled *The Saint on TV*. Sadly by the time it was published the project had failed again but fortunately I was able to pull the introduction prior to publication.

An independent film producer called Brad Krevoy entered the picture and, working with Messrs Moore and MacDonald, picked up a refreshed baton determined to get the Saint back on TV. He asked if I was interested in helping? What do you think I said?

So followed months of trouble.

Long discussions, lengthy e-mails, script drafts and notes, this poor producer discovered the hard way just how happy I was to talk about the Saint, and how long I could witter on for. But eventually we got through it all and I sat in on auditions for the main parts.

And then I spent some time in Los Angeles, San Diego and Switzerland whilst we shot the pilot. Sadly, we couldn't find a suitable home for the show in the UK or US, but you should be able to see the results of our endeavours later this year when it's released as a TV movie.

Eighteen months or so before she died, Audrey Charteris steered me into more trouble. Mulholland Books (an imprint of long time *Saint* publisher Hodder & Stoughton) wanted to reprint some of the original adventures. Of course, I'd be delighted to help, I said, not fully appreciating just how much trouble that would get me into. And when Thomas & Mercer (an Amazon imprint) said they wanted to reprint the books in the US, I recklessly offered to stick my nose in there as well.

Silly boy.

We eventually agreed that Mulholland would reprint thirty-five titles (Audrey wouldn't let them reprint the very first *Saint* book, in line with Leslie's long-standing wishes, and they themselves wanted to limit the reprints to the original Charteris titles, not including the later collaborations) and Thomas & Mercer would reprint forty-nine (they weren't quite so concerned about the collaborations).

Both publishers – and Mrs Charteris – were remarkably receptive to my ideas; getting the talented Andy Howard to do the covers for the UK editions, contributing lots of extra material to help put the stories in context, and getting some relatively well known people to contribute introductions to the books explaining how the Saint and Leslie Charteris had affected them.

With Audrey's passing – she died in September 2014 – I find myself getting into more and more forms of Saintly mischief. Why do I do it? Sure, my tongue is firmly in cheek when I call it trouble, but what drives me more than anything is the desire to read, watch or listen to a new *Saint* adventure, a *Saint* adventure that may not have been written by Leslie but one that perhaps could have been. That's all I really want. And if I can have been involved in the creation of that adventure, then I'll be incredibly lucky.

Like I said, with a bit of luck, watching TV can get you into a lot of trouble.

Afterword • Elaine Spooner

> *"I went to ITC and stayed with ITC for about eight years because in those days it really was the production line of British television at that time. And I enjoyed it. I mean I wish they still made them."*
>
> *Dennis Spooner*
> *Fan Aid convention, Bath, June 1985*

My father's contribution to TV was both hugely significant and prolific, the extent of which was something that very gradually dawned on me as I was growing up during the 1970s and early 1980s. I knew he was a writer; the constant 'tap tap' of the typewriter day and night and seeing his name on television credits confirmed that. I knew he wrote for *The New Avengers*, *The Professionals*, *Bergerac* and much earlier had written episodes of *The Avengers*, *Doctor Who*, *Thunderbirds* and *Stingray*; these were either being broadcast for the first time or were being repeated. I knew he knew 'everybody' (even though I didn't really know who 'everybody' was back then) and whenever we were watching TV or a video, he always had a funny story about whoever was on; around 1982, when I was watching *The Spy Who Loved Me* on video, he casually mentioned that he knew Roger Moore – I was staggered that he knew James Bond.

For some reason my father would always refer to his friends by their full name – which is useful for me now to recall and place all those names from my childhood: Ray Austin, Monty Berman, Sydney Newman, Pat Macnee, Albert Fennell, Terry Nation and Verity Lambert, to name but a few. I had no idea who they were or the part they played in what became TV history; I just knew they were all his TV friends. The exception to this was Brian Clemens, as we saw him regularly, but at the time I didn't connect him with being the man behind *The Avengers*. I remember whenever a maroon Bentley was parked outside our house it meant Monty Berman was visiting. To me, all of my father's friends seemed to have a huge presence and seemed very important – and even though I had no reason to be, I was always a bit scared of them. Although on one occasion, perhaps because a friend was with me and I was showing off a bit, I actually spoke to Monty. I came inside the house and very confidently said "You've left your lights on". He chuckled, put his arm around me and said "They're parking lights". I thought no more about it until years later (when I was about 20 or so) and had actually found out who Monty Berman was, what shows he did and learnt about his legendary approach to budgeting. The notion that Monty Berman would have left his car lights on and risked his battery going flat is quite comical to me now.

My father worked in the States a lot in the early 1980s and was invited out three or four times a year for a number of weeks. He would sometimes stay with either Ray Austin or Pat Macnee. One year he brought home Pat Macnee's autograph for me. I still have it. It says "To Elaine – Best Wishes, Patrick Macnee, *The Avengers* 1982". At the time I looked upon it as being from the man who was in TV shows called *The Avengers* and *The New Avengers* and had worked with my father; it means more to me now as a huge *Avengers* fan. I also remember in 1984 my father coming home with loads of funny stories from filming the *Hammer* House of Mystery and Suspense episode *And the Wall Came Tumbling Down* with Peter Wyngarde.

I vaguely recall going to a few *Doctor Who* and sci-fi fantasy TV conventions in the early/mid-1980s. At one – I think it was Brighton, July 1985 – I remember my father had just finished his talk and he and I were standing on a balcony overlooking where all the attendees were sitting watching the next guest. I started to notice some people pointing at 'us' and nudging their friends to look round. That's when it occurred to me that my father was 'famous'. OK, so it was a room full of *Doctor Who* and cult TV fans, but I was only 13, so it was my idea of famous.

My father died in September 1986 when he was 53 and I was 14. Aside from the normal father/daughter things I later missed out on, I would have loved to have talked to him about his amazing career and all the shows he worked on and created. I knew and watched the aforementioned shows, but wasn't able to properly view all his ITC shows until after he died, when the videos were released, when BBC2 showed all the episodes of *Randall and Hopkirk (Deceased)*, and later when all the DVD box sets were released. I'm thrilled to hear actors, writers and crew talking about my father on the commentaries. It would have been so interesting if he'd been around to do a few commentaries on his shows himself.

I'm such a fan of *The Avengers* and the ITC shows *The Champions*, *Department S*, *Jason King*, *The Baron*, *Man in a Suitcase*, my favourite – *Randall and Hopkirk (Deceased)* – and the ones my father didn't directly work on, such as *The Persuaders!*, *The Saint* and *The Prisoner* (although he did attend production meetings for *The Prisoner*). Even if my father hadn't worked on all these shows, I still would have been a huge fan. I met my husband when we were 20, around the time when Sixties-era TV was having a renaissance. Luckily he was and is a huge fan, too. We always have an ITC or *Avengers* box set on the go and when we've been through all of them, we'll start at the beginning again. We recognise, like I'm sure all fans do, the different directors' and writers' styles. My father's episodes have comedy and a distinct 'Spooner' title; Terry Nation's are usually science fiction, deadly viruses – and didn't he do pretty much the same script for that other show!; Brian Clemens' are always a bit edgier and invariably Nazis make an appearance! And you always know whenever anyone gets into a white Jag it doesn't bode well. We're always going to talks and conventions linked to cult TV and meet such a lot of people that worked with my father, such as Annette André, Ray Austin, Johnny Goodman, Linda Thorson, Richard Bates, Peter Wyngarde and Alexandra Bastedo. I'm so proud and moved when people come up to me afterwards and say how much they enjoy my father's work and how talented he was. Some people even tell me that they spoke to him at conventions when they were younger. He always took time to talk to fans and aspiring writers – it's lovely to read Vanessa Bergman's chapter and learn of the encounters she had with my father.

I love the fact that so many of the people I admire are fans of the ITC shows. Vic Reeves, Bob Mortimer and Charlie Higson remade *Randall and Hopkirk (Deceased)*. Stephen Fry mentions in an article about the BBC and the future of broadcasting that, "ITV gave us… those definite article ITC adventures from Monty Berman and Dennis Spooner". The Smiths' record covers featured ITC actors and in his autobiography Morrissey gives his detailed thoughts on *Man in a Suitcase* and *Department S*. Mark Gatiss is also a fan, particularly of Brian Clemens' work. ITC shows are often affectionately spoofed: *The Comic Strip Presents* did *Detectives on the Edge of a Nervous Breakdown*; Craig Ferguson gave us *The Last Action Series* and the character of Jason King was a key inspiration for Austin Powers. I even remember watching *Newsnight* at the time of the 2005 Conservative Party leadership contest between David Cameron and David Davis; with their vastly different backgrounds *Newsnight* mocked up their own funny rendition of *The Persuaders!* opening sequence featuring the two politicians.

My father loved working for ITC and Lew Grade. And why wouldn't he – it was the golden age of TV and he was being asked to come up with series after series that he and Monty Berman had control of – quite a contrast to the BBC which he called "a bureaucratic monolith". He was asked at the Fan Aid North convention in November 1985 what he thought about his old shows cropping up on TV and he said, "*I'm amazed at how well they hold up. When one first hears that they're going to show them I think 'Oh my god' and I sort of half watch from behind the sofa and eventually come out because they get quite interesting*".

Was my father proud of his shows and what would he have thought of them having a lasting appeal half a century later? A quick email to the charming Ray Austin in the States was met with this reply: "*He was very proud of them and his work on them, plus all of us that were working alongside him. He would have laughed out loud – none of us could have seen us still being out there fifty years on! And on and on and on and so on*". My aunt, Anne Frost, says, "*I'm sure Dennis would be extremely chuffed. Who'd have thought it after fifty years that his work is still going and appreciated by so many now. And on DVD. It's not something anyone would have expected so he'd be surprised, very proud, grateful and honoured*".

Some fifty years on, the ITC shows are still being shown on TV all around the world and still being purchased on DVD, with new incarnations of box sets being released, entertaining the original viewers, those who discovered them as repeats in the 1980s and 1990s, and hopefully gaining a new generation of fans. It's been so entertaining reading all these chapters of everyone's memories and recollections of ITC in their lives – all very different experiences but all with the same love for ITC.

Acknowledgements

We are grateful to each and every one of our enthusiastic writers. They have freely given their time, talents, help and support in bringing this book to life:

Rachael Baez
Greg Bakun
Vanessa Bergman
Matt Courtman
Simon Coward
Chris Dale
Ian Dickerson
Geoff Dodd
Robert Fairclough
Mike Gorman
Alys Hayes
Gabriel Hershman
Annette Hill
Tina Jerke
Neil Jones
Mike Kenwood
Stephen La Rivière
David Mackenzie
Richard McGinlay
Robert Morton
Steve O'Brien
Jon Older
Max Pemberton
Louise Penn
Al Samujh
Sheena Samujh
Linda Kunkle Schley
David Tulley
Jaz Wiseman

Special thanks go to J.R. Southall, our wonderful illustrator Shaqui Le Vesconte, Elaine Spooner for her afterword, and to Annette André for the foreword and for suggesting the book be published in aid of the Born Free Foundation. Thanks also to Kelvin Dickinson for his help in proofing this 1st Reprint edition.

Alan and Rick